WOMEN INTO WIVES
The Legal and Economic Impact of Marriage

Sage Yearbooks in
WOMEN'S POLICY STUDIES

Series Editors

Jane Roberts Chapman and Margaret Gates
Center for Women Policy Studies
Washington, D.C.

Editorial Board

Volume 2
Sage Yearbooks in WOMEN'S POLICY STUDIES

WOMEN INTO WIVES

The Legal and Economic Impact of Marriage

Edited by

JANE ROBERTS CHAPMAN

and

MARGARET GATES

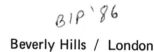

SAGE Publications   Beverly Hills / London

For information address:

SAGE PUBLICATIONS, INC.
275 South Beverly Drive
Beverly Hills, California 90212

SAGE PUBLICATIONS LTD
St George's House / 44 Hatton Garden
London EC1N 8ER

Printed in the United States of America

International Standard Book Number 0-8039-0700-1 (cloth)
0-8039-0701-X (paper)

Library of Congress Catalog Card No. 76-47070

FIRST PRINTING

CONTENTS

Introduction
    JESSIE BERNARD   9

1   Girls into Wives
    RAPHAELA BEST   15

2   Sexual Inequality, Cultural Norms, and
Wife-Beating
    MURRAY A. STRAUS   59

3   Women's Dependency and
Federal Programs
    SUSAN KINSLEY   79

4   Partnership Marriage:
Legal Reforms Needed
    JOAN M. KRAUSKOPF   93

5   Health and Fertility Issues and the
Dependency of Wives
    MARY E. KING, JUDITH ANN LIPSHUTZ, and AUDREY MOORE   123

6   Black Women and the
Family
    DIANN HOLLAND PAINTER   151

7   Child Care for the 1980s:
Traditional Sex Roles or Androgyny?
    MARY POTTER ROWE   169

8 Public Policy and the Family:
A New Strategy for Women as Wives and Mothers
SHEILA B. KAMERMAN   195

9 Homemakers into Widows and Divorcées:
Can the Law Provide Economic Protection?
MARGARET GATES   215

10 A Crisis Perspective on
Divorce and Role Change
JEAN LIPMAN-BLUMEN   233

11 Women into Mothers:
Experimental Family Life-Styles
MADELEINE KORNFEIN, THOMAS S. WEISNER, and
JOAN C. MARTIN   259

Conclusions
JANE ROBERTS CHAPMAN   293

Statistical Appendix   299

The Contributors   317

Dedicated to

HELEN ELIZABETH STULL GATES   GRACE LILLIAN ENOS ROBERTS

INTRODUCTION

JESSIE BERNARD

The first volume of the Sage Yearbooks in Women's Policy Studies—*Economic Independence for Women: The Foundation for Equal Rights* (1976)—dealt with the economic condition of women, a condition which is still characterized by poverty, low wages, tax and social security disincentives, and credit discrimination. The present volume, though independent of the first, is related. It turns the spotlight on women in the family, in which her status, for the most part, is still one of dependency. It takes as a basic premise, therefore, that equal rights for women cannot be achieved until the legal, economic, and social dependency of married women is significantly reduced. The purpose of the present volume is twofold, namely: (1) to dissect the impact of the institutions of marriage and family on women and (2) to present alternative forms of affiliation and family formation, reforms in legal and other institutions, and policy implications for the emergence of egalitarian marriage-family styles.

WOMEN INTO WIVES

Most women who have ever lived have become wives sometime or other during their life. The actual proportion has waxed and waned. John T. Noonan estimates that as many as 60% to 65% of all adult women, including those who would marry later as well as those who would never marry, might be living outside of marriage at any one time in some countries. The proportion of women who married waned in Europe in the 19th century and waxed in the United States in the 20th, until all but 3% or 4% of all adults married at one time or another. For the most part, therefore, the history of women has been the history of wives. Their status has also waxed and waned, declining noticeably with industrialization. Still, the transformation of women into wives has remained the common obligation of parents, church, and school, and it has continued to be the universal experience of practically all women. The transformation has not always been easy to achieve. The process begins early in childhood and extends for as long a period of time as necessary. Even beyond marriage if need be.

"What difference does a piece of paper make?" the young man asks; "we love each other." This is a fairly common position today with young people living together without legal wedlock. Actually, we know that the piece of paper makes a great deal of difference both in the relationship itself and in the law that defines it. We read from time to time, for example, of couples who, after living together for some time, decide to marry and then find, much to their surprise, that the relationship has actually changed. The piece of paper that legally transformed the woman into a wife and the man into a husband has changed their expectations of each other. What was a voluntary gift, freely offered and appreciatively received, becomes an obligation, taken for granted and therefore less appreciated. But even more is changed by the piece of paper. All kinds of legal obligations are assumed; property relations become involved. The piece of paper itself is the end result of a long transformation process that has been going on since the girl was a small child. She was destined to accept it.

Because it is taken for granted at the birth of a girl-child that she will become a wife, we have taken great pains to prepare her for that end. She has had to learn to please men in order to be chosen to be a wife. Whatever men wanted she has had to become—sweet, compliant, complaisant, self-abnegating, subordinate, and, of course, as pretty and sexually attractive as possible. As a wholly secondary goal she might, if she wanted to, do things that pleased herself—provided that they did not in any way deter her from the major goal of becoming a wife. The urgency of becoming a wife has been highlighted by the fact that there have been few times in history when there has been any place for large numbers of women without men—except in convents, brothels, or in the homes of others as put-upon dependents.

Even so, it has taken a lot of processing and "psychological work" to make women eager accepters of the status of wife. The glorification of marriage has had to be built into our society. One way has been to profess great respect, even reverence, for the role of wife, to accord it high moral, if not legal, status. Still, despite the high status professed for it, the wife has, since the 18th century, suffered a relative loss of status. In Congreve's *The Way of the World,* for example, Mistress Millamant bargains with Mirabel about the terms of their marriage, promising that, if he conceded to her demands, she would willingly "by degrees dwindle into a wife"; he, in turn, replies that, if she will meet his terms, he may be "enlarged into a husband." Defoe's Roxana, a successful business woman in her own right, also in 18th-century England, refuses marriage even to a nobleman because "the very nature of the marriage contract was . . . nothing but giving up liberty, estate, authority, and every-thing to the man, and the woman was indeed a mere woman ever after—that is to say, a slave." Blackstone's commentaries on the common law also made quite clear that the wife suffered a profound legal loss when she married. In our own country, foreign observers of the American scene have often commented on the great social and personal freedom enjoyed by young unmarried women compared with the constraints borne by married women. (De Tocqueville in the early 19th century contrasted this American situation with that in France. The observation may still be apt.)

To transform women into wives, it has been necessary not only to glorify the status of the wife (despite its actual disabilities) but also to denigrate the status of nonwife mercilessly. The spinster or old maid has been an object of derision. "Better dead than unwed" was the way the young women of the liberation movement put it in the late 1960s. In addition, since all our institutions, including adult social activities, have been organized on a couple basis, there has been no provision for the unattached. The woman without a man has been deprived of a large measure of social life.

With so much pressure put upon them, it is understandable that women have accepted, even sought, the role of wife with all its disabilities. The alternatives have been grim. Only now have there begun to emerge alternatives attractive enough to make women question the status of wife.

WOMEN INTO HOUSEKEEPERS

In our society, becoming a wife means—or has meant—that a woman changes her occupation from whatever else she has been doing to housekeeping. Or it has meant adding housekeeping to whatever else she has been doing. The double role—which seemed such a liberating idea when it was used at mid-century to counteract the woman's-place-is-in-the-home ideology—has boomeranged. For so long as the two-role ideology does not apply to the husband as well as to the wife, the woman carries a double load which all too often means overload. Nor does the reduction of economic dependency always improve her legal status. In a legal sense she is still disadvantaged in many ways.

WOMEN INTO MOTHERS

For most women, though perhaps a declining proportion, wifehood has also until recently meant motherhood. Even small children know that. Enormous pressures have been exerted on women to make them want to have children. Only within the last few years has it become permissible to state that one does not wish or intend to have children or, as a recent poll indicated, that one would not have children if one had it to do over again. The experience of motherhood makes this understandable. In other writings I have pointed out that the way in which we have institutionalized motherhood in our society is probably the worst possible way to do it—for mothers, for children, and for fathers.

The way in which we institutionalize motherhood not only makes women the exclusive caretakers of children but also makes this care their exclusive occupation. The mother having the exclusive care of children deprives the children of more care by the father and other adults; having this care as her exclusive occupation deprives the mother of the opportunity for wider participation in other activities. Both of these aspects of motherhood underline her dependency.

Indeed, both of these consequences of becoming a wife—taking on a whole new occupation instead of or in addition to one's regular occupation, as well as assuming also the responsibilities of motherhood—have had the effect of increasing the dependency of women. Such dependency can be not only economically but also psychologically dysfunctional.

THE DYSFUNCTIONALITY OF DEPENDENCY: DEPRESSION

Of growing concern to those interested in public health today is the relatively high incidence and prevalence of depression among women in our society. There are numerous theories invoked to explain this disturbing fact. One theory finding considerable acceptance among researchers holds that feelings of powerlessness seem to be associated with depression. The powerlessness theory of depression is borrowed from experiments on animals in which the experimental animal learns to respond in a certain way in order to receive food and then finds, as the experimenter changes the rewarded situations, that there is no way in which the rewards are related to its behavior. Under these conditions the animal will show behavior remarkably similar to depression in human beings —becoming listless, apathetic, withdrawn.

It has been pointed out that women, socialized to accept dependency, are especially vulnerable to such feelings of powerlessness. And there is some reason to believe that married women feel more so than never-married. In *The Future of Marriage* (1972, 1973) I summarized a considerable corpus of research which seemed to indicate that the mental health of never-married women was better than that of married women. The research since that time has expanded our understanding of this phenomenon. It has been found, for example, that never-married women living as heads of households with good incomes show the lowest level of depression, whereas never-married women living as dependents show extremely high levels of depression. This finding suggests that dependency is a contributing factor to the relatively poorer mental health of married, as compared to never-married, women.

CHANGES IN PROCESS

Something is happening to marriage today. This is not surprising; something is always happening to marriage. But the changes taking place today differ in that they seem to be coming exceptionally fast. All of a sudden we have to change a host of preconceptions, assumptions, clichés, stereotypes that we have always taken for granted. We rub our eyes in disbelief. The facts just do not fit the old clichés. Young women not so eager to get married? Can't be.

Marriage better for men than for women? Impossible. The bachelor not so well off? The unmarried woman not so badly off? Women living alone and liking it? Cannot be.

The decline in the first-marriage rate began some years back. For a while it was obscured by the fairly high remarriage rate, which made the overall marriage rate appear high. But now even the remarriage rate seems to have leveled off, so that in 1974 both the number and the rate of marriages fell; the same was also true for 1975. The 1975 figure was 4% lower than the 1974 figure. What this change means is not yet altogether clear. Are these young women merely delaying marriage? Are they substituting other kinds of relationships for marriage? That most women will marry some time or other can still be taken for granted. But exactly what proportion is not certain. Nor is it certain exactly what kind of marriages they will enter.

The decline in the birth rate has also been marked in recent years. Beginning in the late 1950s, the decline has continued until the number, as well as the rate, in 1975 was lower than in 1974. Since in the immediate future there will be more young women than there are today in child-bearing ages, especially 20-29, the number of births may be expected to go up. But the fertility rate, that is, the number per wife, may not. Indeed, an increasing, though still small, number of young women state that they do not intend to have any children at all.

Even more interesting are the changes in opinions, attitudes, and sex-role concepts that are now taking place. Little girls in the primary grades, though they fully expect to become mothers, do not think in terms of excluding all other careers. They take in stride the idea that they will also have jobs. They do not fit the old stereotypes still common in their textbooks of passive, dependent little creatures always having to be rescued by strong, adventurous boys. The fifth-grade girls and boys are already thinking in egalitarian terms. The boys are already beginning to make a bow in the direction of acknowledging the rights of girls. And a woman is quoted in the daily press who cannot see "love and commitment in marriage separate from independence and freedom" (*Washington Post,* November 15, 1976).

Changes are already beginning in the law. And questions are beginning to loom large in policy also. What kinds of policies dealing with marriage do we want? How can we evaluate them? How can we anticipate their consequences? How much will change cost? This book does not pretend to supply all the answers. But it goes a long way toward clarifying the questions.

GIRLS INTO WIVES

RAPHAELA BEST

The data on changes in sex-role socialization on which the present
study is based, cover a three-year period in one elementary school,
Pine Hill, in one of the most affluent counties in the country. The
original data were collected in 1972-1973 when the children were in
the primary (first, second, and third) grades at Pine Hill.[1] The
purpose had been to test the hypothesis that membership or
nonmembership in the boys' peer group affected the learning
process.[2] But it soon became evident that the data were telling us
more about sex roles and socialization than about academic
achievement. The children in the primary grades organized their
worlds in different ways—boys needed groups, girls needed friends
—and the differences had dramatically telling effects on their lives.
The focus is on the group of 40 children who were 8-9 years old and
in the third grade during the first or base year of the study and who
were 10-11 years old and in the fifth grade at the time of this report.

During the first two months of the study, the children had seemed
very much like other 8-9 year old children whom I had known in the
past. The boys fought among themselves to prove they were men;
they played ball games whenever they could, and they played to win;

AUTHOR'S NOTE: I am deeply grateful to Jessie Bernard for the guidance, encouragement,
and constant support that she provided during the three years of this study. She listened for
endless hours as I reported to her what I had learned day by day, week by week, month by
month, and year by year, and she asked the questions for which I tried to supply answers.
The study was begun at her urging, and with her help it reached this stage. It is not finished:
it will be finished only when the children in the study are no longer children who can be
studied.

they proudly displayed injuries, scars, and bloody noses, and the stayed away from girls and girls' activities as much as possible. The girls walked hand in hand from one place to another; they helped the teacher with classroom chores; they argued with friends and they made up; and they chased and kissed the boys as often as possible. These sex differences were by no means casual or incidental. The boys and girls lived in quite different ambiences. The differences were the result of relentless pressures.

THE BOYS

There was a tacit assumption between parents and teachers and between parents, teachers, and boys at Pine Hill that they—the boys—would someday be breadwinners and thus must get a good start in life: that is, that they must get a good education and good grades when they are young in order to assure themselves of good jobs when they are older. It was also understood by parents, teachers, and the boys that successful competition with peers, whether in schoolwork or at play, indicated that a boy would be able to compete successfully with peers when good jobs and high salaries were at stake. Thus, the daily message that the boys received from the school and from parents was: Learn more now to earn more later.

And it was not only the school and parents who made it clear to boys that they were men and expected to behave like men. Daily messages from the media, from books, from magazines, and from the community reinforced the idea that a boy was a man from infancy to senior citizen. "A man can't go out the way he came in, Ben; a man has to add up to something," Willie Loman told his friend in *Death of a Salesman.* The training or education that a boy receives in school is the major way that society contributes to helping a boy to add up to something. The burden of adult status is imposed on the boy much earlier than on the girl. A boy must conform to society's expectations for appropriate sex-role behavior long before that expectation is imposed on girls. Hartly (1959) tells us:

Demands that boys conform to social notions of what is manly come much earlier and are reinforced with much more vigor than similar attitudes with respect to girls . . . and at an early age, when they are least able to understand either the reasons for or the nature of the demands. Moreover, these demands are frequently enforced harshly, impressing the small boy with the danger of deviating from them, while he does not quite understand what they are.

The boys in the primary grades were aware that from the moment of birth a boy is considered a man. "We're not boys, we're men," was a frequently heard response when the teacher referred to them as boys. But it is a role for which society has given the 5-, 6-, 7-, 8-, or 9-year-old boy few clues and no appropriate models. A boy that young cannot bring home a paycheck each week as his father does. A boy cannot topple mountains or lift trains from their tracks as the Bionic man does. A boy cannot even decide for himself when he should go to bed in the evening or whether or not he should go to school on any given day. The major decisions in a young boy's life are made by people more powerful than he, his parents. All a small boy has to prove that he is a man is his gender identity and his peer group.

Since "Daddy's little man" is expected to prove beyond doubt that he is worthy to be called a man, he turns to his peer group—the only source available to him—for clues. The answers that he gets from peers are not enough, for they, too, are searching for a definition of maleness. At Pine Hill the boys developed their own definition. They created their own rules for achieving the status of a Man and they applied those rules for sex-role behavior to themselves and to others. They rewarded the boys who met the criteria that they had established, and they punished the boys who did not. It was a harsh world that they created, but it was also a harsh world that denied them assistance as they groped their way toward an understanding of appropriate sex-role behavior.

From the first grade to the fifth grade, the way in which boys defined maleness affected their relationships with the girls who shared their classrooms. In the primary grades a boy who sought acceptance from his peers could not risk friendship with a girl, for, as David and Brannon (1976:13) tell us, the earliest lessons that a boy learns is: "Don't be like girls, kid, be like . . . like . . . well, not like girls." Two years later, when the third-grade boys were fifth-graders, compromises were being made with girls, and the early definition of maleness as being as unlike anything female as possible showed signs of change.

THE GIRLS

In contrast to boys, girls were being socialized to be women who would please others, to be sweet and good and not make waves, a seemingly simple task compared with the demands placed on boys for constant successful performance in the classroom and on the playground. They were rewarded for helping with classroom housekeeping chores such as washing the boards and sinks and keeping the supply closets neat and tidy. They were rewarded for excellence in school work with praise and hugs and for poor academic performance with encouraging words and hugs. At Pine Hill the academic performance of girls created much less concern than did the academic performance of boys, for it has long been noted among educators that few girls fail to achieve academically in elementary school.

Since girls could be trusted to obey school safety rules and since their behavior rarely created a disturbance of any kind, they were less closely watched than were boys. They were thus learning not only to be dependent but also to be invisible. While boys played on the major playground areas carefully marked for a variety of ball games, the girls played on the fringe areas near the school. And it was the boys' games that were carefully monitered for signs of trouble. The girls faded unnoticed into the background. The consequence was to process them for acceptance of passive adult roles.

There is, however, a hidden danger in socializing girls for dependency and invisibility, for as Jessie Bernard (1975:39) warns us:

> Dependency, a "dispensation from the terms of adulthood" becomes counterproductive when the girl becomes a woman. The helplessness that is so cute in the girl becomes ridiculous in the woman. The inability of the bride to balance a checkbook may be adorable, her tears appealing, but at some point her dependency becomes an incubus rather than a charm, a bore, not to say a nuisance—not to say a real drag on a relationship. For there is a hidden joker in the way we socialize boys and girls.

IMAGES

The messages that reinforced these stereotypical images of males and females came not only from parents and teachers and from the media and the community but also from the very textbooks that the children used in their daily classrooms. Jeana Wirtenburg (1976) has reviewed the available literature and has given us a clear picture of the damaging effects of sexism in textbooks, especially for girls and women. Beginning with Child, Potter, and Levine in 1946 and continuing through 1975, Wirtenburg found that, then as now, "three themes emerge which still characterize the inferior and inadequate treatment of females in textbooks": (1) the invisibility of the female, (2) the stereotyping of the female, and (3) the inferiority of the female.

> Men were shown much more often in occupational roles, as well as in a much wider range of occupations. The few times that women were shown to appear in occupational roles, these were limited to only the most sex-typed occupations (e.g., teacher, nurse). . . . Males exhibited far more aggressiveness, problem-solving, physical activity, cleverness, heroism, elective generosity, unearned rewards, adventurousness, and imagination than did females. Females consistently demonstrated more passivity, dependence, self-sacrificing altruism, goal restriction, domesticity, incompetence, and victimization by the opposite sex, than did males. . . . "Girls collapse into tears, betray secrets, and act upon petty and selfish motives." Besides their lack of character, females are shown to be lazy, incompetent, lacking in ability to think for themselves and to act on their own initiative. Boys are frequently shown rescuing older girls and women from situations, clearly indicating their superiority. [pp. 19-21]

Those images—damaging though they were to both boys and girls—were unchallenged, because the potential danger of the sexism in textbooks had yet to be brought to the attention of teachers in the school. Even today, three years later, book companies have not made a serious attempt to correct the problem, and teachers are not willing to give up their textbooks, for, however sexist they might be, they are considered better than nothing. Only when a book has been "withdrawn" from the approved list of textbooks do book companies listen to demands for change. This, then, was the situation in the base year of this study. The children expounded the traditional beliefs about appropriate male-female roles as they had been taught to do.

This, at any rate, was how it would have seemed on the surface to a casual observer. It was even how it seemed to the teachers of these children. But beneath the surface of stereotypical boy-girl behavior a revolution was in progress. The boys were the first to suspect that something was amiss, for many of the girls did not behave properly. They did not seem to know their place in the scheme of things. The reality of the girls' behavior did not fit the stereotype, and this created considerable conflict for the boys. When they should have been playing with their dolls, they were playing ball with the boys, and often they played the game better than many of the boys. In fact, some of the girls were so successful at playing ball that a boy team captain who valued winning the game more than he valued the stereotypes of what girls should or should not do often recruited the better girl players for positions on his team. But they could just as often be annoyed at the sight of a girl playing ball as was the third-grade boy who said, "Girls should play their own games and leave boys' games alone." There was also the fear that girls might abandon the kitchen if they spent too much time having fun on the ball field. "Girls should stay at home and cook and clean," said another third-grade boy. But now the girls were marching to the tune of a different drummer. "Boys are crazy to think we like to play with dolls or cook and clean," said the girls.

In the past, girls have been permitted a great deal of freedom in their early childhood years, but there came a time when they were expected to exchange their ball and bat for a needle and thread and a cookbook. In the literature beloved by children there is no more vivid example of this than that of *Caddie Woodlawn*, who grew up on the Wisconsin frontier in Civil War days. After 12 years of adventurous life with her brothers—learning to plow rather than to sew—she is told that she must grow up into a woman. On the day that Caddie must give up her exciting, interesting life, she and her brothers play a joke on a cousin from New England, but only Caddie is singled out for punishment. "That a *daughter* of mine should so far forget her hospitality to a guest—that she should be such a hoyden as to neglect her proper duties as a lady! Shame to her! Shame!" But it is Caddie's father who makes it clear to her the role she must accept:

> It's a strange thing, but somehow we expect more of girls than of boys. It is the sisters and wives and mothers, you know, Caddie, who keep the world sweet and beautiful. What a rough world it would be if there were only men and boys in it, doing things in their rough way! A woman's task is to teach them gentleness and courtesy and love and kindness. It's a big task, too, Caddie—harder than cutting trees or building mills or damming rivers. It takes nerve and courage and patience, but good women have those things. A woman's work is something fine and noble to grow up to, and it is just as important as a man's. But no man could ever do it so well. . . . Do you think you would like growing up into that woman now? How about it, Caddie, have we run with the colts long enough?

If that was the message heard by the girls at Pine Hill, they rejected it, for they had heard another message that told them they had a choice: they could continue to run with the colts and still be mothers and wives. They had invaded the boys' world and found it more exciting, more adventure-filled, and more rewarding than cleaning the house or sitting in a rocking chair. They had everything, and they knew it, for later in the fifth grade they were to say, "We're girls but we're boys, too. I mean we're both girls *and* boys." And, indeed, they were. They knew about the women's liberation movement and they said that "We have women's liberation now and things are going to be different." Their determination to share the work and the fun, the costs and the rewards, changed the behavior of the boys. "We'll compromise," they said, "we'll do things together." In this chapter, without for the moment attempting to explain them, we trace the changes noted in the children between the base and last year of this study.

THE GIRLS AND BOYS OF THE PRIMARY GRADES

THE FIRST GRADE: MOTHER'S WORK, WIFE'S WORK

The first-grade children were intimately bound to their homes and to their school. The primary adults in these two worlds—mother, father, and teacher—comprised the center of the world around which they revolved, and throughout the year they remained more adult- than child-oriented. This did not mean they were not aware of their peers—they were acutely aware of each other—but for all of their year in first grade they clung more to familiar adults for protection and reassurance than they did to each other.

The first-grade girls had come to school with firmly established ideas about the kind of work that a mother did and the kind of work that a wife did. They revealed their perceptions of these two roles when they role-played "mother" and "wife" in the popular "house" game. They knew that the mother role was different from the wife role. Both were fun, but they did not overlap. And the role of mother far outweighed the role of wife in their play. In this emphasis they were confirmed and reinforced by their textbooks, in which mother was always a cheerful playmate of children, whereas the role of wife was never discussed. This relative emphasis is understandable in light of the reluctance that adults tend to experience in dealing with the personal relations between the sexes. First, then, the child's concept of the mother role.

Being a mother was fun. The children were firm on that point. How could it be otherwise? Their mothers had been playing with them for years. Being a mother was, obviously, being a playmate. And it was clear that this fun was reserved for girls. The script gave mother all the good lines, so it was not surprising that the first-grade girls argued and fought among themselves for the privilege of playing that role. It was also not surprising that no boys ever indicated a desire to play the mother role, for the fun of being mother was less attractive to them than the authority that they assumed when playing the father role.

The children not selected for either parent role played the "children" in the family, and from their play it was obvious that being a child meant being under their age, six, although they were driven to school each day by their mother. Perhaps they perceived a "child" as being a five-year-old kindergartner and not a six-year-old first-grader. Since they were very young, they could crawl on the floor and misbehave—something no mature first-grader would be found doing. The reward for misbehaving—and it was perceived as a reward—was a spanking, while the reward for being "good" was a hug or a kiss or both. These rewards were greatly appreciated, for they meant that they could touch and be touched.

The children often used the term "housewife," and it referred not to the work of the wife but to the work of the mother. In the "house" game it was "mother" who drove the "children" to school, cooked, washed the clothes, ironed, cleaned the house, sewed, fed the children and put them to bed. When they wrote stories about their future lives, many girls said that they wanted to be "housewives" to take care of their children, to do the housework. A housewife was not a wife who worked at home; she was a mother who worked at home. Here are two of their stories:

> Housewife
> I want to be a housewife.
> I can help my children.
> I can help my children learn to read and write.
> > by Sally

Housewife
Mothers clean the house.
"Time for bed children!"
I will feed my children.
by Karen

In their textbooks and at home, the first-grade girls had been provided with models which provided them with a superficial understanding of a mother's work in the home, but they had no models at all to guide them in understanding a wife's role. All that the girls knew was what they had been able to see for themselves; no one discussed these roles with them. This denial of a girl's right to know about the complex features of the mother and wife roles was as serious a deprivation as the denial of the boy's right to know about the appropriate male role for a six-year-old. They revealed their limited perceptions of these roles in the "house" game, in which a mother played with her children, and a wife hugged and kissed her husband.

As seen through the children's eyes, the wife's role was free of stress, glamorous, delightful, and fun-filled from dusk to dawn. Here is how Christine, a six-year-old "wife," her "husband," and "children" viewed wedded bliss.

Christine had just finished her day as "mother." Her "children" had not wanted to go to bed, so she had had to chase them around the classroom until one by one she had caught them, spanked them, and, with a final word of warning to "stay there," had put them to bed. For fully twenty minutes Tony, Christine's "husband" and "father" to her children, had displayed unusual patience for a boy only six years old, for he had sat unmoving on a chair as he waited for Christine to finish with her obligations to their children and to join him as his wife.

When that moment finally arrived, Christine and Tony joined hands, giggled, and crept behind the large blackboard which hid the coat rack area from the view of the rest of the classroom. There Christine and Tony, snuggled under the dozen or so coats they had pulled over them, hugged and kissed. When their observant teacher noticed that they were not with the other children, she quickly began to look for them. Their giggles and their feet sticking out from under the coats revealed their hiding place. "What are you doing?" she asked as she removed the coats from their bodies. "Playing house," they answered. "Let's play house in the classroom where I can watch you and see that you don't get hurt." The two children joined the other children in the classroom. The "house" game was not resumed, and the children playing the three major roles dispersed to play other games with other children.

With all of the emphasis on motherhood and housework in the books that they used in their classrooms and with their own interest in role-playing in the "house" game, it is surprising that only three first-grade girls opted exclusively for careers as housekeepers and mothers. The rest wanted careers outside the home as well. With the exception of Terri, who said that she wanted to be a football player, all the career choices had one thing in common: they were the so-called helping professions. The first-grade girls had chosen to be teachers, nurses, or pet keepers (pet store owners) so that they could help others.

Although they never role-played "nurse" or "pet keeper," being the "teacher" in the "school" game was second in importance only to being the "mother" in the "house" game. Again, the leading role, that of the "teacher," always fell to a girl, although there were male teachers in the school to serve as role models for the children. Following the pattern set in the house game, unruly pupils were rewarded with spankings, while "good" pupils were rewarded with hugs and kisses. For the boys these two games were important sources of physical contact, for only by pretending to be someone else—children younger and therefore less subject to rigid masculine requirements—could they permit themselves to accept the affectionate gestures doled out by girls. For girls these games were important, for they permitted them to be both nurturing—and therefore feminine—and in charge. Here is how two first-grade girls expressed their reasons for wanting to be a teacher and a nurse.

> Teacher
> I want to be a teacher.
> A teacher helps the children.
> A teacher wants children to learn to read and write.
> by Sally

> Nurse
> I want to be a nurse.
> Nurse helps the doctor.
> Doctor gives medicine to people.
> Nurse helps doctor.
> by Jennifer

Even when Tammy added a touch of glamor to the job done by a nurse, helping was still the important function to be performed —important because it was a female virtue.

Nurse
I want to be a nurse.
Sometimes a nurse
Gets to take care of movie stars.
by Tammy

One first-grade girl, Terri, did not make the traditional and approved career choice for a female. For her sin she suffered the insulting laughter of her peers. Terri was an exceptionally bright child. Testing showed that at six years of age she read on a sixth-grade level. She preferred blue jeans to dresses, ball games to hopscotch, and she preferred playing in her fort in the woods to playing with dolls at home. She was the perfect candidate for the nickname "tomboy." When the children wrote stories about their future careers, Terri wrote:

Football Player
I want to be a football player.
Some of the time one of the players
Has to kick the ball.

When, along with all the other stories written by the children in the class, the teacher read Terri's story the children—both boys and girls—laughed. Some of the boys rolled on the floor and held their sides to emphasize their scorn. A girl football player? Ha! Ha! Ha! But when the teacher read Michael's paper, those same children did not laugh, although Michael claimed that he was already a football player. A boy of six a football player? Why not? Nothing strange about that. Here is Michael's story.

Football Player
I am a football player.
I am in a football game.
I can get a touchdown too.
I play foxy football.

No young voices laughed. No one rolled on the floor to emphasize his or her amusement. Boys and football go together like girls and doll carriages, so there was nothing in Michael's claim that seemed to the children to be out of step with what they knew about the world as it should be. That Michael had never been in a real football game in his life and that his brand of football would be unacceptable to older children were unimportant. The important thing was that football was a male thing, and Michael was a male child. These same children who respected Michael's claim showered hooting disrespect on Terri, who they thought should have known that female children cannot hope to find a place in an exclusively male game or career.

It is not easy to assess how many Terris have been discouraged and even shamed into accepting traditionally approved roles for girls while in their hearts they yearned for the sweat, the competition, and the mud of the football game. Their number is, no doubt, legion, but this Terri will not be among them, for two years later she still staunchly maintained that she would play football when she grew up. She was not a child to give up easily.

THE SECOND GRADE: GIRLFRIENDS, BOYFRIENDS, AND DIVORCE

In the second grade, the "house" and "school" games passed from the scene. Now, a year older, the second-grade children moved their center of interest from their homes and classrooms to the outer world. Older children in the school and in their neighborhood began to have an impact on their lives. Whereas the first-grade children play-acted only mother and father roles, other ways that the sexes related to one another were becoming manifest to the second-graders. Child-child as well as adult-child factors became more salient.

The second-graders at Pine Hill had observed that young adults of one sex were often intensely interested in young adults of the other sex. In their own homes, older siblings spent considerable amounts of time talking on the telephone with boyfriends and girlfriends, and these terms had become household words. Even a few older children at Pine Hill had begun to date, for dating, once considered appropriate only for mature adults, is now practiced by some 10- and 11-year-old children.

It was not strange, then, that the second-grade children should seek to emulate this relationship between the sexes as they struggled to be considered "grown-up." From among their classmates they chose "boyfriends" and "girlfriends," and they referred to one another in those terms. In some cases the boys and girls mutually agreed to use these terms when referring to one another, but in other cases the choices were made unilaterally, with no mention of intent to the chosen children.

In no instance did the use of the terms imply that children of the two sexes would spend more time with one another, for in actual practice the second-grade boys gradually distanced themselves from the girls until they became two distinct groups in the classroom and on the playground. Whereas the first-grade children had sat side by side at the lunchroom tables, the second-grade boys clustered at one end of the lunch table, leaving the other end for the girls.

Still, a considerable amount of time was spent discussing their new status vis-à-vis each other and much good-natured teasing went on among themselves. Boys teased boys, and girls teased girls, and on occasion they teased each other. Some boys, when teased, first denied, then admitted that they had "girlfriends," while the girls never denied that they had "boyfriends." Having a "girlfriend" or a "boyfriend" was not a disgrace; it was not having such a relationship that marked a child unpopular.

Because the primary children sought to reproduce in their play the relationships that they had observed between adults and older siblings, it is interesting to note that they did not play-act divorce. In every classroom at Pine Hill there were one or more children whose parents were either divorced or divorcing. The children spoke freely of parents (usually fathers but not always) no longer living in the home. Why, then, did not the first-grade children play-acting "mother" and "father" roles occasionally divorce rather than engage in hugging and kissing to the exclusion of other kinds of relationships between married people? There are two possible answers. First, perhaps children that young have no clear perception of the kind of behavior permitted divorced or divorcing people, or, second, perhaps they understand that behavior very well and knew that it would not be welcomed or rewarded by their peers as an acceptable substitute for hugs and kisses. Or a third, and perhaps more important, reason might be that neither the first-grade children nor the second- or third-graders had husbands or wives in any but a play-acting situation. When the game ended, the relationship also ended.

Children, then, do not divorce because they do not marry, or, at any rate, most primary aged children do not marry. At Pine Hill in the first year of this study there was an exception to the general rule, for two second-grade children, Jim and Julia, did marry. Not in a church nor by the justice of the peace but by mutual consent. They did not set up housekeeping, but they did set up a system of mutual care and concern. Like many marriages today, this one began with great hope and loving words, but, also like many marriages today, it ended in divorce. For both children there were tragic consequences, but the loss of a wife had longer-lasting negative effects on Jim than did the loss of a husband on Julia.

Jim's first year and a half in school had been marked with failure. He had had difficulty learning to read. The boys in his peer group had not chosen him as a desired companion, and he received few rewards from them, although he tried very hard to prove himself a man. Jim's physical beauty was not an asset to him in his peer relations, but an outsider would have been immediately attracted to this exceptionally handsome boy.

In contrast to Jim, Julia was one of the most popular children in the class. The girls liked her because she was an affectionate friend and often devised new games for them to play. The boys liked her because she was an asset on the ball team, and, as one or another of them often said of her, "She can fight better than any boy except me." In December, this aggressive, tomboyish, dark-haired little girl gave blue-eyed, blond Jim her picture which she had inscribed with the words, "To Jim with love, Julia."

If Jim had had satisfactory relationships with his peers, the boys in his class, he might have accepted Julia's picture without comment and then, perhaps, casually referred to her as his "girlfriend." But Jim needed the recognition that Julia offered him, so he bragged openly about the picture to others. After a few days of publicly acknowledging that they were "in love," Jim asked Julia to be his wife, and Julia accepted. Then, they no longer used the terms "boyfriend" and "girlfriend" to refer to each other. Now they were "husband" and "wife."

When Julia organized a successful chasing game on the playground, she named Jim First Captain of the game and took the Second Captain position for herself. Asked about this, she explained that, since Jim was her husband, he should be the First Captain. Julia's friends, both boys and girls, accepted Jim without question. She was a powerful girl. She could and did enforce her will on others.

About this time, Julia took charge of Jim in the classroom as well as on the playground. She helped him with his seat work and insisted that he finish his assignments each day. It seemed that Jim would have a successful year despite his poor beginning. Then, on a day in late February, Jim came to school seeking answers to questions about divorce. "Are you divorced?" he asked many adults in the school. "Sonny and Cher are divorced," he mused to himself. In the middle of that morning Jim suddenly confronted Julia with the words, "I divorce you! I don't love you any more!"

After a few attempts at reconciliation and just as many rebuffs, Julia stopped seeking to reestablish her relationship with Jim. Jim, meanwhile, had learned exactly how important it had been to him to have a "wife," and he attempted to replace Julia with other girls in his classroom. Now it was Jim's turn to be rebuffed. Not only could he not get another "wife," he could not even get another "girlfriend." When he asked Sherry—his "very last chance"—and she refused him, he knocked her to the floor and kicked her. Deprived of his "wife" by his rash decision to divorce her and deprived of the supportive relationships that he had had with other children vis-à-vis Julia, he became increasingly depressed. A year later Jim was placed in a class for emotionally disturbed children.

Not only had his parents divorced but Jim had had his own "divorce," and both events had happened to him when he was only seven years old. It would be interesting to know whether, after his experience, Jim grown to manhood will better understand the significance of marriage and divorce for adults. It was an experience not many, if any, seven-year-old children have duplicated.

THE THIRD GRADE: COURTSHIP BETWEEN TWO WORLDS

To the extent that it was possible, second-grade boys had segregated themselves from girls on the playground, in the classroom, and in the lunchroom. The third-grade boys, having long since segregated themselves from the female world, went even further and proclaimed their solidarity by forming an exclusively male club with in-group names and secrets. The club members declared that girls should play their own games and leave boys' games alone. They explained that they wanted girls excluded from boys' games to prevent them from being hurt. Their motives were strictly honorable. It was also their unanimous opinion that a girl's place was in the home cooking, cleaning, sewing, and "sitting around."

The boys knew how things should be, so the problem for them, then, was that that was not the way things actually were. Girls were doing the things that boys said they should not do: they were playing ball. They were also not doing the things that boys said they should do: they were not cleaning the house. Nothing the boys said or did changed the reality that girls were doing exactly what they chose to do and were getting away with it.

The girls invaded the boys' world, and they did this in two major ways: by changing gender identity and by courtship. Tracey was the first girl to become firmly entrenched in the boys' world by changing gender identity. Tracey liked the active life in which boys participated, and she regarded the role ascribed to girls as one of "just sitting around and getting fat." She preferred wearing jeans and sneakers to wearing dresses and polished shoes. She was so successful a ball player that three years later she would be named the most valuable player on a Little League team. The only obstacle to her access to the activities she preferred was that she was regarded as a girl by both peers and adults. Tracey solved the problem by petitioning the boys to accept her as a boy. The boys, the gatekeepers to gender identity, could be magnanimous when they held the power. "Okay," they told her, "you can be a boy." Later she asked to be admitted to membership in the all-male club established by the boys. "Okay," they told her, "you can belong." Throughout the four years of this study, Tracey continued to be regarded as a boy by her peers, although they used the pronoun "she" when speaking of her. "She is a boy," they would say.

But Tracey was unusual even among those few third-grade girls who played ball with the boys every day. Other girls entered the boys' world by enticing them to play a time-worn game: a chasing and kissing game. The courtship of boys was carried out through advanced negotiations. A girl would ask a boy of her choice if she could chase him on the playground at Free Play. If the boy agreed, as he usually did, then the unspoken part of the pact was that the girl would be permitted to eventually catch and kiss him. Such an arrangement made it possible for a boy to claim that he had nothing to do with the kissing part of the game. Ronnie, for example, explained his innocence when he was teased about being kissed by Nancy every day for a week:

> I'll tell you how she gets me into it, see. She chases me and I run. Then I get to a place where I can't run no more, like she chases me to the end of the hall and I'm trapped. Then she grabs me and kisses me. Man, that's fun! he exclaimed as an afterthought.

Having removed himself from any blame, Ronnie could admit that being chased and kissed by a girl was fun.

Boys who were chased and kissed by girls often pretended to be their helpless victims, as did Derek who bragged one day, "Michelle caught me and kissed me a hundred times!" Poor Derek had been caught and kissed a hundred times and had been unable to do anything to stop the assault. The boys had had as much fun as the girls when they played the kissing game, but they must have felt that they had much to lose—their macho image perhaps—if it were known that they welcomed the kisses that the girls gave them. Thus, they protected themselves from exposure by laughter, with explanations, and with denials of the pleasure that they received.

The third-grade girls, with nothing to lose, freely proclaimed their love interest in boys who shared their classroom. Much of their talk at lunch and on the playground was about boys. One day Michelle bragged that Derek had permitted her to use his pencil and eraser all morning, while Brenda said that her boyfriend had given her an engagement ring but that she was not permitted to bring it to school for her friends to see. They affectionately teased each other with the old rhymes about love and marriage, inserting a girl's name and the name of the boy that she said she loved into the rhyme. In this way they teased Michelle one day on the playground with their lusty singing.

> Denver and Michelle sitting in a tree
> K-i-s-s-i-n-g
> First comes love, then comes marriage
> Then comes Michelle with the baby carriage.

These girls, like the younger girls in the first and second grades, said that they wanted to be wives and mothers when they grew up. Sonya, who played ball with the boys every day, was no exception. She knew that being a wife was preliminary to motherhood, so she could say, "I want to be a housewife because I want to have a baby." At the age of eight, Sonya was barely past her own years as an infant, and she knew nothing of the problems that come with motherhood, yet she could say that "she wanted to have a baby." It was still viewed as a "fun" thing. Thus, Michelle could say that she wanted to be a "plain old woman wife" because it's fun, and Donna could say that she wanted to be a mother because "it's fun." They knew that having a baby somehow made a girl into a woman but beyond that they knew nothing of babies and they knew nothing of motherhood. The books and filmstrips in their classroom would tell them in detail about the work of a plumber, an electrician, a beautician, a lawyer, and hundreds of other jobs and professions, but not one book and not one filmstrip would tell them about the work required of a mother. These girls would have to learn by doing, and, unlike other learning experiences, they could not then discard it if they did not like it. Motherhood was "for keeps."

In addition to being wives and mothers these girls wanted careers outside the home, as did the younger first- and second-grade girls. But, unlike the younger girls, they made career choices which would be personally satisfying to them. The careers they chose were often not realistic, but they did introduce an important element: the eight-year-old girls were beginning to think that they deserved something for themselves. Life did not have to be only giving; they could receive also. Thus, Monica said that she wanted to be a "storekeeper with lots of candy. I would eat the candy." Another girl said that she wanted to be an actress, while still another said that she wanted to be a pilot because "I like to fly." Liking what they would one day do had for the first time become important in other than a "helping" situation.

Unlike the girls, the boys made career choices that had monetary value attached to them. They wanted good jobs which would earn them a lot of money. In the first and second grades, boys had been nearly alike in choosing policeman, fireman, mailman, and farmer as their career choices. The third-grade boys, with more exposure to career education materials, chose IBM technician, doctor, football player, government worker, and lawyer to "get a lot of money." One boy from a poor blue-collar family, possibly seeing that most high-status jobs required an expensive college education beyond his reach, said that he wanted to be a "robber," to "get a lot of money." When the boys who had chosen to be football players were asked if they had made that choice because playing football was fun, they greeted the question with scorn. "Don't you know how much money football players make? They make a lot of money, man!"

The third-grade children at Pine Hill, like the first- and second-grade children, were traditional in their approach to their future lives as adults. The boys gave serious thought to preparing for jobs that would make a lot of money. The girls looked forward to becoming women when they became wives and mothers. There was nothing in what the third-graders said or did that would account for the emergence two years later of a class of fifth-grade boys and girls who looked forward to a life of understanding and respect for each other and were willing to make concessions to each other at the age of 10 to accomplish that goal.

THE LIBERATED GIRLS AND BOYS OF THE FIFTH GRADE

Donna stood up, put her hands on her hips, and said in a very determined voice, "When I'm 18 years old I'm going to get married. If the boy I want to marry doesn't ask me, I'll ask him. I want to get married when I'm 18, and I'm going to get married when I'm 18. Why can't a girl ask a boy to marry her?" Bolstered by Donna's forthright declaration, Melanie admitted that she also wanted to marry when she was 18. "I'll have a career, too," she added. "I might even have a career first and then get married. I might even wait five months (after completing high school) before I get married."

Taken out of context, the remarks made by Donna and Melanie sound very much like the statements that they had made in the third grade when Donna had said that she wanted to get married and be a mother "because it's fun" and Melanie had said that she wanted to "sit and watch TV all day." They were still interested in marriage, but now the focus was not on housework and children but on love and sex. They liked boys; they were not ashamed to admit it. They wanted husbands whom they could share their love and their lives with. And that is what the boys also wanted. The same boys who had distanced themselves from these same girls in the third grade now found them attractive and interesting to be with. They also looked forward to the day when they could marry and share the intimacies of married life with a girl they loved.

> "Boys get to like girls at the ages of 10 and up," explained Jeffrey. "We get to like girls because they're nice, they're pretty, and they're smart. They're different from us boys." Now Jonathan interrupted to say, "They're better than boys in some ways." Asked what he meant, Jonathan explained, "Well, they're smart, and they do a lot of things." "Yeah," said Tommy, who was the oldest child in a large family, "they do all the housework and we don't have to do it." Jeffrey and Jonathan immediately silenced Tommy with the remark, "Don't say that. The girls might get mad."

Somewhere between the beginning of the third grade and now—two and a half short years—the attitudes of these young children toward the traditional roles for men and women had changed. They had learned to be honest about who they were and what they expected from life. Housework and motherhood had lost their aura of glamor for girls, and boys were willing to admit that they never did think highly of sewing, cooking, cleaning, and changing the baby's diaper. Courtship had always been conducted by

girls, but now the boys were able to admit that they liked it that
way, that they were shy about asking a girl for a date or to marry
them and were relieved to have the girls take over the painful task.
And, far from being reluctant to be led to the altar, these boys
looked expectantly toward the day—hopefully at 18—when they
could marry.

> "Boys usually want to get married at the age of 18," said Jeffrey, while
> the other fifth-grade boys said "Yeah" or nodded their heads to signify
> that they agreed with him. "Usually they don't because their parents don't
> want them to, but they want to. Boys are anxious. Maybe they like the girl
> a lot."

Recent studies have shown that girls are no longer marrying as
young as in previous years and, perhaps, not marrying at all but
opting for other kinds of relationships. The fifth-grade boys and girls
at Pine Hill said that they were eager to marry at 18 or as soon as
they had graduated from high school. Donna and Melanie had
emphatically stated that they would marry at 18 even if they had to
propose to the boy, and most, but not all, of the girls had agreed that
they would also follow this course. Jeffrey and Jonathan, as well as
all the other boys, were somewhat doubtful about their chances of
marrying at 18; they would like to, but they would obey their
parents and delay marriage if they were told to do so. The girls either
could not foresee any parental objection to their marrying at so early
an age or were sufficiently independent of parental control to make
their own wishes prevail.

Only one of the fifth-grade boys responded to Donna's declaration
that she would propose to her boyfriend if he did not propose to her;
Jonathan said, "You can't do that, it's against the law." A chorus of
girls' voices challenged Jonathan: "What law?" Donna told him,
"We've got Women's Lib now and we'll do what we want."
Jonathan's wide grin told the girls that his remark had not been made
seriously, so they did not pursue the issue. Wanting to know how
other boys felt, I asked a more or less leading question:

> "Would you mind if a girl proposed to you? Would it hurt your pride if
> you didn't have the chance to ask her first?" "No," said Matthew, "why
> should it?" "Why should a guy be embarrassed, especially if he were in
> high school or college?" said Paul. Then Jeffrey volunteered the key
> answer to the question. "Some boys are shy," he said without further
> explanation. Wanting to be sure that I fully understood the meaning of his
> words, I asked, "Do you mean that some boys are shy about asking girls to

marry them?" "Yeah," he said without elaborating on the point. "Are they shy about asking a girl to go on a date?" I asked. "Yeah," he replied. "I've noticed that boys are shyer than girls," said Laura. "All my life the boys I've known have been shyer than me." Asked if they agreed that boys are shyer than girls, all the children—both boys and girls—said that they did. Then, as if in defense of the male image, Allan added, "Some girls are shy. My little sister [aged 2] is shy. When someone she doesn't know comes near her she cries."

As third-graders these same boys had perceived themselves as masters of their universe, fearful of nothing, especially girls. Their admission of shyness, of reticence in relation to girls, was evidence of significant change. Some of the change might have been developmental, but that would not explain their progress in relation to fifth-graders of previous years. It would not explain why these fifth-grade boys were willing to relinquish some of their privileges, especially when the issue was something as unattractive as housework.

Motherhood had been the prize sought by the girls in the primary grades who, when they play-acted, practiced those skills—hugging, kissing, sewing, cooking, cleaning, and spanking—that they would later use when they had their own children. It was a glamor job which offered fun not stress, they believed. It was definitely what they wanted for themselves, and as soon as they could marry and have children they would do so. Now that they were older, they frequently had responsibility for younger siblings when their mothers were busy or absent from home for a period of time. A greater share of household tasks was also their lot. They learned through these experiences that small children can often be pesty, noisy, troublesome, and demanding of time that they would prefer to spend in some other way. Washing dishes, setting the table, or even cleaning one's own room took time away from talking with friends on the telephone or going to the bowling alley. "Housework is boring," they concluded from their experiences with the real thing, and they now knew that small children meant additional time spent in accomplishing these boring tasks.

On the subject of housework the boys admitted that they agreed with the girls. Jeffrey sagely summed up everyone's feelings on the subject when he said, "Housework is not too appetizing," and a dozen voices agreed. "Don't we know it!" sighed Elaine. "It's boring," said Laura. Tommy voiced his dislike of housework and his appreciation of girls when he followed their comments with, "Girls are great because they do all the housework so us boys don't have to do it." Children accustomed to having things move in traditional ways probably would have agreed with Tommy. His remark is similar to that of today's feminists who assert that everyone needs a wife. But Tommy was not voicing the opinions of his peers at Pine Hill and they let him know it. The girls said, "Tommy is a dope." The boys again advised him, "Don't say that. The girls don't like it." Tommy could think that if he liked, but he was not to gloat over it. He could even court a girl with the intention of handing over to her the job of keeping house for him for the rest of his life; but, as Jonathan wisely advised, if he told a girl that he preferred to put up with her as a way of getting his housework done, he probably would not find a girl who would marry him.

Since both girls and boys agreed that housework was boring and not too appetizing, who would do it? They would both do it. They would share. "The kids will do it when they're old enough," said Jeffrey, planning far into the future.

WHAT DOES A BOY WANT IN A WIFE?

What kind of woman does a boy of 10 think he will want when he's old enough to marry? We have been led to believe that boys prefer as wives girls/women who are less intelligent, less interesting, and less able than themselves but who are good listeners and have the potential to be good housekeepers and good mothers. Boys/men are reported to prefer girls/women who will remain in the home and be dependent on their husbands for all their emotional needs and their financial support. Perhaps that stereotype has never been true, or perhaps the winds of change have blown across the lives of the 10-year-old boys at Pine Hill, for girls whose qualifications would have fitted the stereotype perfectly would have been ignored by the fifth-grade boys at Pine Hill. The girls whom they most admired were bright, independent, capable people who could take care of themselves and the boys as well. They liked, as Jonathan had said, girls who were smart and could do a lot of things. The girl who made the highest marks on the spelling tests was more likely to be the girl of their choice than Longfellow's repentant speller who told the boy she had bested:

> "I'm sorry that I spelled the word;
> I hate to go above you,

> Because," the brown eyes lower fell,
> "Because, you see, I love you."

In today's fifth-grade class, this young female martyr, so admired by generations of men and women for acknowledging openly that a woman should deny herself and suppress her talents for the man she loves, would find no place in the affections of the boys at Pine Hill. They would have found her ridiculous.

If the change that took place in these children between the third and the fifth grades had been only developmental, then it would be impossible to explain why these fifth-graders were so different in their attitudes from the fifth-graders who had occupied these same classroom desks only two years earlier. A more plausible explanation is that the historical changes taking place in the United States during these years have filtered down to children in the elementary school. There is some evidence for this assumption. The two-year-old sister of one of the fifth-grade boys came to Pine Hill one day wearing a T-shirt that read, "I am a liberated woman." Other T-shirts worn by girls were inscribed simply, "Ms." And, as the girls themselves said, "We've got Women's Lib now, and things are going to be different." One sensed, listening to these children, that things would indeed be different for them when they became adults and in charge of their lives.

Only two years earlier I had played the songs from the record, "Free to Be You and Me," to all the children in the school from grades one through six. In all grade levels there had been boys who had crawled under their desks and under coats hanging on the coat racks to hide their shame and embarrassment from their peers. A male child, however young and misguided, who insisted on having a doll to hug and hold and give a bottle to was an affront to all male children and to their image of manhood. Boys had put their hands over their ears to shut out the sound of the hated story of William, a five year old, whose father had bought him every conceivable male plaything—a baseball, a basketball, a badminton set, a baseball glove—and William loved them all and was good at everything, but William said that he would trade them all for a doll he could love. William gets his doll when his grandmother comes to visit, and she tells William's father that William will one day have a baby of his own and having a doll will help him know how to care for it. When the song had ended and the boys had crept from their hiding places, they expressed their opinion of William: "That boy's crazy to want a doll."

Sandy, one of the sixth-grade girls, addressed a question to Andrew, a sixth-grade boy who had seemed seriously betrayed by William's deviant nature. "What would you do if your wife worked and you had to stay home and take care of the baby?" she asked. "You'd have to know what to do." "I won't have a wife who works" was Andrew's angry reply. "I'm going to have a job when I grow up," Sandy informed him. "I won't marry you," Andrew warned. "I don't care," she replied in a voice that revealed her confidence in herself and in her decision to choose a job over a possible marriage proposal if such a decision should have to be made. Sandy, at least, was far more liberated from the restrictions placed on the female role or even the male role than was Andrew or the other boys who shied at the thought of ever having to change a baby's diaper.

If in 1976 the fifth- and sixth-grade boys did not list "William's Doll" among their favorite songs, neither did they cringe or crawl under their desks when it was played. And it was played often. A copy of the recording was available to them, and they played it whenever they wanted. When the phonograph needle reached the song about William and his doll, the voices that sang their way through "Free to Be You and Me" continued to sing.

WHAT DOES A GIRL WANT IN A HUSBAND?

The boys had spontaneously discussed what they liked in girls/future wives, but the girls had to be asked what kind of husbands they wanted. They were delighted to be asked. "Now that's a good question," said Donna. "Yeah, this is going to be fun," chortled Michelle, gleefully rubbing her hands. Their eagerness showed that this was a subject to which they had given considerable thought and which were anxious to discuss. Why, then, had they remained silent when the boys had talked about the kind of girls they liked? Was this a topic to be discussed among girls/women only?

The fifth-grade girls approached the subject with a firmness of mind that was convincing. They rejected the old stereotype that the girl who married the doctor or lawyer had made the best marriage. They rejected the notion that a woman had everything if she had economic security for herself and for her family. They flatly rejected the image of the "happy housewife." These girls would not spend their lives in the kitchen. They wanted husbands who were "helpful" and who would not think of them only as housekeepers and drudges.

In direct answer to the question, "What do you want in a husband?" Elaine replied, "Well, that they not be crude or common. You know how boys act sometimes?" "Yeah," said all the girls. "I don't like them when they're like that," Elaine continued. Leslie interrupted to suggest "that they be helpful." "Yeah," the rest of the girls responded fervently. "And not to make us do everything we do," Barbara added. Then, the usually quiet Elizabeth said in a strong, forceful voice, "Yeah, not to think we belong in the kitchen."

In the first few minutes the fifth-grade girls had established the fact that they did not want a husband who married merely in order to have a woman to keep his house for him, to have his meals ready when he came home from work, and to wash his shirts. The attractive commercials showing the shame of the wife whose husband's shirt had "ring around the collar" and her subsequent pride when she solves the problem or showing the transcendent joy of the wife whose kitchen tile, stained yellow from months of using the wrong cleaning agent, finally produces a floor so shining that it reflects her face in its mirrorlike surface did not fool these girls. They did not believe the commercials and they did not believe the traditional mythology. Donna succinctly summed up their thoughts on the subject: "Yeah, all that stuff about the 'happy housewife.' I don't believe that, do you?" The other girls indicated that they did not believe it either. "It's a lot of pain," said Elaine.

Apparently what they did not want was more important to them than what they did want, for only after they had expressed their strong aversion to boys/men who would regard them as mere housekeepers could they talk about what it was they did want in husbands. Even then the girls had fewer set requirements for husbands than did the fifth-grade boys for wives.

"A boy should be smart," said Melanie, the most traditional of the girls, possibly thinking of her husband as someone whom she should be able to look up to rather than someone who would be her intellectual equal. Donna brushed aside Melanie's words with a display of annoyance: "Oh, I don't care about that. He doesn't have to be so smart." Laura showed more understanding: "Well, you don't want him walking around saying, 'Uh! Uh!' all the time, do you?" "No boy is that dumb," said the realistic Donna; "I just mean that he doesn't have to be anything special." "Do you mean that he doesn't have to be a doctor or lawyer or something like that?" "Yeah," said Donna; "He can be what he wants to be. It doesn't have to be anything special." "Yeah," said the other girls.

These fifth-grade girls would not be husband hunting among the summa cum laude graduates of an Ivy League university, nor was a man's bank balance the attractive feature that it once might have been. These girls wanted something that their mothers and grand-mothers would have regarded as impossible; they wanted to be regarded as people with equal rights and not as servants to their husbands. Marriage was still attractive to these girls but not under the old system of unequals sharing bed and board.

THE FIFTH-GRADE GIRLS AND MOTHERHOOD

The same realistic attitudes that prevailed when the girls discussed husbands and their roles in the family were in evidence when they discussed motherhood. They still intended to have children after they were married, but they no longer believed that being a caretaker to children was fun. They had learned about motherhood the hard way—by taking care of younger siblings in the family—and they now knew the costs that mothers pay to care for their children. Caring for younger siblings took time from other more attractive activities; they were confined to the house when they would prefer to be outside with friends; and it meant constant attention to the needs of those siblings who were too young to do anything for themselves. As Elaine expressed it, being a mother was a "lot of pain."

> "How many children do you plan to have?" I asked. "Two," said Elaine. "One," said both Elizabeth and Melanie. "I want an equal number of boys and girls," said Laura, "so if I have two girls I'll have two more kids to get two boys." Worldly wise Donna interjected, "You can't do it that way," but no one listened. "We used to live beside this woman who had 13 kids," said Elizabeth. "Gosh, what a lot of pain," exclaimed Elaine. "My mom just had four and that's a lot of pain. She can't hardly take care of even four. I do a lot of the work. Those kids are really messy, and I have to clean up after them and pick up their toys."

Two years earlier these same girls had all indicated that they would have children because it was fun. Then, they would have a lot of children, because a lot of children meant a lot of fun. Now they talked not about the joys that they would experience with their children but of the pain that they had already experienced caring for younger siblings. Yet they spoke of marriage and motherhood as if they were inevitable, as if there were no other choices that they could make. They hated the caretaker role, but they said, neverthe-less, that they would someday be mothers. Some of the girls even indicated that they believed that they could change the order of things so that all their children would take part in caring for the members of the family. And they criticized the boys who, though they said they wanted children, would not say that they would help take care of them.

> "I'm going to have a lot of fun before I get married," said Elaine; "I'm going to travel and do what I want to do before I get in pain with my children and my husband hanging on me all the time." "Me too," said Elizabeth. "I don't believe that 'happy housewife' stuff either. The kids are always causing trouble and hanging around. 'Mom, can I have a cookie?' 'Mom, can I go out and play,' and then they come in with mud on their feet. 'Mom, fix me a sandwich.' "

> "Elaine and me have everything hard," said Donna. "When I get old enough to have kids they're gonna get everything equal. I mean, if I have two kids, the oldest is not gonna have everything to do for the youngest." "I have three kids at home," said Elaine, "and I do everything for them and then I don't get to play. I have to set the table *and* wash the dishes, see," she concluded.

> "I've been doing everything since I was in first grade," said Leslie. "I had to, I was the oldest. My mom, she doesn't sit around and do nothing, but still I do a lot. Sometimes my dad goes to the car show, and then my mom has to mow the lawn. We should have some rights. My brother, David, he's in the second grade now, and he should start doing some of the work, but my mom says he's too young. I've been doing it since I was in first grade."

Though they were only 10 years old, they saw that Dad had more privileges than Mom and that Dad went to the car shows while Mom stayed home and mowed the lawn. They would not settle for the same kind of married routine. "We should have some rights," Leslie said, and all of the girls agreed. They were not going to sit home with the baby and the housework while their husbands had all the fun. They wanted husbands and marriage, but the terms would have to be different.

Would you want to have twins?" I asked, remembering that at one time having multiple births was considered a special event. "NO!" they shouted.

> "I read about this woman who had six babies at one time," Laura told us. "She had to heat six bottles. She had to put six babies in the bathtub. She had to wash diapers for six babies." "That's a lot of pain," said Elaine.

Then I reminded the girls that Jeffrey said that he wanted to have two kids and he wanted the boy to be the older so he could get a good start in life. Did two seem to be a good number of children to have? They did not answer the question. "Yeah, that's what he said," agreed Donna, "but did you notice that he didn't say anything about wanting to help with the kids? They want us girls to do all the work, and we're not going to do it!"   ·

The girls' message was clear. They would not settle for husbands who sought to confine them to their homes to the exclusion of participating in the outside world. They would have children, but they expected their husbands to share in caring for those children as well as sharing in the household tasks. A boy/man who did not agree with that philosophy of married life would not find a wife among these girls. The boys at Pine Hill were hearing the message, and they were willing to make concessions.

THE FIFTH-GRADE BOYS AND FATHERHOOD

The boys gave almost as much thought to their future roles as fathers as the girls did to their future roles as mothers. Both boys and girls viewed their roles as hard work, but there was a difference. For the girls it was the actual care of children that was hard work; for the boys it was earning enough money to clothe and feed them that was hard work. The girls had a close-up view of motherhood, whereas the boys had a far-off view of fatherhood. Fatherhood was hard work, but it wasn't pain.

> "Are you planning to have a lot of children?" I asked Tommy. "No, not a lot, but some," he said. "I'm going to have three," volunteered Jonathan. "I hope I'm going to have two boys and a girl. I want the girl to be the oldest and the boys twins, but if it comes out the other way I don't care. I want the girl to be older so the boys have a little bit of respect."

> "I only want one or two," said Jeffrey. "Kids are expensive. I want the boy to be older so he can get a good job and get a good start into life. Boys have to have good jobs for the wife and the kids and the dog and the fish and the turtle and the cat." "That's a lot of young ones," Tommy pointed out. "Boy, are you going to have to work hard to support all of those!" "I know it," Jeffrey agreed.

The care of twins posed no problems for the boys who did not have to think of diapers and bottles and formulas and baths. True, two babies require more money to maintain than one baby, but, at the age of 10, few children are able to think realistically in terms of dollars and cents. A little money seems like a great deal of money to them. Boys, like girls, had their share of household tasks—taking out the garbage, cleaning the garage—but they did not experience the care of young children. On the subject of housework, boys and girls were in agreement—"it's boring," "it's not too appetizing"—but the care of children was still viewed as a female thing. It was the girls who picked up toys scattered around the house by younger siblings, and the boys did not yet offer to help.

OPTING FOR NON-MOTHERHOOD

Tracey continued to be unique in the group of girls with whom she ate lunch each day and whom she counted among her friends. When the fifth-grade girls met to discuss marriage and motherhood, Tracey listened for a few minutes and then got to her feet looking uncomfortable and said, "I think I'll go back to my class. I don't belong here." Marriage was not of interest to Tracey at the age of 10, and neither was romance and motherhood. Later it might be, but for now Tracey did not intend to surrender her identity as a boy.

"Is Tracey still a boy?" I asked after she had left the room. "Yeah," they said. Then Donna, with an understanding and wisdom far beyond her 10 years of age, said, "Well, we're all boys. And we're girls, too. You know what I mean? We're both boys and girls. We don't want to be just girls; we want to be both." "Why?" "Well, boys get to do a lot of things. We're going to do a lot of things, too." "What kind of things?" "Well, I'm going to travel and I'm going to have a job." "Yeah," echoed Elaine, "I'm going to travel a lot. I'm going to travel all over the world. I'm going to do a lot of things."

The other girls agreed. They would be girls, but they would be boys also. Being a boy meant greater mobility: they could travel if they wished and when they wished. It meant more varied choices of leisure time activities: if men went to car shows, then they would go to car shows. It meant greater job opportunities: their career choices now covered the same range as did the career choices made by boys. They would enjoy the same privileges as men, but they would also fall in love with men, marry, and have children.

Could a boy be both a boy and a girl? He could if society did not laugh at him, but in 1976 there are still many people who would laugh at him and/or destroy him. The boys knew this. They did not choose to fight against such odds.

And what of Tracey? What choices would she make? Would she marry and have a family someday? "Well, maybe," she said in direct answer to the question. Then, as if to change the subject to one she was more comfortable with, she said, "I'm going to play Little League ball this summer. I can't wait until school's out." "When did you know that you wanted to be a boy?" I asked.

"Starting in kindergarten I decided that I wanted to be a boy. Boys' games are more fun than girls' games. Really, there are no girls' games except for playing with dolls—ugh!—or playing hopscotch. Dolls aren't exciting, and you don't get exercise. You just sit around. It's like my sister; she's so fat. She plays with dolls all the time." Then, thinking that she had been unkind to her sister and knowing that I was recording our conversation, she said, "Take that out. Just say she's plump. Boy, is she plump!"

"When I was littler, every day at recess we played Greek Dodge, and that's more fun than just sitting around. Everytime when we go home we go into this yard and play all these games. Everyone on the street plays. That's fun."

There had been no critical fingers pointed at Tracey or smirking giggles behind white linen handkerchiefs. Tracey may never be a mother, but it will be her choice, and she will not lose her friends because she made that choice. The children liked Tracey and accepted her as she was. "Tracey's really nice, and she's smart, too," Elaine complimented her and explained to me. "Thanks, 'Laine," Tracey answered with a broad smile.

WILL SHE BE PRETTY?

Looks. In 1974 the producers of *A Woman Is*—a Channel 4 TV show shown locally in the Washington, D.C., area—filmed the Finney family in their home and neighborhood. The two Finney daughters, aged 8 and 10, were shown applying their mother's makeup to their young faces while discussing boys they knew. They hoped that the boys would think they were pretty, that they would like them because they were pretty. Mrs. Finney said that she often stressed to her daughters the importance of making the most of their other attributes so that they would later be able to make choices about what they wanted to do with their lives, but the girls remained convinced that being pretty was prerequisite to being successful—that is, to being popular.

The 10- to 11-year-old girls at Pine Hill did not use makeup, nor did they indicate any interest in lipstick or eye shadow. They did not wear frilly dresses or shoes with heels. Their usual attire was pants, a shirt, and sneakers, exactly like those worn by boys. They were, however, proud of their appearance, and their jeans, jackets, and shirts were often decorated with birds, butterflies, and flowers. But so was the clothing worn by boys. If their clothing was not decorated, they often painted on their own designs. Wearing butterflies and bows was no longer the prerogative of girls only, but of boys too; and children of both sexes were proud to be complimented on their appearance.

When the boys were asked what they liked in girls, they stressed—as the men in their world also did—that they liked girls who were pretty. But, also in keeping with tradition, no girl mentioned that a boy who would interest her had to be handsome. There was, however, a break with tradition. The girls who had so often heard boys insist that girls/women had to be beautiful in order to be desirable now made a counterdemand on boys.

> "I'm going to criticize the boys now," said Donna. "They always want us to be pretty. How about them being cute? They never care about hurting our feelings telling us we *have* to be pretty. Now we're going to hurt them back." "That's right," said Leslie. "Boys don't care what a girl *is* as long as she's pretty. She can be real mean, but if she's pretty they don't even notice. Of course, if she did something real bad to him I guess he'd notice, but mostly they just don't care if she is pretty enough." "I agree," said Elizabeth. "If we have to be pretty, then they'd better be cute." "Would a boy have to wear makeup on his face to be considered cute?" I asked. "That's silly. No one cares about that anymore," said Donna. "They'll just have to be naturally cute."

The girls knew that being a pretty girl or a cute boy was not the basis on which to judge a person with whom you wanted to spend a lifetime, but if the boys wanted to play the game that way, then the girls said they would play it that way too. But, they added, they hoped that the boys would see how silly that was and change their thinking about what qualities of a girl were important and what were not important.

Bras: A status symbol. If wearing makeup was considered unimportant, wearing a bra became a desired status symbol regardless of need. But the playful manner with which girls wore their bras was a decided break with past tradition. A girl of 10 or 20 years ago would have worn her bra just as proudly, but she would not have drawn attention to it; only her best friend would have known. Pine Hill's 10- to 11-year-old bra-wearers played a game with their bras which served the purpose of drawing attention to the fact that they

had breasts. Whether they did or not was not the issue; even the most flat-chested girl had the potential for breasts, and, when one girl began to wear bras, they all wore bras.

The name of the game they played was "snapsies." One girl would pull the bra strap of another girl as far back as her outer clothing would permit and then release it so that it snapped loudly against the wearer's back. At this sound the heads of all the children in the classroom would turn in the direction of the two girls, and their giggles could be heard throughout the classroom. It was not the sound of the bra strap that brought forth the giggles. They laughed because they shared a secret: the girls wearing the bras had breasts.

The children at Pine Hill were always interested in women's breasts. Even first-graders would search the pages of *National Geographic* for pictures of women naked to the waist. Although there was a certain amount of suppressed giggling among the children who viewed the pictures, there was also an awesome interest that sent them back time and time again to the same magazines. When one child discovered a picture in a magazine, the news would spread throughout the school until everyone but the kindergartners knew where to find it.

With ongoing fascination with the female breast among the children, it was not at all surprising that a group of fifth-grade girls as liberated and unashamed of their sexuality as these girls should be so unreserved in bringing attention to their own developing bodies.

> Donna carried a large notebook clutched closely to her chest. "I'm going to have to carry this around all day," she said. "Why?" I asked. "Look," she said as she quickly dropped the notebook from her chest and just as quickly replaced it. "What am I supposed to look at?" I asked, completely bewildered. "Look again," she instructed as she dropped her notebook for a longer time. "I'm so embarrassed. Have you got any ideas about what I can do so I don't have to keep this in front of me all day? I won't be able to get any work done." Then I understood. Donna, slender as Twiggy but only half as tall, had forgotten to wear her bra.

By the middle of the morning Donna had established the fact that she had forgotten to wear her bra and she was able to put her notebook back in her desk. It had served its purpose.

KISSING

In grades one through six, whether by prearrangement or by role-playing or by theft, children had found ways to get kissed by children of the other sex. Among fifth-graders both girls and boys were interested in maintaining the kissing tradition. Kissing was great fun, and they did not want to abandon the old ways, for girls had always been made to seem to be the aggressors, and boys the innocent victims. Their position in this matter made them losers, for the sixth-grade boys, a year older and no longer shy kissed the lips of fifth-grade girls in public and in private, but mostly in public.

Sixth-graders Kristen and Barry had met on the stairway leading to the second floor. Kristen was returning to her classroom, and Barry was headed for the libary. After an initial comment or two between the two children, which could not be heard from the first floor, the two children kissed mouth to mouth, then giggled and parted. Kristen raced up the steps, and Barry skipped down them. "Are you and Kristen in love?" I asked as he passed me in the hall. "Did you see that?" he wanted to know. "Yes." "Are you mad?" "Well, it's not exactly a school-approved activity, but I suppose it's better than fighting." "I'm glad you have that attitude, because Kristen and I kiss all the time," Barry said as he proceeded toward the library.

The interest in kissing a child of the other sex became so intense among the fifth-grade girls and the sixth-grade girls and boys that a substitute teacher decided to allow them to play Spin the Bottle in the classroom as a way of showing them that there was no special miracle about kissing and that adults do not necessarily disapprove. The experiment boomeranged. The children loved the game so much that they wanted to play it all the time, and it took a major effort on the part of their regular classroom teacher to persuade them that kissing was not part of the school curriculum and, therefore, could not take place in school.

The children were interested both in taking part in kissing activities and also in being observers when other girls and boys kissed. Some children even offered to pay for the privilege of watching two children kiss.

The school librarian had gone to a meeting, and the library was dark. Some of the fifth- and sixth-grade children, considered mature enough to handle themselves in an unsupervised situation, had been permitted to go to the library to work on research projects. Fifth-grader Donna sat at a table with sixth-grader Craig. The conversation turned to girl-boy affairs. Then Mark told Craig and Donna that he would give them a quarter per minute for the length of time that they could hold a kiss without breaking apart. Donna and Craig accepted and held a kiss for two minutes before they had to break apart to catch their breath. Mark paid them 50 cents, but Donna refused to accept her part of the money. "I don't know why, but I just don't want it," she said. "I'll buy her a present with the money," Craig told the children who had gathered to watch.

MONEY

The time-worn idea that a woman should "marry up"—that is, marry a man who can support her in luxury—was not a popular one among the fifth-grade girls at Pine Hill. They stated quite firmly that the man they married did not have to be anything special like a doctor or a lawyer. It was more important to them that their future husbands should agree to mow half the lawn and that they share recreational activities—such as going to the car shows on Sunday—as well. Money was not an important issue to these girls, but the willingness to share was. Asked if they would expect their boyfriends to pay for them when they went on dates, the girls said no. "I'll pay for myself," Elizabeth said, and the other girls agreed.

Most of the girls intended to go to college or to some kind of business school after graduating from high school. They would have jobs or professional careers, and their husbands would have jobs or professional careers. Just as they intended that their husbands should share housework and child care, they intended to share the financial burden. At the age of 10 and 11, few children have any real idea of the importance of money in their lives. Nor do they fully realize that some jobs and professions offer greater financial rewards than others, although among them they had parents in a wide range of occupations from the most honored in our society to those of blue-collar workers. Their confusion about careers can be seen in the wide, and often unrealistic, choices of careers made by both girls and boys.

Donna, for example, had listed as her career choices, "architect, secretary, policewoman like Angie Dickenson, owner of a donut shop, teacher." Under her list she had drawn a few decorative lines and then had written in large manuscript letters, "CAREER-MARRIAGE-HOUSEWIFE." Another girl had chosen, "oceanographer, doctor, paleontologist, work at a restaurant." Among the boys, only one child, Tommy, made only one career choice. He said that he wanted to be a pilot, and it is interesting that this was the same career choice that he had made on an interest inventory in third grade. Matthew, in contrast to Tommy, said that he wanted to be "a psychiatrist, surgeon, truck driver, lawyer, President of the United States, football player, electrician, ham [radio] operator, cop, architect, or a librarian at the Library of Congress."

The one difference between the girls' career choices and the boys' career choices could be found in an important omission from the boys' list. All the girls except Tracey had listed marriage and motherhood-housewife, but not one boy had considered marriage and fatherhood important enough to be considered a career. The omission did not go unnoticed by the girls. "Did you notice," they asked, "that they didn't say anything about marriage?"

WOMEN'S RIGHTS: A CAMPAIGN ISSUE

In November the fifth-grade class held elections for the office of class president. Three children had been nominated to run for the office: Donna, Jonathan, and Jeffrey. Donna and Jeffrey quickly got their campaign under way, and they worked long hours to win. They appointed campaign managers, and they appointed workers to help the campaign managers. The campaign committees made posters that were hung in the halls of the school, and they made paper buttons which other children in the school wore indiscriminately. Donna ran her campaign on an issue of interest to television watchers, Truth in Advertising, while Jeffrey chose to be the Law and Order candidate.

By the middle of the week following the nominations, Donna and Jeffrey had their campaign speeches written, and both looked forward to victory on the following Monday. A poll of the voters taken by sixth-graders showed that Donna was favored to win, with Jeffrey a close second. Jonathan trailed far behind in the polls, with no apparent support from anyone. He had not even bothered to assign a campaign manager. Then, on Thursday, with only two school days until the election, Jonathan appeared at school carrying posters and campaign buttons which read, "Jonathan fights for Women's Rights." He had stayed up most of the previous night making them, and they were an immediate success. In his campaign speech he said:

> I believe that women should have equal rights with men. If a woman does the same job as a man, she should get the same pay. Women should be allowed to get as much education as a man gets. Also, if a woman is good enough to be your boss, she should have the job. How would you feel if someone said you couldn't have a job as a boss just because you're a man? That's not right. So, if I'm elected, I will see to it that women are treated

as equals with men. So vote for me, Jonathan, because Jonathan fights for women's rights.

Jonathan won by a landslide vote. Later, when he was asked why he was able to win when he entered the campaign so late, he said, "I think it was my campaign speech. People want equal rights for women, so I fought for women's rights and won."

Then Jeffrey raised an issue that would have been laughed out of school only two years earlier. "I think boys and girls should play together more, so that when we grow up we can get along together better," he said. Then he continued, "We'd have more respect for each other, and we'd get along together better." The wisdom of Jeffrey's words did not escape the other children, and they agreed that boys and girls should do more things together now, so that later they would be better companions, better husbands and wives for each other. If recent historical events have made this impact on the thinking of these 10-year-old children, they might indeed look forward to happier futures than generations of children before them.

Only two years earlier, when in the third grade, these same boys had put forth the argument that "girls should play their own games and leave boys' games alone." They had presented the moral issue. "It isn't right for girls to play boys' games. They should be home cooking and cleaning the house." And they had presented the problem of girls being the weaker sex and boys the protector of women. "Boys' games are too rough for girls," Paul had said. "Girls get hurt easy." Girls should be protected by being excluded. Jeffrey's declaration that boys and girls should learn to play together and to respect each other was positively revolutionary, and yet 20 young 10-year-olds cheered his words.

Laura had a question that she might someday ask as an adult woman: "What if the girls wanted to play one thing, and the boys wanted to play another?" Again Jeffrey's answer reflected an historical change in male attitudes toward females. "We'd compromise," he said. "Sure, we'd compromise!" Jonathan assured her. Girls and boys playing together and learning to compromise when their ideas conflicted. It was a new world and, hopefully, a better world.

THE STORY ENDS HERE: BECOMING A HOUSEWIFE

Given their choice of subject matter for a creative writing assignment, girls wrote about boys, and boys attempted to write about girls. The boys abandoned the idea when they found that they were unable to express themselves on paper without feeling "silly." Instead they chose to write about safer subjects like scuba diving and Unidentified Flying Objects. Tommy explained, "I was going to write about my love life, but I don't have any love life, so I thought I'd write about the Loch Ness Monster." Neither the girls nor the boys attempted to write about careers. It might have been that they had said all they could about careers, since that topic was a favorite one for teachers to assign children as writing projects. Laura's story covered the life of a girl from kindergarten to adulthood.

The All-Age Book with Boys

Introduction

Well, let's start in Kindergarten. I'm 10, and it's best starting when you're young. I'm starting this book April 2, 1976. It will be about girls in different stages of their lives with boys. *The story ends with becoming a housewife.* [Emphasis added.]

Kindergarten

In kindergarten you go through a stage when you start to like boys, but boys don't like you. They run around and call you cooties.

First Grade

In first grade you still like boys, and then they sure hate you. And they interfere with your work, and you really go down in your work. Boys really hate you until second grade.

Second Grade

In second grade you like boys and they like you. They chase you and try to kiss you but are not serious about it. Then your work kind of goes up again. You think you're really serious about liking boys, but you're not serious yet. You'll have to wait until fifth grade.

Third Grade

In third grade you really felt no need for liking boys, but you still liked them, and they still liked you, and that's when their work goes down. You are the age when you really don't get serious but kind of. You do your work most of the time, but sometimes you care for the boys. They call you almost every day, and sometimes you get sick of them when they act dumb. But most of the time they give you tic tacs and are very nice.

Fourth Grade

In the fourth grade you like the boys, and they like you. They do as much to get near you as they can. They sit near you. They do lots of funny things to get your attention. Like making funny noises, hitting you; they keep on bothering you, and they brag in front of you.

Fifth Grade

In the fifth grade you get a little mature and a little serious in liking boys. Then is the time boys start sticking up for you. And they start buying you stuff like candy, a coke, ice cream, lunch, and lots of other stuff.

Sixth Grade

In the sixth grade you are mature and kind of serious about boys. The boys in sixth grade are nice to watch. I guess all boys are nice. The boys in sixth grade take you places and buy you things. But the one thing is they get jealous very easy. So, girls, watch out when you get into sixth grade.

Seventh Grade

In seventh grade you ARE serious and mature. Boys visit you, and I think all they do is talk. In school they take you to your classes and all over the place. They like to be with you as much as possible. They don't get as much jealous as they did in the sixth grade; only a little.

Eighth Grade

In the eighth grade you like the boys, and they like you. They are very shy when it comes to girls. They don't know what to do. If you want to talk to them, you would have to be the one to start to talk. And the girls get jealous when they talk to different girls.

Ninth Grade

In ninth grade you like boys, and they like you. That is when you get a little shy, and they get over their shyness. That is when they meet you at basketball games or dances, and he is usually with a friend, and most of the time you have a friend with you, too, because you are both very shy at that age.

Tenth Grade

In tenth grade you like boys, and they like you. That's when you start to go on dates alone. You go places like the movies, dinner, lunch, and parties. And you both are not shy at all. And when you get in tenth grade you should not have to stay home and clean house all day. You should have fun but not take things that are bad for you, like drugs.

Eleventh Grade

In the eleventh grade you start to go with boys, and you are just good friends with lots of boys. And the same with boys. You go lots of places with just one boy and sometimes with friends. You see him almost every night, and he tries to be with you as much as he can.

Twelfth Grade

In the twelfth grade you have your boyfriend over for dinner and then to help you with the homework. You go to the ice cream parlor, and he treats. Then you go home to TV downstairs. And you should always have a good time if you have the right date. If you don't have a good time, something is wrong.

College

In college you have to get used to staying away from home. And having roommates. Then you are worried about getting good grades and finding jobs after school. And thinking about when you're going to get married and with whom.

Marriage

When you get married you have to be worried about when and what you are going to fix for dinner and when to clean the house. And you have lots of things to do and to think of. And *you should be sure you're ready to make the big step into a woman.* [Emphasis added.]

Housewife

A housewife has to know what she is doing, because you have to clean the house, feed the kids and get them to school, and fix dinner and change the baby, and then feed the hungry DAD. And you married the boy you were once afraid of, and now you have some boys of your own. And you have little girls going through stages like you once were.

by Laura

Footnote: How I got this information is: I learned it from my mom and from talking about it with my sister and her friend. The part about kindergarten to fifth grade I got because I've gone through those stages.

COMMENTS ON WOMEN'S LIBERATION AND SEXISM IN TEXTBOOKS FROM THE BOYS AND GIRLS OF THE FIFTH GRADE

In the various states of our country the National Organization for Women (NOW) has had task forces assigned to examine textbooks used in schools for evidence of sexism. One such task force was reported by the *Washington Post* (May 23, 1976, p. B3) as objecting to the "sexist insults" found in the stories in a second-grade reader, *The Dog Next Door.* The task force was particularly offended by "No, No, Rosina," the story of a small San Francisco girl who sneaks on board her father's fishing boat despite his shouted warning that "A woman on a fishing boat brings bad luck." At the end of the day her father and brothers, who, judging from the pictures in the book, are only a year or two older than Rosina, have a huge catch of fish. Rosina points out that she did not bring bad luck to the fishing expedition and that, in fact, they caught more fish than usual. Her father has a long serious talk with her, after which she apologizes to the entire family. However, since she is such a "small woman," she is permitted to go with her father just "one more time."

The *Washington Post* reported that a visitor to an elementary school in the Washington area read parts of "No, No, Rosina" to a few second-graders. One child, a girl, "listened carefully and then said that boys had told her that there were things she could not do because she was a girl. 'It wasn't fair not letting her go on the boat,' she said." Another child, a boy, was "asked whether it was bad for girls to fish. He nodded enthusiastically. 'Yeah,' he said."

The day after the *Washington Post* printed its story about the report of the NOW task force, I read "No, No, Rosina" to the fifth-graders, because *The Dog Next Door* is the most popular textbook in elementary schools with which I am familiar. I did not mention the NOW report or the newspaper article.

"Did you like that story?" I asked. Donna jumped from her seat and waved her hands in the air to emphasize her words. "That's what Women's Liberation is all about," she shouted. "What do you mean?" "Well, her father said that women are bad luck on boats, but she went out on the boat and she didn't bring bad luck; she brought good luck, and that's what Women's Liberation is all about—changing things that people believe about us that aren't true." "Why do you think Rosina's family believed that women on boats bring bad luck?" I asked. "They never tried it before," yelled Donna and Melanie simultaneously. "They closed their minds to the whole situation," said Melanie; "they didn't want to find out whether it was true or not."

Then Jonathan asked, "Who wrote that story?" We checked the book. It had been written by a woman, Patricia Miles. "When was it written?" Jonathan persisted. We consulted the book again. The copyright date was 1964. "Maybe that explains it," said Jonathan. "Maybe she grew up in a place where she wasn't hardly allowed to do anything. If she had been a women's libber she wouldn't have ended the story like that; only letting Rosina go on the boat one more time. She probably wouldn't have written the story at all," he concluded.

While the discussion was in progress, the principal of the school walked into the classroom with a copy of the *Washington Post* article in his hand. "Have you seen this?" he asked. The paper mentioned that the NOW task force had written a story about a black boy that they called "No, No, Roosevelt." He "wants to go to a white school but is told that, if he goes, he'll poison the water and everybody will get sick." "That's stupid to believe anything like that," said Tommy. Then Donna emphasized for one more time, "We've got Women's Liberation now, and things are going to be different."

WAVE OF THE FUTURE?

It is not easy to determine how much or how little the fifth-grade students of Pine Hill resemble fifth-grade students elsewhere in the same geographical area. It is even more difficult to judge how similar or how different they are from fifth-grade students elsewhere in the United States. However, there is some evidence that in this area of the country the generation of children now enrolled in elementary schools have been affected by the historical changes taking place in our society with regard to male-female sex role behavior—more so than were the children of 10 or even 5 years ago.

The first piece of evidence is the changes that have taken place in teacher behavior and attitudes. In discussing with teachers their attitudes on such topics as marriage, children, equal pay for equal work, alternative styles of living, abortion, rape, sex role behavior, and sexism in textbooks, I have found them open, aware, and sensitive to the issues. I could not have made that statement even four years ago during the base year of the study. At that time, one of the teachers at Pine Hill, a woman, said that she wanted her girls to be girls and her boys to be boys. She did not want boys and girls in her classroom to play the same games. She wanted them to wear clothing appropriate to their sex. Another teacher, a man, said that women should not be permitted to compete with men for high paying jobs since it is the duty of men to support women, and, thus, it is men who need the most income. Women, he said, only need to work for "pin money."

That was 1972. In 1976 a teacher at Pine Hill, a man, read the NOW report which brought to his attention the sexism in a series of textbooks used in the school. He wanted the books removed immediately rather than chance having a child, girl or boy, suffer from the effects of sex discrimination. Another teacher, a woman, who for her classroom in 1972 had requested building blocks and wheeled toys for the boys and dollhouse equipment for the girls, enrolled in a course on sex role stereotyping in schools. The fact that the majority of teachers on the staff had developed strong feminist attitudes might have been due to the influence of young women who had joined the staff.

But were the teachers in other schools equally sensitive to the issue of sex discrimination? In the spring of 1976 I taught a course on Women in Today's Society to a large group of teachers and other school staff people. All the class participants were keenly interested in learning how to eradicate the effects of sex discrimination in their schools and indicated that they were working hard to achieve greater awareness among children.

One other fact points to this situation as not being unique at least in this part of the country. Many mothers of small children at Pine Hill were returning to college, business school, and nursing school so that they could eventually enter the job market. "I hate housework," one mother of four children told me. "I told my husband that I'm going back to school, and I'm going to get a job, and I'm not going to stay home and just clean house anymore." At this writing this woman is a student in a local university. A teacher in the school reported that her mother had started her college work only after her last child was out of the home. At the age of 58 she had received her master's degree in psychology. These women are only a small part of the ever-increasing numbers of women in this area who have returned to school after having devoted many years exclusively to their families.

It has been suggested, and I admit that it may be true, that my close contact with these children influenced their thinking. Although I tried not to impose my biases on the children, the fact is that I probably did influence them to some extent.

These, then, were the forces that impacted on the attitudes and behavior of the fifth-grade children at Pine Hill. Thus, it was to be expected that both the boys and girls should congratulate Laura when she won the 60-yard dash and broke the school record for that race. And that two girls in the class, Donna and Tracey, should be voted "most likely to succeed," in a private poll taken by the children during the last month of school. The next closest winner had been Jonathan, and he had trailed Tracey by six votes. At least among their peers, Donna and Tracey had not been judged by their gender but by their ability.

NOTES

1. There were 320 children, Head Start through sixth grade, attending Pine Hill. Another 40 children were in special education classes housed in the school. There were no minority group children attending Pine Hill during the first year of the study. However, during the second year a few black, Oriental, and Spanish-speaking children enrolled in classes then classified as second and third grade.

2. A more extensive discussion of the children at Pine Hill can be found in Best and Bernard (forthcoming).

REFERENCES

BERNARD, J. (1975). Women, wives, mothers: Values and options. Chicago: Aldine.

BEST, R., and BERNARD, J. (forthcoming). Winners, losers and girls: Peer power in the child's world.

BRINK, C.R. (1935). Caddie Woodlawn. New York: Macmillan.

DAVID, D.S., and BRANNON, R. (1976). The forty-nine percent majority: The male sex role. Reading, Mass.: Addison-Wesley.

HARTLEY, R.E. (1959). "Sex-role pressures and the socialization of the male child." Psychological Reports, 5:457-468.

WIRTENBURG, J. (1976). Biases against minorities and females in textbooks: A review of the literature. Washington, D.C.: U.S. Commission on Civil Rights.

2

SEXUAL INEQUALITY, CULTURAL NORMS, AND WIFE-BEATING

MURRAY A. STRAUS

The research of Wolfgang (1956), Driver (1961), Bohanan (1960), Curtis (1974), and others has made it clear that, in a great many societies, one is more likely to be murdered by a member of one's own family, and especially by a husband or a wife, than by any other category of person. But even criminologists are not aware of the extent to which physical violence of all types occurs within families. In other papers, my colleagues and I have documented the available knowledge, which suggests, among other things, that for many people a marriage license is a hitting license, that physical violence between family members is probably as common as love and affection between family members, and that, if one is truly concerned with the level of violence in America, the place to look is in the home rather than on the streets (Gelles, 1974; Gelles and Straus, 1976; Owens and Straus, 1975; Steinmetz, 1974; Steinmetz and Straus, 1974; Straus, 1971, 1974b).

The intriguing question is why the social group that the society most often looks to for warmth, intimacy, help, and love is also

AUTHOR'S NOTE: This paper is reprinted with permission from *Victimology*, Vol. 1, No. 1, Copyright © 1976 by Visage Press, Inc. This is a revision of a paper presented at the International Institute of Victimology, Bellagio, Italy, July 1-12, 1975. I would like to express my appreciation to Bruce Brown and Richard Gelles for their careful reading and comments on drafts of this paper. The writing of this paper was supported in part by National Institute of Mental Health grant number MH-15221 for research training in family and deviance and grant number MH-27557 for a study of "Physical Violence in American Families."

characterized by cruelty and violence. Gelles and Straus (1976) have
identified a large number of explanatory factors which, together,
constitute a theory of intrafamily victimization with respect to
violence. These factors include such things as "time at risk," the
semi-involuntary nature of family group membership, the age- and
sex-determined role structure of the family, the level of emotional
involvement, the privacy of the family as an institution, and the
frequent high level of stress resulting from all of the above factors.

Wives as Victims. Whatever the validity of the factors mentioned
by Gelles and Straus, by themselves these factors do not explain a
striking aspect of intrafamily violence. This is the fact that wives are
much more often the victims of violence by their husbands than the
reverse. The existence of this pattern is demonstrated in a variety of
studies, of which the most dramatic are those of homicide. Perhaps
the starkest measure is the differences in number of deaths caused by
husbands as compared to those caused by wives. Wolfgang's (1956)
study of 588 homicide victims found that 41% of the women victims
were killed by their husbands as compared with only 11% of the
male victims who were killed by their wives. Some other studies cited
by Wolfgang show even higher rates of wife murder. The highest of
these is von Hentig's analysis of 1931 German data which showed
that 62% of women victims were wives killed by their husbands
compared with only 14% of men killed by their wives.

It might be argued that these figures overstate the case because
they are based on all homicides, no matter what the personal
relationship. If the percentages are based only on murders in which
the victim and offender were married to each other, then about half
are by husbands and half by wives (Wolfgang, 1956, 1958; Curtis,
1974). But in my opinion, the latter figures do not accurately reflect
the situation. This is because whether or not an altercation becomes
a murder is heavily influenced by whether knives or guns are used,
and wives—as a result of their lesser physical strength—more often
use knives and guns, and moreover, more often do so in self-defense.
This can be seen from Wolfgang's data on "victim-precipitation"
(defined as homicide in which physical force was first used by the
victim): of the husband-wife homicides for which there was
victim-precipitation, almost all were cases of husbands who precipi-
tated the attack. Finally, and most directly relevant for the present
concern with wife-beating, is Wolfgang's data on the degree of
violence involved in husband-wife murder. Wolfgang defined a violent

homicide as one involving two or more acts of stabbing, cutting, or shooting, or a severe beating. He found that "Among the 53 husbands who killed their wives, 44 did so violently." It is clear, then, that there is a striking imbalance in the extent to which wives are victims of violence by husbands.

What could account for this imbalance? One factor might be the greater physical strength of men. However, that could not account for the fact that murders of wives by husbands were more brutal and more violent than murders of husbands by wives (Wolfgang, 1956:269). In fact, the greater strength and skill with weapons on the part of men would lead one to expect *fewer* stabs and shots if the difference was based on physical strength and skill. Much more than differences in physical strength seems to be involved. The balance of this paper is an examination of some of these factors accounting for the high degree to which wives are the victims of physical violence by husbands. Specifically, we will attempt to show that wife-beating is not just a personal abnormality but rather has its roots in the very structure of society and the family; that is, in the cultural norms and in the sexist organization of the society and the family.

CULTURAL NORMS LEGITIMIZING INTRAFAMILY VIOLENCE

The norms and values relating to intrafamily violence pose something of a paradox. On the one hand there is what we have called the "myth of family nonviolence" (Steinmetz and Straus, 1974; Straus, 1974b), which reflects cultural norms and aspirations for the family as a group characterized by love, gentleness, and harmony. On the other hand, there also seem to be social norms which imply the right of family members to strike each other and which therefore legitimize intrafamily assaults, at least under certain conditions.

Cultural contradictions and discontinuities of this type are present in every society to a greater or lesser extent (Benedict, 1938; Embree, 1950; Ryan and Straus, 1954).[1] Physical aggression or violence is a prime example of this in American society. Although there are clear norms and values restricting violence and emphasizing the value of peace and harmony—especially between family members—simultaneously there exists a high level of actual violence and also norms glorifying aggression and violence. In respect to the family, the legitimation of violence is sometimes explicit or even mandatory—as in the case of the right and obligation of parents to use a necessary and appropriate level of physical force to adequately train and control a child. In fact, parents are permitted or expected to use a level of physical force for these purposes that is denied even prison authorities in relation to training and controlling inmates. In the case of husband-wife relations, similar norms are present and powerful, but largely implicit, unrecognized, or covert.

INFORMAL MANIFESTATIONS OF CULTURAL NORMS PERMITTING OR APPROVING MARITAL VIOLENCE

Ingeborg Dedichen, who lived with Aristotle Onassis for 12 years, describes an incident in which Onassis beat her severely until he quit from exhaustion:

> The following day instead of apologizing, Onassis explained "All Greek husbands, I tell you, all Greek men without exception, beat their wives. It's good for them." And then he laughed. [Shearer, 1975:4]

Most of the American or English public reading this would dismiss it as another Greek peculiarity. But, just as Onassis' statement is an exaggeration for Greek men, our denial of this norm is an exaggeration in the other direction. Once one is aware of the possibility that there may be norms legitimizing marital (and especially husband-to-wife) violence, instances such as the above pop up constantly. One amazing example is the ancient (and incredibly sexist) joke told on the BBC women's program "Pettycoat Lane" in the spring of 1974. One woman asked another why she felt her husband didn't love her anymore. Her answer: "He hasn't bashed me in a fortnight."

At a higher literary level, plays provide many examples of the marriage license as a hitting license norm, including several by G.B. Shaw, and the recent play about a lesbian couple, "The Killing of Sister George," in which June makes threatening motions toward Alice:

> Alice: Don't touch me. You've got no right.
>
> June: I've got every right.
>
> Alice: I'm not married to you, you know.

The above are, of course, only literary reflections of the cultural norms which can be observed in everyday life. These range from casual remarks such as the railway conductor who, when asked for help with a stubborn seat, did so and remarked to the woman(!): "Some of these seats are just like women: you have to kick them to make them work" (protest letter to the *New York Times,* July 14, 1974, p. 5). Other examples appear in the media with at least tacit approval of their contents, as in the following section of the widely read column by Ann Landers (October 29, 1973):

> Dear Ann Landers: Come out of the clouds, for Lord's sake, and get down here with us humans. I am sick to death of your holier-than-thou attitude toward women whose husbands give them a well-deserved belt in the mouth.
>
> Don't you know that a man can be pushed to the brink and something's got to give? A crack in the teeth can be a wonderful tension-breaker. It's also a lot healthier than keeping all that anger bottled up.
>
> My husband hauls off and slugs me every few months and I don't mind. He feels better and so do I because he never hits me unless I deserve it. So why don't you come off it?—REAL HAPPY.
>
> Dear R.H.: If you don't mind a crack in the teeth every few months, it's all right with me. I hope you have a good dentist.

A number of husband and wives interviewed by Gelles expressed similar attitudes, so that Gelles developed a classification of types of "normal violence," including such categories as "I asked for it," "I deserved it," "She needed to be brought to her senses," etc. (Gelles, 1974:58). Other examples occur in connection with police calls concerning family disturbances, with wives as well as husbands often asserting their right to hit each other because they are married (Parnas, 1967; *Yorkshire Post,* May 23, 1974, p. 9). These same attitudes are also widely shared by officials of the criminal justice system (see next section). Sometimes this presumed right to hit is linked to the race or social class of the couple, as shown in many of Parnas' examples (1967) and in an English judge's remark that "if he had been a miner in South Wales I might have overlooked it" (London *Daily Mirror,* January 29, 1974, p. 1). This remark made headlines, but only because Welsh miners (not women) protested.

A final example is a marriage counseling case cited by Straus (1973:120) in which the husband hit his wife on numerous occasions. He and his wife felt that he could not help himself because, in the heat of the tremendous arguments, he "lost control." The counselor, however, demonstrated to the couple that this was not simply a reversion to "primitive" levels of behavior, but in fact was under normative control. He did so by asking the husband, "Why didn't you stab her?" This brought out the fact that there was an implicit, unrecognized, but nonetheless operating norm which permitted the husband to hit his wife but not to stab her. This unrecognized norm legitimizing intrafamily violence, unless it produces severe injury, is remarkably parallel to the California "wife-beating" statute cited below.

LEGITIMATION OF HUSBAND-WIFE VIOLENCE BY THE COURTS AND POLICE

There is considerable evidence that even though laws giving husbands the right to "chastize" an erring wife are no longer with us, the underlying spirit of such laws lingers on. That spirit is now primarily extralegal, but there are important ways in which it is still embodied in the legal system.

Immunity from Suit. One of the most important of these legitimizations of husband-wife violence is to be found in the doctrine of "spousal immunity," which, to this day in many jurisdictions, prevents a wife from suing her husband for assault and battery. In other jurisdictions, the law has only recently been changed. Truninger (1971:269) cites the following example:

> In Self v. Self (1962) the wife alleged that "the defendant husband ... "unlawfully assaulted plaintiff and beat upon, scratched and abused the person of plaintiff," and that as a result plaintiff "sustained physical injury to her person and emotional distress, and among other injuries did receive a broken arm." The husband's motion for a summary judgment was granted by the trial court.

> On appeal, the California Supreme Court reversed the trial court's judgment, thus overruling several older California cases supporting interspousal immunity. The rationale of courts retaining the common law spousal immunity doctrine was that it was needed for preservation of the family. The fear was that allowing the tort action "would destroy the peace and harmony of the home, and thus would be contrary to the policy of the law."

Failure of the Police to Act. As Truninger also points out, it is doubtful whether a wife gains much, other than the principle, from an ability to sue her husband for assault and battery, because the actual operation of both the civil and the criminal justice systems put enormous obstacles in the way and, in any case, typically do nothing to prevent immediate repetition of the offense while the case is being adjudicated. An arrest is usually the only way in which a violent spouse can be removed from the home, but it is extremely rare for the police to make such arrests. In fact, the training manual of the International Association of Police Chiefs recommends that arrests *not* be made in such cases (1965).

The guideline mentioned above is probably more closely followed than any other in the training manual, because it so clearly fits the experience and values of the police. In general, the police seem to share the implicit legitimacy of spousal violence, provided that the resulting injuries or destruction is within limits. Some police departments have informal "stitch rules" whereby the wound requires a certain (high) number of stitches before an officer makes an arrest (Field and Field, 1973:229). Parnas (1967) cites case after case of the police avoiding arrests in situations in which there would be no doubt of an arrest were the parties not husband and wife. Almost any policeman can cite numerous examples of husbands' claiming the right to strike a wife, and many police themselves believe this to be the law (Truninger, 1971:271; Coote, 1974).[2]

Failure of Prosecutors to Act. Despite the repeated occurrence and frequent severity of marital violence, it is endured for long periods—often many years—by large numbers of women. Some of the reasons why so many wives tolerate this situation follow from the variables analyzed in this paper. Other factors have been identified in Gelles' paper "Abused Wives: Why Do They Stay?" (forthcoming). But sooner or later the situation brings large numbers of women to the point of desperation. Some respond to this by ultimately killing the husband, some leave, and some attempt to secure a warrant for the arrest of the husband. For obviously different reasons, each of these alternatives is typically unsatisfactory. If the wife attempts to bring charges, she faces being "cooled out" at every step by officials of the criminal justice system. This is graphically illustrated by Martha and Henry Field's tabulation of the approximately 7,500 such attempts in Washington, D.C., in 1966:

> Invariably, the police had told them that, in order to protect themselves, they had to "get a warrant from the district attorney." They announced typically, "I have come to get one." To them this implied an automatic process, like dropping nickels into a vending machine, and they expected a routine procedure culminating in the issuance of a warrant for their husband's arrest. Their heightened feeling of precipitate danger reinforced this expectation, and their sense of grievance and desperation was further

solidified by the long wait they endured before talking with the initial screening policeman or the district attorney. Of these seventy-five hundred women, less than two hundred left have secured their objective. [Field and Field, 1973:232]

Finally, even when the circumstances are such that the police and district attorney cannot avoid bringing charges, few such cases get to trial:

A survey of the assault cases in the District of Columbia showed that over three-fourths of the cases not involving husbands and wives went to a disposition of the merits of guilt or innocence. The enforcement pattern was reversed in husband-wife cases. Only about one-sixth of all arrests involving marital violence ultimately ended at trial or with a guilty plea, and the crime charged by that time was invariably a misdemeanor rather than a felony. [Field and Field, 1973:224]

Victim Compensation. Another way in which the law continues, in effect, to legitimize the assault of wives by husbands crops up in connection with the workings of boards and commissions which have been set up in England and a few American states to compensate victims of crimes. The English board has explicitly ruled against compensation when the victim is a spouse (Williams, 1974), and this also seems to be the case with the California law (Edelhertz and Geis, 1974:278; Truninger, 1971:270).

The Legal System and Cultural Approval of Intrafamily Violence. The situation described in this section is well summarized by the phrase used as the subtitle of the Fields' article (1973) on the criminal process in cases of marital violence: "Neither Justice Nor Peace." A situation as pervasive as this is not likely to be a result of historical accident. Nor is it likely to be a consequence of the many difficulties in dealing with marital violence and the low rate of success achieved by invoking the criminal law. These difficulties and uncertainties, after all, do not deter the police and courts from invoking criminal adjudication processes for many crimes with an even lower rate of success in control such as prostitution. Rather, the failure to invoke criminal penalties reflects historical continuities in the cultural norms which make the marriage license a hitting license. This is almost explicit in the California Penal Code section on wife-beating, which prohibits an assualt only if it results in severe physical injury. But the most explicit contemporary legal expression of the right of husbands to use physical force is found in the immunity of husbands from prosecution for rape of a wife.

EXPERIMENTAL AND SURVEY EVIDENCE ON
APPROVAL OF MARITAL VIOLENCE

There is a slowly growing body of empirical research on intrafamily aggression and violence, some of which provides evidence on the cultural norms we are considering. The survey conducted for the U.S. National Commission on the Causes and Prevention of Violence found that about one-quarter of the persons interviewed said they could approve of a husband or wife hitting each other under certain circumstances (Stark and McEvoy, 1970). That figure is probably a considerable underestimate because of the existence of opposite and more socially acceptable antiviolence norms and because of the implicit or covert nature of the proviolence norms.

The contradictory and covert nature of the norms approving marital violence makes experimental and observational studies particularly appropriate because these do not depend on the willingness or ability to verbalize norms and values. Unfortunately, the observational studies have, for practical reasons, all been of parent-child violence (Bellak and Antell, 1974). But there have been experimental studies of marital aggression, or studies which bear on marital aggression.

The first of these studies also reflects the more general phenomenon of male hostility to women:

> One of the least recognized indices of male hostility to females is the reaction of men who watch a violent act against women, rather than committing or initiating it themselves. Three psychologists from Michigan State University staged a series of fights that were to be witnessed by unsuspecting passersby. The researchers found, to their amazement, that male witnesses rushed to the aid of men being assaulted by either women or men, and that men helped women being hit by other women. But not one male bystander interfered when a male actor apparently beat up a woman. [Pogrebin, 1974:55]

In addition to the interpretation of these findings as reflecting male hostility to women, it also seems likely that it reflects the norm permitting assaults between spouses. That is, it is possible that male bystanders did not come ot the aid of a female victim of a male assailant because they inferred that he was the woman's husband. This, in fact, is the reason given for not intervening by a number of those who stood by as Kitty Genovese was murdered (Rosenthal, 1964). The plausability of this conclusion is further enhanced by its congruence with experimental studies of "bystander intervention," such as the experiments reported and summarized by Bickman (1975). Bickman concludes that the social definition of what actions are right for the bystander is a more powerful determinant of intervention than the severity of the crime or concern for the welfare of the victim.

Closely related is an unpublished experiment by Churchill and Straus in which the subjects were given a description of an assault and asked to indicate what punishment they felt was appropriate. In the course of the assault, the victim was knocked unconscious. In half the descriptions the assailant was described as the woman's husband. In the other half, the subjects responded to the identical description except that the couple were described as "going together" for a year. The mean punishment score when the victim was not married to the assailant was 4.15, compared to only 2.65 when the victim was the wife. Moreover, this experiment probably understates the difference because it specified that the unmarried couple had been going together for a year. It is likely that the difference would have been much greater if the unmarried couple had not been described as having a quasi-marital relationship.

A final set of experiments bearing on this issue is based on observing couples interact in a standardized and conflictive laboratory task. The data for couples was compared with the data for unmarried couples in the same task situation. A study by Ryder (1968) found that strangers were treated more gently and more nicely than were spouses. Similarly, using an experimental task which required the couple to reach a decision, Winter, Ferreira, and Bowers (1973) found that unrelated couples listened respectfully to one another whereas married couples were often rude to each other. Although there is a long distance between "rudeness" and violence, it seems likely that what is manifested in these two experiments is the beginning of the journey which for many couples ultimately ends in violence (Straus, 1974a).

SEXIST ORGANIZATION OF SOCIETY AND MARITAL VIOLENCE

The cultural norms and values permitting and sometimes encouraging husband-to-wife violence reflect the hierarchical and male-dominant type of society which characterizes the Western world. The right to use force exists, as Goode (1971) concludes, to provide the ultimate support for the existing power structure of the family, if those low in the hierarchy refuse to accept their place and roles. Nine of the specific ways in which the male-dominant structure of the society and of the family create and maintain a high level of marital violence are described in this section.[3]

1. Defense of Male Authority. In the context of an individualistically oriented urban-industrial society, the ascription of superior authority to males is a potent force producing physical attacks on wives. This is because, in such a society, male-superiority norms are not clearly understood and are in the process of transition and because, in such a society, the *presumption* of male superiority must be validated by superiority in "resources," such as valued personal traits and material goods and services (Rodman, 1972). If every man were, in fact, superior to his wife in such resources as intelligence, knowledge, occupational prestige, and income, there would be a concordance between the ascribed authority and the individual achievements which are implicitly expected to accompany that authority in individual-achievement-oriented societies. Clearly that is often not the case, despite the societal structure which gives men tremendous advantages in accesses to these traits and resources. Consequently, many men must fall back on the "ultimate resource" of physical force to maintain their superior position (Goode, 1971; Straus, 1974b:66-67). A graphic illustration of just this process is the case of Joe and Jennifer reported by LaRossa (1975). Statistical evidence is given by Allen and Straus (1975), who found that among working class husbands who were high in resources, there was no correlation between power and violence. However, among those working class husbands who were low in resources, the correlation between male power and violence was .49.

2. Compulsive Masculinity. Talcott Parsons (1966) has argued that, in modern industrial societies, the separation of the male occupational role from the family and the predominance of the mother in child-rearing creates a fundamental difficulty for males with respect to achieving a masculine sexual identity:

> The boy has a tendency to form a direct feminine identification, since his mother is the model most readily available and significant to him. But he is not destined to become an adult woman. Moreover he soon discovers that in certain vital respects women are considered inferior to men, that it would hence be shameful for him to grow up to be like a woman. Hence when boys emerge into what Freudians call the "latency period," their

behavior tends to be marked by a kind of *"compulsive masculini-ty."*. . . Aggression toward women, who "after all are to blame," is an essential concomitant. [p. 305]

Although Parson emphasizes a particular family constellation to explain the generally high level of male aggressiveness in Western societies, it also seems likely to be an important part of the reason why so much male aggressiveness is directed against women, and wives in particular. Similarly, although space limitations prevent giving the details, Parsons' analysis also shows that the origins of female aggressiveness are partly to be found in the particular structure of the family in industrial society and that much of this aggressiveness is specifically focused on men, and especially hus-bands, as the agents of their repressed position in society.[4] The climate of mutual antagonism between the sexes, which is partly an outgrowth of the factors described by Parsons, provides a context which is not only conducive to attacks by husbands on wives but probably also involves a number of other related phenomena; there is growing evidence, for instance, that in many instances "rape is a power trip, not a passion trip" (Bart, 1975:40; Burgess and Holmstrom, 1974). Moreover, as in the typical homosexual rape in prisons (Davis, 1970), the degradation and humiliation of the victim is often a major motivating force.

   3. Economic Constraints and Discrimination. The sexist economic and occupational structure of society gives women few alternatives. The jobs open to them are lower in status, and, despite antidiscrimi-nation legislation, women continue to earn less than men in the same occupations. Without access to good jobs, women are dependent on their husbands. If there is a divorce, almost all husbands default on support payments after a short time, even if they can afford them in the first place. (See Chapter 9.) Consequently, many women continue to endure physical attacks from their husband because the alternative of divorce is living in poverty.

   4. Burdens of Child Care. The sexually based division of labor in society assigns child-rearing responsibility to the wife. She therefore has the problem of rearing the children, but at the same time society does not provide either economic provision for her to do so or child-care centers that can take over part of the burden so that she can earn enough to support her children. The combination of occupational discrimination, lack of child-care facilities, inadequate child support from either the government or the father, all coerce women into remaining married even when they are the victims of violence.

5. *Myth of the Single-Parent Household.* Another of the cultural norms which helps to maintain the subordination of women is the idea that children cannot be adequately brought up by one parent. Thus, if a woman is to have children, she must also have a man. To the limited extent that research evidence supports the view that it is bad for children to grow up in a single-parent household, this view exists only because of the confounding of poverty and social ostracism with single parenthood. Although it seems likely that, if social pressure and constraints were removed, most women would want to live with a man and visa versa, there is an important minority for whom this is not the case and who, in effect, live in a state of forced cohabitation. Thus, the fact that innumerable and (under present conditions) unnecessary social and economic constraints prevent the single-parent family from being a viable social unit forces many women into accepting or continuing with a subordinate and stressful relationship.

6. *Preeminence of the Wife Role for Women.* Under the present system, being a wife and mother is the most important single role for a woman. Indeed, American cultural norms are such that one cannot be a full woman unless married. A man, on the other hand, has the option of investing much or little of himself in the husband-father role depending on his interests, ability, and circumstances. In short, the stigma of being a divorced man is tiny compared to that of being a divorced woman—to which a special term with somewhat immoral overtones has in the past been attached: divorcée. This forced dependence on the wife role as the basis for a respected position in society makes it difficult for women to refuse to tolerate male violence by ending the marriage.

7. *Negative Self-Image.* Under the present social structure, women tend to develop negative self-images, especially in relation to the crucial trait of achievement (Horner, 1972; Truninger, 1971:260), and therefore also feelings of guilt and masochism which permit them to tolerate male aggression and violence and, in some extreme cases, to seek it out. Full sexual equality would eliminate this as a sexually structured pattern of behavior, even though it will remain on an individual-to-individual basis. Only a deemphasis on individual competitive achievement will fully eliminate this problem.

8. *Women as Children.* The concept of women as the property of

men is no longer part of the legal system of industrial countries. However, elements of this concept linger on in the folk culture and in certain aspects of the law, such as the statutes which declare the husband the head of the household and give him various rights over his wife, such as the right to choose the place of abode.[5] In addition, there is the related concept of women as "childlike." In combination, these two aspects of the sexist orientation of society give husbands a covert moral right to use physical force on their wives in a fashion analogous to that of the overt legal right of parents to use physical force on their children (see Gelles, 1974:58, for examples).

9. *Male Orientation of the Criminal Justice System.* Not only is much male violence against wives attributable to the sexist orientation of society, but the crowning blow is that the male-oriented organization of the criminal justice system virtually guarantees that few women will be able to secure legal relief. To start with, the long delays in obtaining court orders and "peace bonds" make them useless in securing immediate relief from the danger of another assault. But even without these delays, many women cannot attend court because of the absence of child-care arrangements during the long hours of waiting for a case to come up and the frequent repetition of days when the case is rescheduled. Among the other impediments to securing legal protection against assaults by a husband are those previously described in the section on "Legitimation of Husband-Wife Violence by the Courts and Police": immunity from suit, the failure of police to act against husbands, the cooling out of complainant wives by police, prosecuting attorneys, and judges, and the denial of compensation by public compensation review boards.

SEXUAL LIBERATION AND
THE REDUCTION OF MARITAL ASSAULT

Although Goode believes that force or its threat is ultimately necessary for the existence of society, he also concedes that "the amount of force now applied in these various areas of family life" is not "either necessary or desirable" (1971:42). One of the ways in which the amount of force necessary to maintain a viable pattern of family life can be reduced is to lower the degree of inequality found within the family. The immaturity of children imposes a limit on the extent to which they can be given equality with their parents. But the particular economic and physical conditions which may have justified a subordinate position for women in previous historical eras are clearly no longer present.

The goals of the women's liberation movement are centered on eliminating each of the violence-producing inequities which were discussed in the previous section. Since these are fundamental factors accounting for the high level of physical assaults on women by their husbands, it is clear that achievement of the goals of the feminist movement is tremendously important for any reduction in the level of marital assault victimization.

In addition to these fundamental structural changes, the objectives of the women's movement also include various short-run contributions. For example, the ideology of the feminist movement itself encourages women to resist all forms of oppression, and especially physical violence. In England, over the past three years there has been an explosive growth of "battered-wife shelters." These provide immediate physical escape for wives, particularly for those with young children, who might otherwise have no alternative to being victimized by their husbands. Finally, the women's movement has been perceptive in recognizing that superior male physical strength and skill are important parts of the process by which male dominance is maintained. It is this recognition which partly accounts for the emphasis on karate and other self-defensive training. It is unlikely that this will, in fact, protect women from assault, anymore than the ability to respond physically protects men from assault by other men. Moreover, the karate approach serves to institutionalize the role of physical violence in social interaction and hence increase the likelihood of still further violence. Nevertheless, the emphasis on physical self-defense training is an important *symbolic* step toward the eventual elimination of violent repression of women. But this eventuality will only come about if it is possible to overcome the more fundamental problems of sexual inequality described in the previous section. Fortunately, the most recent emphasis has shifted from training in the use of physical force to training in nonaggressive "assertiveness," which is an important step in the direction of sexual equality.[6]

At the same time, the difficulties of the period of transition cannot be overlooked. The *long run* consequences of a more equalitarian society may be to lessen the frequency with which wives are victims of assault by husbands. But, as Kolb and Straus (1974) and Whitehurst (1974) have suggested, the *short run* consequences may be the opposite, because a sizable number of men will not easily give up their traditional sex-stereotyped roles. Like traditionally oriented women, such men are conditioned by their culture to perceive only the prerogatives and advantages of the traditional male role and to ignore the burdens, restraints, and disadvantages. Thus, a less violent world, and less violence in the family, requires male liberation as well as women's liberation.

NOTES

1. I should make clear that such cultural contradictions are by no means entirely undesirable. In fact, cultural contradictions help prevent society from stagnating, open possibilities for social change, and allow for a measure of individual autonomy; without them, we might well be slaves to the dictates of culture.

2. Programs to inform and train police to better deal with family disturbances have been initiated in several cities. See Bard, 1969, 1971.

3. There are, of course, many other factors which contribute to the existence and maintenance of norms permitting intrafamily violence. Owens and Straus (1975), for example, present data on the correlation of childhood experience with violence (including victimization) with proviolence attitudes and values. See also the more general discussion of the influence of the general positive evaluation of violence in society in Huggins and Straus, 1975, and in Straus, 1974a, 1974b.

4. See the discussion of the sex myth in Steinmetz and Straus (1974:10-13) for other ways in which the pattern of male-female relationships built into the society helps to create antagonism between the sexes and hence the association between sexuality and violence.

5. It is pertinent that even in a state known for its social and familial experimentation, the California State Bar Association voted as recently as 1971 *not* to repeal such legislation (Truninger, 1971:276).

6. The combination of sexual equality, a female assertiveness, and sexual liberation might also go a long way toward eliminating rape. Many rapes are an illegitimate extension of techniques used by men to deal with culturally prescribed resistance of women to sex (Kirkpatrick and Kanin, 1957). If women were to escape the culturally stereotyped role of disinterest in and resistance to sex and to take on an assertive role in expressing their own sexuality, rather than leaving it to the assertiveness of men, it would contribute to the reduction in rape in three ways. First, and most obviously, voluntary sex would be available to more men, hence reducing the "need" for rape. Second, and probably more important, it would help to reduce the confounding of sex and aggression which is built into our culture (Steinmetz and Straus, 1974:10-13). Third, to the extent that sexism in societal and family structure is responsible for the phenomena of "compulsive masculinity" and structured antagonism between the sexes, the elimination of sexual inequality would reduce the number of "power trip" and "degradation ceremony" motivated rapes.

REFERENCES

ALLEN, C.M., and STRAUS, M.A. (1975). "Resources, power, and husband-wife violence." Paper presented at the annual meeting of the National Council on Family Relations.

BARD, M. (1969). "Family intervention police teams as a community mental health resource." Journal of Criminal Law, Criminology, and Police Science, 60(2):247-250.

――― (1971). "The study and modification of intra-familial violence." In J.L. Singer (ed.), The control of aggression and violence. New York: Academic Press. Also reprinted in S.K. Steinmetz and M.A. Straus (eds.), Violence in the family. New York: Dodd, Mead, 1974.

BART, P.B. (1975). "Rape doesn't end with a kiss." Viva, June, pp. 39-42, 100-102.

BELLAK, L., and ANTELL, M. (1974). "An intercultural study of aggressive behavior on children's playgrounds." American Journal of Orthopsychiatry, 44(4):503-511.

BENEDICT, R. (1938). "Continuities and discontinuities in cultural conditioning." Psychiatry, 1:161-167. Reprinted in C. Kluckhohn and H.A. Murray (eds.), Personality in nature, society, and culture. New York: Knopf.

BICKMAN, L. (1975). "Bystander intervention in a crime." Paper presented at the International Advanced Study Institute on Victimology and the Needs of Contemporary Society, Bellagio, Italy, July 1-12, 1975.

BOHANNAN, P. (1960). "Patterns of murder and suicide." Chap. 9 in P. Bohannan (ed.), African homicide and suicide. New York: Atheneum.

BURGESS, A.W., and HOLMSTROM, L.L. (1974). Rape: Victims of crisis. Bowie, Md.: Robert J. Brady.

COOTE, A. (1974). "Police, the law, and battered wives." Manchester Guardian, May 23, p. 11.

CURTIS, L.A. (1974). Criminal violence: National patterns and behavior. Lexington, Mass.: Lexington Books.

DAVIS, A.J. (1970). "Sexual assaults in the Philadelphia prison system." In J.H. Gagnon and W. Simon (eds.), The sexual scene. Chicago: Aldine.

DRIVER, E.D. (1961). "Interaction and criminal homicide in India." Social Forces, 40(2):153-158.

EDELHERTZ, H., and GEIS, G. (1974). Public compensation to victims of crime. New York: Praeger.

EMBREE, J.F. (1950). "Thailand—A loosely structured social system." American Anthropologist, 52:181.

FIELD, M.H., and FIELD, H.F. (1973). "Marital violence and the criminal process: Neither justice or peace." Social Service Review, 47(June):221-240.

GELLES, R.J. (1974). The violent home: A study of physical aggression between husbands and wives. Beverly Hills, Calif.: Sage.

――― (forthcoming). "Abused wives: Why do they stay?"

GELLES, R.J., and STRAUS, M.A. (1976). "Determinants of violence in the family: Toward a theoretical integration." In W.R. Burr, R. Hill, F.I. Nye, and I.L. Reiss (eds.), Contemporary theories about the family. New York: Free Press.

GOODE, W.J. (1971). "Force and violence in the family." Journal of Marriage and the Family, 33(November):624-636. Reprinted in S.K. Steinmetz and M.A. Straus (eds.), Violence in the family. New York: Harper and Row, 1974.

HORNER, M.S. (1972). "Toward an understanding of achievement-related conflicts in women." Journal of Social Issues, 28(2):157-175.

HUGGINS, M.D., and STRAUS, M.A. (1975). "Violence and the social structure as reflected in children's books from 1850 to 1970." Paper read at the annual meeting of the Eastern Sociological Society.

KIRKPATRICK, C., and KANIN, E. (1957). "Male sex aggression on a university campus." American Sociological Review, 22:52-58.

KOLB, T.M., and STRAUS, M.A. (1974). "Marital power and marital happiness in relation to problem-solving ability." Journal of Marriage and the Family, 36(November): 756-766.

LaROSSA, R. (1975). "Marriage close up: A study of couples expecting their first child." Unpublished Doctoral dissertation, University of New Hampshire.

OWENS, D.M., and STRAUS, M.A. (1975). "The social structure of violence in childhood and approval of violence as an adult." Aggressive Behavior, 1(2).

PARNAS, R.I. (1967). "The police response to the domestic disturbance." Wisconsin Law Review, (fall):914-960.

PARSONS, T. (1966). "Certain primary sources and patterns of aggression in the social structure of the Western world." Pp. 298-322 in Essays in sociological theory (rev. ed.). New York: Free Press. (Essay originally published in 1947.)

POGREBIN, L.C. (1974). "Do women make men violent?" Ms., 3(November):49-55, 80.

RODMAN, H. (1972). "Marital power and the theory of resources in cultural context." Journal of Comparative Family Studies, 3(1):50-69.

ROSENTHAL, A.M. (1964). Thirty-eight witnesses. New York: McGraw-Hill.

RYAN, B.F., and STRAUS, M.A. (1954). "The integration of Sinhalese society." Research Studies of the State College of Washington, 22(December):179-227.

RYDER, R.G. (1968). "Husband-wife dyads versus married strangers." Family Process, 7(September):233-237.

SHEARER, L. (1975). "Ingeborg Dedichen: She was the great love of Aristotle Onassis." Parade, July 20, pp. 4-5.

STARK, R., and McEVOY, J., III (1970). "Middle class violence." Psychology Today, 4(November):52-65.

STEINMETZ, S.K. (1974). "Occupational environment in relation to physical punishment and dogmatism." In S.K. Steinmetz and M.A. Straus (eds.), Violence in the family. New York: Harper and Row.

STEINMETZ, S.K., and STRAUS, M.A. (eds., 1974). Violence in the family. New York: Harper and Row. (Originally published by Dodd, Mead.)

STRAUS, M.A. (1971). "Some social antecedents of physical punishment: A linkage theory interpretation." Journal of Marriage and the Family, 33(November):658-663. Also reprinted in S.K. Steinmetz and M.A. Straus (eds.), Violence in the family. New York: Harper and Row, 1974.

——— (1973). "A general systems theory approach to a theory of violence between family members." Social Science Information, 12(June):105-125.

——— (1974a). "Leveling, civility, and violence in the family." Journal of Marriage and the Family, 36(February):13-29, plus addendum in August 1974 issue. Reprinted in Nursing Education, 1974, and in R.W. Cantrell and D.F. Schrader (eds.), Dynamics of marital interaction. Dubuque, Iowa: Kendall/Hunt, 1974.

——— (1974b). "Cultural and social organizational influences on violence between family members." In R. Prince and D. Barrier (eds.), Configurations: Biological and cultural factors in sexuality and family life. Lexington, Mass.: Lexington Books—D.C. Heath.

TRUNINGER, E. (1971). "Marital violence: The legal solutions." Hastings Law Journal, 23(November):259-276.

WHITEHURST, R.N. (1974). "Violence in husband-wife interaction." Pp. 75-82 in S.K. Steinmetz and M.A. Straus (eds.), Violence in the family. New York: Harper and Row.

WILLIAMS, D.B. (1974). "Compensating victims of crimes of violence: Another look at the scheme." Pp. 147-153 in I. Drapkin and E. Viano (eds.), Victimology: A new focus. Vol. 2: Society's reaction to victimization. Lexington, Mass.: Lexington Books.

WINTER, W.D., FERREIRA, A.J., and BOWERS, N. (1973). "Decision-making in married and unrelated couples." Family Process, 12:83-94.

WOLFGANG, M.E. (1956). "Husband-wife homicides." Corrective Psychiatry and Journal of Social Therapy, 2:263-271.

——— (1958). Patterns in criminal homicide. New York: Wiley.

3

WOMEN'S DEPENDENCY AND FEDERAL PROGRAMS

SUSAN KINSLEY

In public debates over government programs affecting the family, rarely has the dependence of wives been an issue. Yet nearly every one of these programs in some way promotes that dependency. Behind many federal laws or programs that impinge upon family life is the assumption that the husband is—and should be—the primary wage earner and that the wife is—and should be—primarily a housekeeper and mother. Policy makers have consistently had a clearer vision of "proper" family roles than of the best means of achieving any of the primary goals, such as "fair" taxation or support for needy families. In assuming that society does and should operate according to traditional sex roles, policy makers have often created programs that fail to work as planned when couples deviate from the traditional family patterns. Furthermore, role assumptions implicit in public laws reinforce the family conventions that they have presumed, both financially and psychologically.

This chapter analyzes three areas of federal involvement—income tax, social security, and public welfare. These programs and their enabling legislation illustrate several ways in which the often unstated assumptions about proper family roles have permeated public policy and helped sustain the dependent status of wives.

In order to appreciate how federal policy has promoted dependency, one must understand the relationship between that dependency and the traditional roles. At the core of a wife's dependence on her husband is her inferior earning power. A wife can be "dependent" upon a husband earning more than she even if she is capable of surviving financially without him. As long as she is not able to get a job with pay and prestige at least equivalent to that of her husband, she must rely upon him to maintain her standard of living and social status. Her dependence on him is reinforced by her attachment to her current life-style and the relative disparity in their earning power.

A wife who does not consider herself a breadwinner is likely to be less aggressive than her husband in pursuing job opportunities, raises, and promotions, especially when they involve overtime, geographic mobility, or inflexible hours. She is less likely to undertake long or arduous training to escape a dead-end job. However, she is more likely to encounter job discrimination, because employers, like herself, expect less of her than of her male counterparts. Furthermore, a wife who is the primary housekeeper and child-rearer has less time and energy to devote to a job than a man who has a wife to do these things. Psychologically and physically, the woman's family role contributes to her inferior ability to earn money outside the home.

Over the past three decades, the participation of American wives—and particularly mothers—in the job market has increased dramatically without a corresponding adjustment in home work patterns. At the outset of World War II, fewer than 1 married woman in 6 and only 1 out of 10 women with children under 18 held paying jobs. In 1976, over two-fifths of all wives—and mothers—were employed. During that same period, opinion surveys have charted an impressive reversal in the public's attitude toward working wives. They have gone from the unacceptable exception to the approved norm (Gallup:131). At the same time, several studies indicate that roles within the family have not changed (Hedges and Barnett, 1972:10). A recent survey of households in Syracuse, New York, revealed that husbands averaged about 1.6 hours a day on household tasks whether or not their wives worked. Wives employed more than 30 hours a week averaged an additional 5 hours a day on home chores. Another study found that, even when husbands spend substantial amounts of time working around the home, chores still tended to divide along sex-stereotyped lines. Women still perform the services requiring every day attention—cooking, cleaning, shopping, child care—while the men could schedule their more occasional services—such as yard and maintenance work—into available time.

Women's increased participation in the labor force has not improved their earning potential. In fact, the income gap between women and men has widened, rather than narrowed, in recent years as more women have entered the work force. Several facts indicate that adherence to traditional family roles is a large factor in this differential. Family responsibilities are a major reason why married women leave the work force. In 1970, over half of the 6.5 million women stopping work cited home or school responsibilities as the cause. About one-third of the 2.7 million women who wanted work did not seek a job for the same reason. Women with small children are also more likely to work part-time (Hedges and Barnett, 1972:11).

Job segregation by sex has been identified as a major cause of the income gap between men and women (Bergman, 1971). Segregation of family duties undoubtedly sets the model for segregation in the work force. Government action is thus by no means the only reason why families continue to follow sex-stereotyped roles. But public policy has undoubtedly played a part, and the following discussion sets forth just what that part has been.

PUBLIC WELFARE

There are no groups whose basic family patterns the government can influence more than those unable to support themselves: the old, the disabled, the unemployed, and the chronically poor (those who, whether employed or not, are unable to earn a living wage). And nowhere is government advocacy of sex roles more blatant and effective than in its public assistance program known as Aid to Families of Dependent Children (AFDC). Congress has, in practice, established two categories within AFDC: one for men, stressing self-sufficiency, and one for women (wives and mothers), emphasizing dependence.

AFDC provides direct cash relief to needy families with several stipulations. The stated purpose of the program is to prevent poverty from depriving children of their own parent's care. Over 97% of the recipients are female-headed families (U.S. Department of Labor, Women's Bureau, 1975:230). Program administrators have historically aimed at improving the quality of family life rather than family prosperity. In practice, the government has assumed a role quite similar to that of the traditional husband. As one critic of the program has put it, "You trade in A man for THE man" (Tillman, 1972:51, 52-53).

The Work Incentive Program (WIN) stresses job placement and training—shrinking the welfare rolls by making families self-sufficient. Only AFDC recipients are eligible for WIN. Although fewer than 3% of AFDC recipients are male, 30% of WIN's registrants are men (U.S. Department of Labor, Women's Bureau, 1975:231).

The predominance of female-headed households among those receiving public help underscores women's dependent status within the family. Because many women are not trained or educated with the expectation of becoming self-supporting breadwinners, women who lose their husbands fare much worse than men who lose their wives. While women head only 12% of all families, they head 45% of all households with income below the poverty line (U.S. Department of Labor, Women's Bureau, 1975:141).

The disproportionate number of men in WIN follows legislative design. Most adults receiving AFDC funds must register for WIN. However, women are exempt if their husbands have registered. In other words, Congress has assumed that a married woman somehow needs work less if she has a husband. Similarly, selection of participants for the program follows a list of priorities set by Congress. Men head that list. Women can be accepted only after all registered men are placed. Because WIN slots are limited, most mothers on welfare—even those who might want jobs—are excluded.

As if the priority system were not enough to keep mothers out of the job program, the federal government has added a strong financial incentive for administrators to include men over women in WIN. The state that administrates the program must provide mothers enrolled in the program—but not fathers—with enough money to cover their child-care expenses. One WIN administrator has estimated that this provision costs about $100 per month for each woman (C. Walker, 1971:288). With limited funds, WIN can reach more people when its administrators accept fewer women.

Behind the government's approach is the attitude that people are on welfare because they have failed—they have the wrong values, the wrong approach to life. Women end up on welfare because they have failed to get a man to support them and their children. Men are on welfare because they have failed to find or retain work. Neither has properly fulfilled the traditional role. The ultimate solution, judging from current welfare policy, is to push the welfare poor into traditional sex roles—that is, find the woman a husband (or provider) and find the man a job.

Several AFDC provisions reflect this attitude. If an official of the program concludes that the welfare recipient does not need state assistance, he or she can cut off funds even in situations in which the family income falls far below the poverty level. If a woman has a husband (even if he has deserted her) or a husband substitute—a "man in the house" in welfare language—the state administrators have often decided that she is ineligible for funds. If a woman is an unwed mother, recent amendments to the law require her to name and locate the father of her illegitimate child in order to qualify for AFDC aid. If she can, she must make the man support her. If a man on welfare refuses to work, he too is ineligible. Of course, he is not expected to find a wife to support him. A woman who refuses the aid of "her man" is not considered to deserve public assistance any more than a man who refuses to accept employment.

The stipulations accompanying welfare aid are aimed at preparing the man or woman for the role that will overcome his or her present failure: to assist the man in finding sustained work and to help the woman become a dependent mother and housewife. In effect, the government plays the part of the person's former source of money: for the man, the government resembles the employer, demanding a willingness to work in exchange for payments; for the woman on welfare, the government, in many ways, assumes the characteristics of the traditional husband. As one former AFDC recipient has described the system:

> The truth is that AFDC is like a super-sexist marriage. You trade in a man for *the* man. But you can't divorce him if he treats you bad (because you need the money). He can divorce you, of course, cut you off any time he wants. But in that case, *he* keeps the kids, not you.
>
> THE man runs everything. In ordinary marriage, sex is supposed to be for your husband. On AFDC, you're not supposed to have sex at all. You give up control of your own body. It's a condition of aid. You may even have to get your tubes tied so you can't never have children just to avoid being cut off welfare.
>
> THE man, the welfare system, controls your money. He tells you what to buy, where to buy it, and how much things cost. If things—rent, for instance—really cost more than he says they do, it's just too bad for you. He's always right. Everything is budgeted down to the last penny; and you've got to make your money stretch.
>
> THE man can break into your house any time he wants to poke into your things. You've got no right to protest. You've got no right to privacy when you go on welfare. [Tillman, 1973:52-53]

The final irony of the government's philosophy and approach to the welfare poor is that it fails to meet its basic goals precisely *because* it assumes that mothers and fathers should conform to traditional roles. A study of welfare recipients in Detroit notes a substantial difference in the problems of male and female welfare recipients (Wicker, 1973:35):

> Contrary to stereotype, the women do not have large numbers of children, but they do tend to be the only workers in their families and they work for the lowest wages. The men, on the other hand, usually make much better wages and sometimes are helped by a working wife or older child, but have such large families that they cannot adequately support them.

In that situation, job training and placement for female recipients might eventually take them off the welfare rolls, while it is not likely to help the men, who really need a direct relief to assure their children adequate support and care.

INCOME TAX

The income tax, in its present form, supports the traditional, dependent role of wives through several provisions which discourage them from entering the work force. The code's work-disincentive derives from the fact that it fails to fully recognize the value to a family of a wife's unpaid household services and the cost of replacing those services when she works outside the home. On top of the work disincentive, the tax code reinforces the traditional family model—including the dependent wife—by defining her as a family member rather than defining her on the basis of her own achievements and abilities. Congress has reached both results by failing to recognize the prevalence—much less the necessity—of the working wife. Three aspects of the code should be noted: (1) limits on deductions allowed for child care, (2) aggregation of family income, and (3) income-splitting.

CHILD CARE DEDUCTIONS*

Although the present tax provisions for child care are the most liberal ever enacted, few families are able to deduct the entire cost of replacing a mother who seeks paid work, and many families receive no tax relief at all. Section 214 of the tax code allows couples

*See editor's note p. 85.

earning a combined income under $35,000 with dependent children under 15 years to deduct up to $400 a month from their taxable income when both spouses work.

The system, however, is full of holes through which many deserving families fall. First, the deduction is available only to couples who itemize their deductions, which eliminates most low-wage earners. Second, only families in which both spouses work "substantially full-time" are eligible for the deduction. This disqualifies women who work part-time or who are in school to train for better job opportunities. Third, the law discounts any payments to live-in relatives. This section, for example, deprives a woman living with her son, daughter, niece, or other relative of an opportunity to be paid for her child-care services. Fourth, deductions are also only available to the parent who claims the children as dependents for tax purposes. This provision hurts the divorced woman who has custody of children most of whose support is paid by their father. In this situation, neither parent can claim the child-care deduction even though the woman needs it in order to be able to leave home and earn her own living. Finally, Congress has placed a ceiling of $35,000 on the amount that a couple can earn and still qualify for the child-care deduction. While a couple earning that amount of money can probably afford to replace the wife's services, child-care expenditures nevertheless eat into a working mother's net income and reduce her financial incentive to seek paid work.

(Editors' Note: As this chapter was going to press, Congress amended the tax code, replacing the child care deduction with a child care credit. The new provision eliminates many objectionable aspects mentioned above, although the amount of relief remains inadequate. Taxpayers at all levels of income can now subtract 20% of their child-care expenses from the taxes they pay. However, the new law limits the credit to $800 ($400 per child)—still well below the estimated $1,000-$2,800 a year cost of care for one child. In addition, the poorest people receive no credit at all since they have no taxes against which to credit their expenses.)

AGGREGATION

Since 1948 Congress has designated the family—rather than the individual—as the unit upon which it calculates tax liability. Under this system, two couples who have equal *aggregate* income pay the same tax rate on their combined earnings regardless of who actually earns the money. That is, a husband and wife, each earning $15,000 a year, are in the same tax bracket as a husband and sole breadwinner earning $30,000 a year. The work disincentive for housewives built into this system comes into play when a woman accustomed to living on her husband's earnings contemplates entering the work force. She pays the same tax rate on her first dollar of earnings as her husband paid on his last. If his last $1,000 of income fell into the 25% tax bracket, her *first* $1,000 of earnings would be taxed at 25% and the rate would rise from there. As a result, her paycheck may not add much to the family's spendable income.

Tax scholars and analysts commonly justify taxing the family's rather than the individual's income along the same lines. One of many commentators on this subject has put it this way:

> So long as family harmony prevails, equal-income couples can purchase equal quantities of goods and services and probably make their economic decisions in substantially identical fashions. These common characteristics have been regarded by most theorists as more important in fixing tax liability of equal-income couples than differences in ownership of property, even though technical ownership may become crucial if the marriage is dissolved. [Bittker, 1975:1395]

In other words, aggregation assumes that a wife's social and economic opportunities relate to the family's income, not her own. But this is not true. Consider Mrs. T., a woman without marketable job skills whose husband makes $60,000 a year. Certainly, she can purchase as many goods as Mrs. L., a wife making $30,000 on her own, the same amount as Mr. L. Mrs. T's. social and economic opportunities, however, hardly match those of Mrs. L. For one thing, Mrs. T. must continue her marriage to maintain her spending level. Mrs. L. depends upon no one to maintain her income. Even married, Mrs. T. has none of the status that one derives from one's job. Mrs. L. not only has $30,000 a year to spend but also has the independence and personal recognition that accompany her job.

Yet, the aggregation aspect of the tax code implicitly assumes that these women are equal. Although the code's provisions are written in sex-neutral terms, it is obvious that Congress envisioned the wife as the natural beneficiary of her husband's job and income status. By doing so, Congress has lent credence to the model of the psychologically and financially dependent wife.

INCOME-SPLITTING

Not only has Congress set tax liability in terms of family rather than individual income, it has also created the myth that half the combined marital earnings—for tax purposes at least—belong to either spouse. Under the theory of income-splitting, the IRS divides their aggregate earnings in half in order to determine their tax *rate,* then multiplies the tax liability by two to determine their total tax bill.

This system benefits single-breadwinner families but penalizes two-earner couples. Through the income-splitting device, the married, lone breadwinner earning $30,000 a year "enjoys" a tax rate only slightly higher than that of a single person earning half that much. A married woman (or man) who actually earns half the family income, however, pays a higher tax rate than a single person earning *the same amount.* In addition, married people filing a joint return pay taxes on a higher proportion of their income than do their single counterparts, since Congress limits a married couple to one standard deduction or low-income allowance per family. Two single people could claim two deductions.

By penalizing the two-earner family, of course, Congress implicitly discourages such an arrangement. The total effect of the three tax provisions on the wife considering employment can be substantial. In 1973, one economist offered Congress the following hypothesis as an illustration (Blumberg, 1973:229):

> Mrs. X is married to a young executive making $15,000 a year. She is offered two jobs: an industrial job that promises long hours and pays $15,000, and a teaching job with flexible hours and a salary of $10,000. Since Mrs. X feels she must bear primary responsibility for the home duties, she considers only the teaching job. She calculates that it would cost $2,400 a year for day care for her child, $1,000 a year for suitable wardrobe, $500 a year for lunch, $600 for commuting and $500 for miscellaneous expenses (e.g., larger reliance on convenience foods).

After Mrs. X deducts the increased family expenses and federal taxes (at her husband's marginal rate), as well as increased state, local, and Social Security taxes (which, as will be shown later, also bear more heavily on working couples), she ends up adding only $1,592 to the family coffers. A wife whose sole objective in taking a job is to increase the buying power of the family might understandably conclude that working is not worth the effort.

SOCIAL SECURITY

The social security system involves both a tax and a benefit system. As a tax, the social security tax discourages wives from working, while, as a public assistance scheme, it reinforces women's dependence upon their husbands. Like the tax code, the social security system promotes dependency through its assumption about family roles. Payments to qualified retired workers, a majority of whom are men, are earned through years of social security tax contributions. The dependent spouse benefit is "earned" by virtue of being married to an insured worker.

Many of the principles at work in the tax code are present in the social security system. The social security tax, because of its regressive nature, tends to bear most heavily on the secondary wage earner. In 1976, workers paid social security tax on the first $15,300 of income. The government took 5.85% of all earnings below that level. Thus, people earning less than $15,300 a year—including the vast majority of working wives—paid a greater proportion of their income to the social security fund than did those earning over $15,300. In 1973, 3% of working women earned more than $15,000 a year compared to almost 16% of men (U.S. Department of Labor, Women's Bureau, 1975:128). Like the tax code, social security assessments discourage wives from working by taking a disproportionate share of their paychecks.

Second, social security taxes, like personal income taxes, penalize the two-earner family. Because social security exacts a greater share of the income of low-wage earners, two coequal "breadwinners" each earning $15,000 will pay twice as much social security tax as a single breadwinner earning twice as much.

While social security taxes come from the paychecks of working people, social security *benefits* flow not only to retired workers but to their families as well. Workers, therefore, subsidize the benefits of dependent non-wage earners. This produces a situation in which a working wife's social security payments help to provide retirement benefits for dependent wives of male workers. At the same time, the working wife's payments fail to improve her own benefits over those that she would have received if she had never worked or contributed to the system. In fact, one-sixth of retired working women can collect more as dependents than they can on their own earnings record.

While thus providing incentives for wives to stay home, the social security system magnifies the dependent status of women already reliant upon their husbands' earnings: the nonworking or secondary wage-earning wives. First, by keying social security payments to a retired person's former earnings, Congress has created a system in which a retired working wife may benefit more as her husband's dependent simply because he has earned more. The more one makes while working and the longer one has worked in jobs "covered" under the act, the more money one's family receives upon retirement. Because some married women have never had paid employment or have worked in jobs that have traditionally paid less or have worked fewer years or in noncovered jobs, most of them receive at least part of their social security benefits as "dependents" of their husbands (U.S. Department of Labor, Women's Bureau, 1975:175-176).

On top of this, Congress has conditioned these wives' payments upon the continuation of their dependency. Until 1965, a woman who contributed her services to the family through unpaid housework received *no* benefits if her husband divorced her. That year Congress amended the act to provide wives social security payments if the divorce occurred after 20 years of marriage. Even so, the divorced woman receives social security benefits only when her ex-husband retires, and only if she has not remarried. The system forces her to continue to depend upon a man to whom she is no longer even married. If she divorces before 20 years of marriage, she receives no benefits despite her years of contribution to the family's well-being.

As with the tax code, the social security system promotes dependency by defining women as family members rather than as individuals, by ignoring the prevalent phenomenon of the working wife and by failing to recognize the value of housework. The penalty against two-worker families derives mainly from the fact that Congress sees women as dependent family members, not as individuals. Two-earner families suffer because the unit paying taxes—the individual—differs from the unit receiving benefits—the family. If wives never worked, as the law seems to assume, no discrepancy would exist; the husband's earnings would be the family's income. Similarly, the provisions which exacerbate the dependence of nonworking wives derive from the program's assumption that housework is not valuable. If the social security system in some way taxed families and credited wives for their unpaid work in the home, they could earn benefits regardless of whether they stayed married or dependent. Several proposals along these lines have been introduced in Congress. These include schemes which would tax the "imputed" income of the housewife (the value that the family derived from her services in the home) and plans which would credit half a working spouse's social security payments to the other spouse.

Likewise, if Congress had based benefit levels upon an individual's own productivity—whether paid or not—not only might wives' self-reliance increase but also the ability of the program to perform as designed would also improve. Social security is supposed to operate like a pension plan or insurance program; the taxes credited to a worker's record are intended to finance the benefits received upon retirement. But, the social security taxes do not fully pay for the benefits given to retirees. A major factor is undoubtedly the fact that so many dependents who pay no social security taxes receive benefits nonetheless. A system that taxed all adults who were to receive benefits could go far toward making both the social security system and wives self-supporting.

CONCLUSIONS

The interplay between public law and public opinion is a dynamic one. Laws not only codify social attitudes prevalent at the time of passage but also lend credence to those views long after the basis for their popularity has disappeared. Congress enacted the joint tax return, welfare, and social security legislation during a period when the traditional family role model accurately described the majority of American marriages and correctly reflected public opinion. That traditional family, however, is no longer the norm; most wives work outside the home during some, if not most, of their married lives. Yet, these conventional role assumptions remain an integral part of legislative schemes, and the public programs to which they gave birth have slowed the emancipation of American wives from their traditional dependence upon their husbands. Each program, in its own way, pressures wives to follow different work patterns than their husbands—from the tax code's subtle economic penalty of two-earner couples to AFDC's outright coercion.

Because these assumptions pervade public programs in so many

subtle and deeply ingrained ways, simple solutions are inadequate. It
seems possible that reform aimed at ridding programs of their
traditional assumptions might promote the independence of wives
more successfully than a campaign aimed at more specific purposes
—e.g., encouraging women to enter the work force or men to
undertake housework. At any rate, educational campaigns to change
work patterns would be ineffective without policy changes to lend
them legitimacy.

REFERENCES

BELL, C.A. (1973). "Women and Social Security contributions and benefits." Paper
    prepared for hearings on the Economic Problems of Women, Joint Economic
    Committee, 93rd Congress, July 25.
BERGMAN, B. (1971). "The economics of women's liberation." Proceedings of the
    American Psychological Association, September.
BITTKER, B.I. (1975). "Federal income taxation and the family." Stanford Law Review,
    27(July):1389.
BLUMBERG, G. (1971). "Sexism in the code: A comparative study of income taxation of
    working wives and mothers." Buffalo Law Review, 21:49.
——— (1973). Testimony at the hearings on the Economic Problems of Women before the
    Joint Economic Committee, 93rd Congress, 1st Session, Pt. II, p. 229.
BRODY, W.H. (1975). "Economic value of a housewife: Research and statistics note" (U.S.
    Department of Health, Education, and Welfare, publication no. 75-11701, August 28).
GALLUP, G. (1972). Gallup Poll: Public opinion, 1935-71 (3 vols.). New York: Random
    House.
HAUSMAN, L.J. (1969). "From welfare rolls to payrolls? The welfare system as a
    manpower and rehabilitation system." In A.R. Weber, F.H. Cassell, and W.L. Ginsburg
    (eds.), Public-private manpower policies. Madison, Wisc.: Industrial Relations Research
    Association.
HEDGES, J., and BARNETT, J.K. (1972). "Working women and the division of household
    tasks." Monthly Labor Review, April, pp. 9-14.
NUSSBAUM, J.M. (1973). "The tax structure and discrimination against working wives."
    National Tax Journal, 25(2):183-191.
TILLMAN, J. (1973). "Welfare is a women's issue." Pp. 51-53 in F. Klagsburn (ed.), The
    first Ms. reader.
U.S. Department of Labor, Women's Bureau (1975). 1975 handbook on women workers
    (Bulletin 297). Washington, D.C.: Author.
WALKER, C.M. (1971). "Sex discrimination in government benefit programs." Hastings
    Law Journal, 23(November):277.
WALKER, K.E. (1975). "Economic contributions of the homemaker." Unpublished speech
    given at the Women's Bureau's 55th anniversary conference on "Women in the economy:
    Full freedom of choice," September 12.
WICKER, T. (1973). "The poor and the work ethic." New York Times, July 13, p. 35.

4

PARTNERSHIP MARRIAGE
Legal Reforms Needed

JOAN M. KRAUSKOPF

The family is a revered and valued institution in our society, and so also is the dignity and worth of each individual, man or woman. Law serves best when it serves the values of society. We need a law of the family which furthers family stability and which at the same time accords equal value and opportunity to wife and husband. The role of wife, mother, homemaker is valued perhaps more than any other single role in our society, but valued also is the opportunity for a woman to assume productive roles outside the home. We need a law of the family which enables women to choose either role, exclusively or at different times, without inequitable consequences. Neither the tension between furthering family welfare as distinguished from individual welfare, nor the tension between furthering the welfare of women as homemakers contrasted with women as wage earners is accommodated well by the current family law. Changes are needed both in the common law jurisdictions which base their law on that developed in England and in the community property jurisdictions which base their law on that developed in Spain.[1] The family law of all states would best implement the generally accepted values in our society if it were based on a partnership model of marriage.[2]

THE EXISTING LAW OF THE FAMILY

The legal relationships of a married woman and man in the common law states are governed by traditions originating in or influenced by feudalism and Christianity (DeFuniak and Vaughn, 1971; Sayre, 1943; Johnston, 1972). The law was summarized over a hundred years ago by the Ohio Supreme Court (Phillips v. Graves, 1870:380):

> Whatever may be the reason of the law, the rule is maintained, "that the legal existence of the wife is merged in that of the husband, so that, in law, the husband and wife are one person."

> The husband's dominion over the person and property of the wife is fully recognized. She is utterly incompetent to contract in her own name. He is entitled to her society and her service; to her obedience and her property. . . .

> In consideration of his marital rights the husband is bound to furnish the wife a home and suitable support.

Only control of the wife's separate property has changed since that court spoke. Four characteristics dominate the law of husband and wife today: Husband as head of the family; husband entitled to the wife's services; separation of assets; husband obligated to support wife.

HUSBAND AS HEAD OF THE FAMILY

In most states, the legal head of the family is the husband, and, in fact, some states have recently reenacted statutes to that effect (California Civil Code, 1970:§5101). The rationale usually given has not changed since 1898 (Haggett v. Hurley, 1898:563): "To insure the unity and preservation of the family, there seemed to be thought necessary a complete identity of interests, and a single head with control and power. The husband was made that head, and given the power, and in return was made responsible for the maintenance and conduct of the wife." Jeremy Bentham justified male dominance because the man is stronger (Johnston, 1972:48). Wide legal authority to determine the standard of living of the family, the child-rearing method, the household management, and the family domicile is given to the husband. The law gives him "almost unbounded discretion as to expenditures and style of living" (Crozier, 1935:33).

HUSBAND ENTITLED TO THE WIFE'S SERVICES

Second, a wife must provide her husband with her services as a companion and household servant as a consequence of marriage

(Crozier, 1935; Johnston, 1972; Karowe, 1974; Weitzman, 1974; Krauskopf and Thomas, 1974; Clouston v. Remlinger, 1970). Only a few years ago a Connecticut court thus described the wife's duties to the husband (Rucci v. Rucci, 1962): "to be his helpmeet, to love and care for him in such a role, to afford him her society and her person, to protect and care for him in sickness, and to labor faithfully to advance his interests." The court further stated that she was to perform "her household and domestic duties . . . without compensation therefor. A husband is entitled to the benefit of his wife's industry and economy." Since services in the home belong to the husband, if the wife does activities at home such as babysitting, sewing, or telephone solicitation for a fee, she may find that the earnings actually belong to the husband, not her (Tyron v. Casey, 1967). Today the legal consequences of the wife's obligation to render services to the husband appear most often when an outsider has negligently injured the wife, such as in an automobile accident. It is the husband, not the wife, who has the legal claim against the wrongdoer for the value of the household services that the injured wife is unable to perform (Wallis v. City of Westport; Krauskopf and Thomas, 1974:561).

An important factor in connection with the responsibility to render household services is that the wife is not entitled to any share in the family assets for her services. She may be the best housekeeper and most considerate and compassionate mother and wife, but she is not entitled to an allowance, to a claim on the husband's earnings, to wages, or to a share in any of the property that she has indirectly helped the husband to earn. The wife's entire economic worth can be absorbed in her wifely role, but she is entitled to no economic reward for her service. So long as a woman spends all her energy and time in the home, where the law assumes she should be, her economic dependence on her husband is assured; and, as noted by Johnston (1972:1066), assured also is male dominance of the marital unit. The obligation to perform labor without compensation creates an economic relationship between wife and husband like no other since the days of slavery; in economic terms the wife is the husband's property (Crozier, 1935:28).

SEPARATION OF ASSETS

Until the latter half of the 19th century wives could not make contracts, could not bring law suits, could not own and control their own earnings or property. Everything they owned was subject to the control of their husbands. Some authorities (Johnston, 1972; Karowe, 1974:54) suggest that the movement for reform came either from fathers who wanted to leave property to their married daughters free of their husband's control or from husbands who wanted to cut off their own creditors by placing property in their wives' name. Whatever the reasons, by the end of the century each state had enacted a Married Women's Property Act. Although they varied from state to state, these acts generally gave married women the right to own and control their separate property, including their earnings from employment outside the home. However, as described by Karowe (1974:55), "These new freedoms were in the main empty rights for most women. . . . They did not change her ownership of her own labor." Most wives did not earn; most wives expended all their energies in child-bearing, child-raising, and a multitude of essential tasks in the home. The culturally and legally defined role of wife was to contribute to the marital unit by performance of household services, even to producing soap, candles, yarn, cloth, medicines. As Clare Booth Luce (1973) so aptly described her, "Woman was the first industrialist." However, the reformed law did not require recognition of that contribution in monetary terms. It remains true that for most wives the law, by permitting her to control her own property, does not put the wife on an equal basis with the husband because only he, in fact, earns (Younger, 1973:213). Yet it has been widely recognized that "the wife who spends almost all her married life in homemaking and child rearing contributes significantly to the family's economic welfare by making it possible for the husband to earn income and amass property during the marriage" (Levy, 1968:165).

Because the law gives the homemaker no property rights during the marriage, she is totally dependent upon the husband's charity. In over half the families with small children, the husband earns all the funds; if he titles the family home and auto and bank accounts in his name, they are his alone. The common law courts presume that all household goods which do not have documentary title are the husband's (DiFlorida v. DiFlorida, 1975; State ex rel George v. Mitchell, 1950). In a recent Illinois case (Norris v. Norris, 1974) a farming couple who started out their marriage with nothing acquired considerable net worth in 20 years, but at the termination of the marriage the wife received only her personal belongings and clothing.

The court noted that the ordinary services of a wife cannot be taken into account in deciding whether she has any property rights in the assets acquired during the marriage. Those "ordinary" services included the hard work of a farm wife, including preparing five or six meals a day for farmhands. When a Missouri farm wife tried to prevent her husband from disposing of their personal property, livestock, and canned goods (which she had probably grown and canned), she was told by the court that she had no property rights to them (State ex rel George v. Mitchell, 1950).

Even the wife who does earn money outside the home may find herself with no claim at all on the family assets. She may use her earnings for family expenses and thereby enable the husband to save more of his earnings. If the husband invests his savings in assets titled in his name, he may be allowed to retain them all for himself (Fisher v. Wirth, 1971; Popper v. Popper, 1975).

Only at termination of the marriage by death does a wife in common law jurisdictions receive a right to any share of her husband's property (Johnston, 1972; Kulzer, 1973). At termination by divorce many courts have been given the power to award property to her.[3] Although numerous writers are calling for recognition of "marital property" rights for the spouses during an ongoing marriage, none have been created in the common law jurisdictions (Karowe, 1974; Kulzer, 1973; Krauskopf and Thomas, 1974; Weitzman, 1974). The current legal doctrine of separation of assets means that a husband may retain for himself all property or income over that needed for family support even though the wife's legal obligation to perform household services may prevent her from acquiring assets of her own.

HUSBAND'S DUTY OF SUPPORT

Unenforceable by the Wife. In return for having complete control of his wife's property and earnings and in return for her services, the husband has the legal duty to support his wife. The predominant feature of this so-called duty is that the wife has no way to enforce performance of the obligation while she lives with the husband. Very simply, there is no legal action that she can bring to require the husband to provide adequate support for herself and the children, unless she is willing to leave him and set up a separate household. As head of the household, the husband determines how much of his funds shall be spent for the family. The courts will not undermine his authority nor allow themselves to be budget makers for family units. The legislatures have created no basis for a legal action until the parties are separated. In a well-known case of this sort, McGuire v. McGuire (1953), the wife attempted to increase the level of support given her and was completely unsuccessful. The husband insisted that his family live in a house without a bathroom, kitchen sink, or adequate furnace, even though his assets were valued at over $100,000. Neither would he give the wife money for church or charities. In this case, the court ruled that the husband was not required to supply the wife with a higher level of support. Commonwealth v. George (1948) was a case involving a wife's request for some control over finances, because she was embarrassed to "have to ask for fifty cents." She was not successful.

A wife's legal right to support from her husband is little more than symbolic so long as the courts give the husband complete control of the household and refuse to make orders which would benefit the wife. The wife's right to support is an empty phrase so long as she is denied direct action against the husband. She is not entitled to an allowance, any control over family finances, or a claim against the husband's income or property.

Private Agreements Unenforceable. Attempts to achieve enforceable rights by private agreements have been unsuccessful (Warren, 1925; Krauskopf and Thomas, 1974:67). Husbands and wives, aware of the failure of the law to accord the wife specific or enforceable rights to support, have sought to do so by private agreement. They have been unsuccessful in these attempts. The common law duty of support is imposed by operation of law as an incident of the marital status, rather than as a legal obligation based on contract. The courts adopt the view that the legally imposed incidents of marriage cannot be modified. As the United States Supreme Court in Maynard v. Hill (1888) held:

> The consent of the parties is of course essential to its existence, but when the contract to marry is executed by marriage, a relation between the parties is created which they cannot change. Other contracts may be modified, restricted, or enlarged, or entirely released upon the consent of the parties. Not so with marriage. The relation once formed, the law steps in and holds the parties to various obligations and liabilities.

A few states, such as Ohio, freeze this judicially announced concept in statutes: "Husband and wife cannot, by any contract with each other, alter their legal relations, except that they may agree to an immediate separation and make provisions for the support of either of them and their children during the separation" (Ohio Revised Code, 1972: § 3103.06).

The husband's duty of support is considered essential to the preservation and stability of the marriage. As a consequence, a private contract between the husband and wife which changes the nature of his support obligation is invalid. One decision (Garlock v. Garlock, 1939), invalidated a contract for a defined level of support made between a husband and wife. The court regarded such an agreement as interfering with the necessary flexibility of family finances. But the decision had the affect of giving the husband arbitrary power in deciding how he will support the family, since a wife is unable to force support payments through the court.

Rights of Third Parties. One means through which a third party may seek enforcement of support payment is an action for necessaries, which is a right belonging to a creditor with whom the wife has done business. Under common law, if a wife is living with her husband, she may pledge his credit in order to purchase necessaries for herself or the family. However, this has been inaccurately described as a remedy afforded her if the husband neglects to support her (Ewell v. State, 1955; Attebury v. Attebury, 1974). An action for necessaries is actually a right available to the creditor, not the wife. Nothing in the law places any obligation on merchants to sell to the wife on the husband's credit. The wife must persuade the merchant to supply the goods. Very few are persuaded. Major stores always require the husband's consent, which he is completely free to refuse. An Iowa court decision reveals that even in the days of the friendly neighborhood grocer a wife could not supply her needs through this device. The court said (Graves v. Graves, 1873):

> The wife may find it difficult, if not impossible, to obtain a continuous support in this way, since such dealers and professional men would be unwilling to supply their articles or services if thus compelled to resort to litigation in order to secure their pay. Here then is a plain legal duty of the husband for the violation of which no adequate remedy ... can be had.

In reality, the merchant's burden of proving his cause of action is so heavy that he will not supply the wife with her needs unless the husband has personally agreed to pay. It is the burden of the merchant to prove that the items that he supplied were necessary and related to the standard of living set by the husband. However, since the standard of living of each family differs, it would be difficult for a merchant to determine if an article is "necessary." In addition, it must be determined by the merchant that the husband was not already supplying necessaries to the family. It is also possible that the wife has wrongfully left her husband; the remedy exists only when the wife is living with her husband or when he has wrongfully abandoned her. Obviously, pledging the husband's credit as a means to enforce the right to support is not an adequate remedy.

The family expense statutes, passed along with the married women's Property Acts in many jurisdictions, provide another third party means of enforcing support obligations. The statutes may have been passed in order to assure creditors that, in the event that the wife's property was unseizable through the husband, they would still be paid. Both the husband's and the wife's property under these statutes is directly subject to the obligation for family support. In some states the family expense statute (Illinois Revised Statutes, 1959, ch. 68, 15) creates a *personal* obligation of both husband and wife to pay the family expenses. The family expense statute does nothing to create direct personal rights for support in either spouse, but it represents a move toward equality of responsibility for family expenses.[4]

Criminal nonsupport laws are an additional statutory means to enforce support by third parties. It is a criminal offense in almost all states for a husband to refuse to support his wife. These statutes cannot be used as an effective remedy for the enforcement of the common law duty of support because of two serious limitations on this offense. First, the majority of statutes cannot be applied to the wife who is living with her husband; both desertion and abandonment *and* failure to support must be ascertained (Clark, 1968; Jones, 1959). In other words, the husband may stay at home and starve his wife, but he may not desert her and starve her. This reflects the traditional hesitancy to accord legal sanctions for matters within the ongoing family. Second, the statutes commonly provide that the wife must be "necessitous" or destitute—in that she is not receiving the bare essentials of life from anyone else—in order for the conviction to be sustained (American Law Reports, 1925). The most crucial fact is that no prosecutions are brought when the wife still lives with her husband. The assumption that a man living with his family and capable of support is, in fact, supporting them is so strong that it would be nearly impossible to obtain a conviction. In other words, even a statute worded so that it applies to a man living with the family is not enforced by prosecutors.

Summary. During the time that the husband and wife are living together, the husband's common law duty of support is only what he wants it to be. Because the husband owns her labor in the home, the wife is not entitled to remuneration. Because the husband is the head of the household, her "right to support" is not a right to be maintained at a level commensurate with either her efforts or the amount of the husband's earnings or assets. As the Citizen's Advisory Council on the Status of Women succinctly stated (1972): "A married woman living with her husband can, in practice, get only what he chooses to give her." The wife's dependence on the will of the husband is nearly absolute.

FAMILY LAW CONSEQUENCES

FAMILY ECONOMICS

Since the family and the homemaker are so revered in American society, it is tragic that the law fails to afford them economic protection while husband and wife live together. The ineffectiveness of the duty of support and the separation-of-assets theory of property result is no economic security whatever for the dependent homemaker-wife-mother. When first examined, it is difficult to fully grasp the uselessness of the right to support. On review, one sees that if a woman decides to live with her husband, she loses control over the decision to stay home and care for the home and the children. If the wife decides to stay with the man who spends his money foolishly, then she must resolve to live on what he gives her. If she and the children require more funds to live adequately, she is forced to obtain employment or to leave her husband. The courts pronounce that woman's place is in the home, that she is the center of family and homelife, that her highest role is to serve husband and family (Bradwell v. Illinois, 1872; Hoyt v. Florida, 1961), and that as a wife she is obligated to serve her family through household services. The law thus molds and encourages women to fulfill the full-time homemaker role, but that same law refuses to give her economic protection. Not only have women been ignorant of the necessity to improve the law, they have been positively harmed by the naive and false belief that marriage means economic security (Citizen's Advisory Council, 1972). To attempt to obtain court protection, the wife must break up the family and seek a separation or divorce decree. Neither wife nor family is protected by this law.

A concomitant of the separation of assets theory is that there is no legal recognition of the economic worth of the homemaker's services. In a society in which worth is measured in dollar terms and in which property means power, the wife's efforts are treated as worthless and the wife herself is without power because she is without property. The old saw, "Behind every great man there is a great woman," is especially true in middle-class upward-striving American families. The two-person career, in which the wife vicariously achieves satisfaction through a myriad of efforts which further her husband's career, is common (Papanek, 1973; Bernard, 1972; Weitzman, 1974). In any home in which a wife does most of the housework, child care, and day-to-day management, she indirectly enables the husband to earn and amass property. She may indeed, through her economies, directly save his earnings for investment. No matter how significant these contributions, they are not likely to be rewarded by the law.

A final economic consideration is that the woman engaging full time in the culturally valued homemaker role loses the opportunity to develop her own earning power. Earning power grows with seniority, with experience, with enhancement of the earning skill. Day by day and year by year in the homemaker role, the woman falls farther behind in earning power. When her full economic worth is eaten up by marital duties, she has neither property nor earning ability. And yet the common law system accords her no rights for that sacrifice. The wage-earning husband may retain all his earnings in excess of what he chooses to use for family support, and, in addition, he gains pension and social security rights and that all-important growth in earning power.

Such a legal system creates incentives for women to deprecate the homemaker role and to leave it, even when it may be disadvantageous to them and the children. In earlier times, when no other alternatives for women existed, this could not happen. Today the combination of effective contraception and increased employment opportunities makes it possible for women to literally walk out of the home. Women no longer have to remain in a servant-owned-property status. If the goal of the law is to encourage wives and mothers to remain in the home, the law of the last century will not do. Today family law does not serve its own goals, but is counterproductive to both family stability and enhancement of the homemaker role.

FAMILY MANAGEMENT AND SERVICE

The rigidly defined and unequal roles and obligations of husband and wife are anachronistic and antagonistic to basic values very dear to many Americans.

For many women the most significant inequity of the common law is crowning the husband as head of the household, with full authority and power over its management. The law has done so on an unfounded belief that unity and preservation of the family require a single head with power and control. That belief has been questioned vehemently since the time of John Stuart Mill. One of the world's authorities (Rheinstein, 1972) on the law of the family and divorce has pointed out that good marriages require the common effort of both parties. A family needs the joint effort of two persons interested in its survival as a social unit. A spokeswoman for the American Home Economics Association (East, 1974) objects to the current legal status of wives, because it penalizes both husband and wife and fails to provide an atmosphere in which each individual can function effectively. The companionship, partnership marriage is the marriage of modern-day society. The legally subservient status of the wife labels her as a second-class participant in the venture.

The statistics tell us that a great deal of the time that wives in large numbers once devoted to household services are now being devoted to earning wages. A value currently accepted in our society is that each person should be accorded equal opportunity to develop his or her own capacities and that a married woman, in particular, should be free to engage in productive roles outside the family. Yet the common law obligates the wife to serve her family only with household services; it is inflexible in assuming that a married woman carries out only one stereotypical role in any family and throughout her married life. The most striking phenomenon of recent times is that high percentages of married women are employed for major portions of their married life. In the United States, 40% of the work force is female (U.S. Department of Labor, 1970). Of the married women living with their husbands, 41% were employed in 1970, up

from only 16% in 1940 (Kreps, 1971). In Missouri, over 50% of the
mothers of school-age children have outside employment, and 34%
of mothers with preschool children also work (Missouri Commission
on the Status of Women, 1973). "Since the period immediately
preceding World War II, the number of women workers has more
than doubled, but the number of working mothers has increased
eightfold" (U.S. Department of Labor, 1972).

An article by Clare Booth Luce (1973) entitled "Woman: A
Technological Castaway" reveals that tasks that were once done in
the home by women are now performed elsewhere:

> Today all the weaving, almost all the preparation and production of food,
> and the manufacture of all household equipment and utensils are "man's
> work." Man is now the weaver, baker, butcher, candlestick maker,
> pot-and-pan manufacturer of society. There is almost no productive
> domestic task, once traditional and "natural" to woman, that man has not
> taken over.

The result has been that women have been taking jobs in order to
make a contribution to the family financially, whereas previously
their contribution was made through household services.

To require only the husband to make monetary contributions
when both partners are earning wages is unrealistic. This traditional
approach ignores the changing societal role that has been forced
upon women by the technological revolution. More than 30 years
ago, Sayre (1943:864) emphasized that, when both husband and
wife were contributing earnings and performing household tasks, a
legal requirement that each individual contribute to the marriage as
he or she is able would be more realistic.

In addition to the need to help their families economically, there
are other reasons why married women choose to spend large portions
of their married life in the professional work force. In contrast to the
expected early death of a woman one hundred years ago, today's
young American wife expects to live to be over 75 years old. She
looks forward to more years in which to do more things. Second, the
young wife and husband today want only two children. The relative
effectiveness of birth control converts that desire to fact. The woman
today is having fewer children and so is free to do other things which
interest her. Even if mothers remain full time in the home until both
children reach 18 years, this is only 20 years out of an expected 57
years of adulthood, leaving 37 years without the responsibility of
children. In addition to the technological revolution creating

incentives for women to develop careers outside the home, the prospect of 30 or 40 years of adult life free from the demanding motherhood role opens new vistas for women. For the first time in history all women in this country have the opportunity to enter a role other than that of full-time mother and homemaker. The law is out of step with reality in failing to recognize that women not only do perform other roles in society but will do so increasingly. Legal recognition that a woman may properly play a role besides wife and mother may help to resolve the identity crisis of today's women.[5]

CONTRACTUAL LIMITS

Perhaps most ludicrous is the refusal of the courts to recognize the validity of contracts between husband and wife for money payments and property divisions. This limitation put on the husband and wife to define by contract the legal incidents of their marriage is unnecessary. When they cannot contract, husband and wife are forced into a status with legal connotations which are needless and not conducive to the stability of the family unit. Some young people have preferred to live together outside wedlock rather than be subjected to these demeaning connotations. Others wish only to be able to define the parameters of their marriage. All contractual bases for the responsibilities of support and household tasks cannot be justifiably invalidated even if some marital contracts are so far removed from the traditional concepts of marriage as to be unacceptable for legal validity. When contracting is the only means for either party to enforce the marital rights, this is particularly true. There is an inherent injustice in limiting an individual's right to control his private affairs by contract when no social advantage is demonstrated.

DEPENDENCY

The actual economic dependency of a homemaker is not inequitable in itself but is made so by the law. The refusal to value homemaking services in economic terms unfairly brands her as a socially nonproductive person. The supposed right to be supported by the husband without regard to her contributions to the family categorizes her as a parasite. In these times, when we are especially cognizant of the respect and feeling of accomplishment that each person needs and when there is widespread concern about the disintegration of families, it is folly to disregard in law the important contribution that a homemaker gives to her family. The second inequity is that the denial of compensation for homemaking contributions places the wife's financial dependency at the mercy of her husband. The dependency is wholly arbitrary so long as the legal system will not define and enforce his obligations to her.

A more far-reaching inequity that spreads from these antiquated concepts of a wife as a nonproductive person is that they shape the view that women have of themselves in society. Paulsen (1956:709) suggested that these legal concepts gave a reality to a cherished myth: "In the best of worlds Alice does not leave after breakfast for a job which may bring more money into the household than her husband's earnings. It is best if she is the protected homemaker and he the protecting provider." In the marital contract, women supposedly receive the right to financial support in exchange for domestic service. The woman's "true" role is defined *only* as housekeeper and mother, making any productive work outside the home seem secondary to a woman's "real" function. Consequently, women tend to *automatically* define their roles as home-related and do not aspire to other roles. Their dependency is increased by an ill-informed and, therefore, not truly free choice. Weitzman describes it well (1974:1197):

> The legal rules we, as a society, have developed for regulating alimony, custody, and child support thus give priority to and reinforce women's domesticity and dependency. We have offered the young woman support and alimony—a legal guarantee of financial security if she gets married and performs her marital role well. We have told her that she need not develop her individual capacity, for her economic security will be dependent on her husband's (not her own) earning ability. Thus our society encourages girls to sacrifice their own education and training to further their husbands' careers. Both the middleclass college graduate who foregoes graduate school to put her husband through medical school, and the high school graduate who foregoes college to build a family, are doing what we, through the law, have encouraged them to do. Of course, as already shown, the law's guarantees are illusory. In reality, a woman's "right" to support and security for her family depends on the goodwill of her husband (in both marriage and divorce). But by the time the woman discovers that the law's guarantees are hollow, it is too late; she has typically passed the point where she could easily choose a different course.

Having chosen dependency, the traditional legal rules serve to keep the wife dependent. All the work of the household is legally the wife's responsibility, so that if she does attempt to become financially capable, the law imposes a cultural expectation that she must continue to carry the full burden of home. Thus, the law discourages her from venturing into a financially rewarding career. Even within the ambit of family responsibility, the legal characterization of husband as head of household with the responsibility for support and control of property impels him to handle the business and financial aspects of the household, thus limiting the homemaker's experiences outside the home itself.

Perhaps most devastating for the wife who wishes to develop earning power is the job discrimination she faces. In spite of the laws forbidding employment discrimination on the basis of sex (Krauskopf, 1972), women receive less pay and are refused job accessibility because they are not by legal definition the breadwinners in the family. Kulzer (1973:215) noted that the discrimination is often justified by the observation that wives are entitled to be supported by their husbands and therefore do not really need the jobs; to hire women means to take jobs away from breadwinners. The low return for the effort invested is enough to discourage the wife, who does not currently need the money, from obtaining training or employment. Thus, we have a vicious circle of dependency forever revolving: channel women into a protected and dependent role; use their dependency and protection as a rationalization for keeping them dependent; channel them into the role because they are dependent.

The ultimate tragedy is played out when that economically dependent woman is left unprotected as the law and husband so often leave her. Today we have millions of unskilled and undereducated women employed because their husbands provide too little money for the family or because they have no husband providing support. The United States Commission on Civil Rights reported (1974:5) that the median income for a husband-wife family in 1972 was $11,900 compared to $5,340 for families headed by a woman; that the median income ($6,205) earned by white female heads of families was 62% of that earned by white male heads of families ($11,504). Of the 6.6 million female-headed families, 34% are below the poverty level. The entire society pays the price for the induced dependency of wives and the ultimate failure to protect them once they are made dependent.

It is time to recognize that the "cherished myths" which relegate the woman's role only to household services is so behind the times that the law should cease doing so. We should give appropriate legal acknowlegement not only to the woman's equal role in the home as childbearer and homemaker, but also to the fact that it is proper and valuable for her to engage in other societal roles.

LEGAL REFORM

LEGISLATIVE GOALS

Reform of the current inequitable laws through legislative action is most feasible if it serves the values and interests of a large portion of our populace. The high value placed upon the family unit in our society is such that the legal system should require a commitment from its members to serve that family unit. The law should establish that the unit is of primary importance and should consider that the primary duties of husband and wife are to serve the family. Paul Sayre (1943:875) made this point over 30 years ago:

> If . . . we do nothing to assert a duty to each other in the case of husband and wife and a duty in both of them to the family as a unity, we . . . [impair] the most valuable elements of unity within the family for all cultural life. The unit is now the family and duties of husband and wife should be interpreted in terms of service to the family and thereby, of course, service to each other.

Within that framework of service to the family the parties should be free to choose roles, to develop individually, and to enjoy equal opportunities, all of which are values currently esteemed in American society.

One theory for reform is that of complete individual treatment of the persons involved so that marriage is solely a personal and not an economic relationship at all. This ideal was propounded long ago by an expert in property law (Powell, 1936:15) and by one of the world's leading feminists, Simone de Beauvoir (1953:479), who said, "The couple should not be regarded as a unit, a closed cell; rather each individual should be integrated as such in society at large." This theory of complete economic independence can work only if each spouse separately acquires property. As has been illustrated under the separation of assets law in which both husband and wife can control their individual wages, legal equality has no real value if the opportunity to earn money is not equal. However, quite a few married couples may decide to have one spouse stay at home, although equal wage-earning opportunities may be available to women. Furthermore, some women may need to be in the home and unemployed during pregnancy and after the child is born. As one writer (Younger, 1973) pointed out:

> However, if she spends her married life performing domestic services for her family, she will have no earnings during that period nor the prospect of making any when the marriage ends. The law's treatment of her, although equal to that accorded her husband, does not put her on a par with him—he, in fact, earns. Because she does not, the law should give her something to compensate for this disparity.

Equality as individuals without economic rights derived from the marital relation itself undermines both the societal desire to further homemaking and family stability and the societal desire to enhance individual opportunity because it penalizes the spouse in the homemaker role. Kulzer notes (1973:225) that "de Beauvoir would seem to turn the old oppression on its head and forbid them to be housewives, notwithstanding that some would like to be." Surely equal treatment as individuals cannot achieve equality in fact so long as one spouse is to be free to choose the homemaking role. What is needed is a system that equalizes the economic position of both spouses, thereby protecting the homemaker spouse and allowing for free choices of roles. What is needed is legal recognition of the homemaker role as a contributor to the marital economic unit.

MODELS FOR REFORM

Equal Rights Amendment. Were the ERA to be ratified, a state right or obligation based solely on sex would be invalidated. In the area of family law under the ERA, equal management rights and family obligations would be required in every state for both husband and wife. The concept of a husband-headed household based on common law would be invalidated. Passage of the ERA would lead to a modification of the husband's nominal obligation to support and the wife's duty to perform household tasks so as to allow a choice of roles by which to fulfill the obligation to serve the family (Krauskopf, 1975). State law could require the spouse who is the wage earner to support the homemaker spouse. The Senate Judiciary Committee's final report (U.S. Senate, 1972) on the Equal Rights

Amendment states: "when one spouse is primary wage earner and the other runs the home, the wage earner would have a duty to support the spouse who stays home in compensation for the performance of her or his duties."

The ERA alone will neither decrease nor increase the enforceable rights of a married woman living with her husband. The amendment would operate like de Beauvoir's individualism theory because it would not require a change in the common law separation of assets doctrine. A man or a woman would continue the right to retain whatever he or she acquired, but additional legislation would be needed to give one spouse rights in the marital assets titled in the other spouse's name alone.

Furthermore, there is no reason to suspect that the ERA will make the courts more interested in becoming involved in the finances of a family. That being the case, an individual living with his or her spouse and legally entitled to support will not be able to enforce this right. This means that a woman performing household services in the home, married to a man whose employment is away from the home, will be able to receive only the level of support determined by her husband. The assets accumulated will belong only to him, and her option is to plead for her deserved share. Equality with no legal means of enforcement is, thus, an empty word.

Since the ERA will have such a small impact on the economic rights of the wife in the home, critics of the amendment who are fearful that it would undermine the accepted homemaker role should be reassured. But proponents of the ERA should also concern themselves with this fact, because their hope that the amendment will raise a woman's economic status in the home will not be realized.

Community Property Law. The community property system is based primarily on equality. DeFuniak describes the historical development of the concept of equality (DeFuniak and Vaughn, 1971, § 11.1). He traces the development of the community property system to the Visigothic tribes:

> In adopting the concept of a community of goods, the law was realistic. It had regard for the industry and common labor of each spouse and the burdens of the conjugal partnership and community of interest. With the feeling in mind that during marriage the time and attention of husband and wife should be directed toward furthering the goals—economic, moral, social—of the marriage, the community was instituted as the most suitable vehicle for accomplishing these goals.

Thus the policy of community property was to establish equality between husband and wife in the area of property rights in marital property acquisitions, in recognition of and to give effect to the fundamental equality between the spouses based on the separate identity of each spouse and the actual contribution that each made to the success of the marriage. Note the striking difference between this and the common law doctrine of the merger of the identity of the wife into that of the husband.

Woman was considered an individual, and marriage a partnership, under community property law. An equal share of the gains and financial assets of the partnership was given to the partners to the marriage, husband and wife.

Professor Robert Sedler (1972:431) is among many legal writers who have recognized the advantages of the community property concepts. He comments:

> Under a community property system, each partner contributes his or her efforts within the home or outside, or by a combination of both, to the well-being of the marital enterprise. Each partner thereupon has the right to share equally in the wealth acquired by the joint efforts. . . .

> Under a true system of community property, in which the management would be entrusted to the partners jointly, many of the dependency problems which accompany the present legal structure of marriage could be eliminated. The contribution of the woman, if she chooses to stay at home and take care of the children, would legally be considered the equivalent of the man's. Secondly, the community property system would be more conducive to an arrangement by which both partners would share the household and child care responsibilities equally or by which the wife would be the sole "breadwinner." It would enable the parties to make their own arrangements concerning the contribution of each to the marital enterprise, would equalize those contributions and would eliminate any notion of "head of the household."

Another advantage of the community property system and the economic partnership was pointed out by Harriet Daggett (1939):

> Thoughtful students of modern marriage have expressed the view that the wife in the home should feel that her efforts are materially rewarded. The sense of satisfaction derived from the fact of remuneration would prevent, in cases where it is not necessary or desirable, the seeking of outside employment in industrial areas and elsewhere with the consequent dissatisfaction and disintegration of the family as a unit. Furthermore, the wife who is unable to earn money outside of the home would not have the feeling, despite her drudgery, of being a liability rather than an asset. The husband and children are more apt to put a higher estimate upon the efforts of the woman of the household if her job is evaluated in terms of dollars and cents. She, in turn, has a greater interest in conserving and

augmenting the family finances and takes greater responsibility in these matters.

Unfortunately, the community property system has not provided equality between husband and wife in practice. The common law system may now be less discriminatory against women than the present community property system,[6] because in many of the eight community property states, the couple's community property is subject to the sole management and control of the husband. The wife has no right to share in the disposition of marital funds, including her individual income (Younger, 1973). Therefore, adopting the present community property system would not lead to an equal partnership between husband and wife.

MARITAL PARTNERSHIP MODEL: A PROPOSAL

It is proposed that a family or marital partnership model for law reform will best serve the predominant values of society: family and homemaking, equality, and individual freedom of choice and opportunity. Such a marital partnership law would be based on true community property law principles and business partnership law principles, which are remarkably similar. During the year 1973-1974 four analyses of family law were published in respected law journals, each one recommending law reform of this kind (Karowe, 1974; Krauskopf and Thomas, 1974; Kulzer, 1973; Weitzman, 1974). Three reform features were salient in each of these recommendations: (1) basic unalterable legal obligations of the marital partnership, (2) modifiable legal economic rights and obligations of the partnership, (3) wide freedom to choose by contract the characteristics of the marital partnership.[7]

BASIC LEGAL OBLIGATIONS OF A MARRIAGE PARTNERSHIP

The law should treat husband and wife as a marital unit, with each partner owing a fundamental obligation to the family created by the marriage. The basic social unit is now the family, and the purpose of marriage itself is to create that unique unit; therefore, both husband and wife should have a duty toward the family as a unit. All vestiges of the common law concepts of merger, husband as head of the household, and wife's sole duty to perform household services should be removed and supplanted with a mutual and equal obligation of service to the marital unit, whether it includes children or not. The term "service" can include both financial and nonmonetary contributions to the marriage, so that a money-making spouse could satisfy his or her duty by contributing to the family financially, whereas the homemaker spouse could satisfy his or her obligation by services in the home. A parallel to this obligation is the business partner's duty of loyalty to the partnership and fellow partners, which in turn is an application of the duty of a fiduciary, one who undertakes to act for the benefit of another, to serve that other in preference to his personal interests. The obligation of parents to support and care for their children is now firmly established in law and should remain unalterable by the parents alone. Both service to a wife-husband unit and to a unit with children could be made basic obligations by a statutory requirement of this type: *Husband and wife are marital partners, equally obligated to serve the best interests of the family created by their marriage.*

Statutory reform should also make unalterable an obligation of spouses to outside creditors for debts incurred for family expenses. In a vast credit economy such as ours, creditors should not be insulated from reaching family property for the payment of normal family expenses. The law of business partnerships makes all the partnership property subject to payment of partnership creditors and, in addition, makes each partner personally liable to pay debts (Uniform Partnership Act, 1969, § 15, § 40). Since that is a profit-making enterprise which each partner enters for the purpose of making a profit, it may be more justifiable to place a personal responsibility for payment of debts on each individual than it would be in a marriage partnership. Currently, some states have family expense statutes which do make both marriage parties personally responsible, while other states only place a charge on the property of the spouses (Krauskopf and Thomas, 1974:571). Since the spouse buying the items would be personally liable, further protection to the creditor by a charge on the property alone may be sufficient. The charge on property could be established by statutory language to this effect: *The reasonable and necessary expenses of the family shall be chargeable by creditors upon the property of the family (marital partnership) and upon the separate property of both husband and wife, or either of them.*

MODIFIABLE LEGAL OBLIGATIONS OF A MARITAL PARTNERSHIP

Equal Rights to Management and Marital Property. In the absence of a contract, the law should postulate a democratic family unit with wife and husband having equal legal status and equal economic power within the family unit. This is what a true community property regime would be if joint control of assets were guaranteed. This is the business partnership model required by law in the absence of a differing agreement. The Uniform Partnership Act (§ 18(e), § 26) gives each partner equal rights in the management and conduct of the partnership business and equal rights to share the profits and surplus. A partner excluded from partnership business or possession of its property has a right to a court accounting of the partnership affairs (Uniform Partnership Act, 1969, § 22). There is no more reason than in a business partnership to legally specify one marital partner as dominant or to legally delineate what roles each is to play in serving the family. The various rationales for male dominance in the family partnership would be thought ludicrous if applied to a business partnership of a man and woman. They amount to a scheme for keeping women "in their place" (Krauskopf and Thomas, 1974). A legal model of equality, with freedom for the spouses to contract otherwise, is more in accord with modern values.

Although the law should set up the underlying tenets of equality and the sharing of responsibility between spouses, the law should not try to further dictate the private social relationship of the partners in the marriage. The roles that husband and wife should play in the family or even outside the family should not be dictated by law. These decisions should be left to the partners in the marriage according to their own discretion. Family laws are not effective to compel the assumption of the role of homemaker by the wife or breadwinner by the husband, but merely make life more difficult for the woman or man who assumes a nonconforming role. As Sedler (1972:419) made so clear, the right of both women and men to choose their life's work is what constitutes the basis for freedom and liberation.

A statutory basis for equal rights to management and property in a family could be worded in this fashion: *Husband and wife are entitled to share equally in the management and assets (marital property) of the family created by their marriage.*

Enforceability of Property Rights. In regard to the assets of the marital partnership, legal control can be effective, and this is where the greatest need for legal reform lies. Business partnership law allows for dissolution of the partnership and equal division of the profits and surplus acquired in the course of the partnership. It is also possible to obtain an accounting and division of profits during the progress of a business partnership. However, if business partners cannot agree to a periodic private accounting and division of their profits, they usually end their partnership. In order to discourage termination of marriages, it is essential that the marital partnership law provide not only for property rights at termination by divorce or death but also for recognition of each individual marital partner's rights during the ongoing marriage. In 1963, the Committee on Civil and Political Rights of the President's Commission on the Status of Women expressed approval of the partnership model for the marriage relationship. The committee concluded that during marriage each spouse should have a legally defined right in the earnings of the other spouse and in the property acquired by such earnings.

However, enforcement of the economics of the parties to the ongoing marriage is the subject matter that legislatures and courts have been so loath to regulate. The consequences have been dire, especially in creating incentives to end the marriage in order to obtain support orders or court decisions as to property rights. Generally, married couples do not call on the courts to work out their problems unless their private, extralegal procedures break down. If the courts and legislatures are genuinely interested in marital stability and harmony, they should establish the legal economic rights of the marital partners and intervene on request to enforce those rights. Certainly, the family and its members are entitled to as much legal protection as a business partnership and its members can achieve in an action for accounting. The legal model should provide specifically for enforcement of rights in language similar to this: *The rights and obligations of husbands and wives as they relate to control and ownership of family property are fully enforceable in a court of law. No court shall refuse to enforce any of the property rights created by law or arising out of a marriage contract solely because husband and wife are cohabiting at the time suit is brought.*

Marital Property Defined. However, provision for enforceable equal rights to marital property is not sufficient alone, because the common law jurisdictions have no legal framework of "marital property" for an ongoing marriage. The proposed legislation must define what is to be included in "marital property." As is true in community property states, this should be all property acquired by either of the spouses during the marriage, with the exception of that acquired without personal effort such as gifts or inheritance or the increased value of property owned prior to the marriage. All else would be separate property unless the owner spouse wanted it to be included in the marital property. All earnings and any assets acquired with the earnings of either spouse would be made marital or family property. In a business partnership any partner alone has the legal authority to incur debts and to use partnership funds for purchases so long as the transactions are in the ordinary course of partnership business (Uniform Partnership Act, 1969, § 9). Marital partners should have that same authority. A prototype for legislation creating these rights could be worded: *All property acquired by either the husband or wife during the marriage, except that which is the separate property of either, shall be deemed the family property of the husband and wife and shall be subject to their joint ownership, management, and control. Husband and wife are agents for one another in the ordinary course of family affairs.* At this point the statute, like that in Washington (Washington Revised Code Annual, § 26.16.030, 1961), could list certain transactions which require the concurrence of both spouses.

Separate Property Defined. This statutory scheme would make all marital property subject to family uses, but does nothing to give each of the spouses separate or individual property. The marital partnership legislation should recognize that each of the members of this marital unit are, indeed, individuals who ought to have some independent financial means if there are otherwise adequate assets for family needs. A business partnership agreement solves this problem by providing for a salary for each partner or for a periodic accounting at which time profits are divided. In most marriages, the spouses either formally or informally would make a somewhat similar arrangement. For those families that do not voluntarily make such an arrangement, the law could make such a provision in one of two ways. First, as recommended by Krauskopf and Thomas (1974:587), the law could provide that each spouse be entitled to a reasonable portion of the family income periodically as his separate "allowance" and that, if the parties could not agree upon a reasonable amount, a court should so order. A slightly different solution, recommended by Karowe (1974:78), is that periodically the living expenses should be deducted from the marital assets and the "excess" shared equally between the partners as their separate property. Under either approach, day-to-day living expenses would draw first priority on income. The "allowance" approach would give next priority to a modest amount of income for each separately, leaving as a last priority matters of capital investment such as down payment on a home, purchase of an automobile, or special savings funds such as those for college or travel. In contrast, the "excess" approach would probably cause a portion of income for capital and unusual expenditures to be set aside prior to a determination of excess. Under the latter system there may be less chance of funds remaining for individual portions. It also requires a third party determination of what is proper for long-term capital goals for this couple. The "allowance" approach avoids the necessity of that determination since the allowance takes precedence over long-term financial commitments. Of course, a combination of the systems could be utilized which would be similar to a business partnership that pays each partner a modest monthly salary and, in addition, shares among the partners the excess after all expenses, including agreed-upon capital investments, have been paid. Whichever system is followed, Mrs. McGuire and Mrs. George would not be left to beg their husbands for 50 cents! A statutory model for separate property rights in a marital partnership using the "allowance" feature follows:

Separate property includes:

(a) That property of either spouse which he or she owned before the marriage and the increase in value thereof;

(b) That property received individually by either spouse during the course of the marriage by way of gift, inheritance, or devise;

(c) That property which is the portion of the family's periodic income in excess of normal family expenses and which is set apart to each spouse as her or his "allowance" by agreement of the spouses or, in the event the spouses fail to agree, by court order upon a finding that individual ownership of such portion of the family income is fair and equitable under all the circumstances.

CONTRACTUAL OBLIGATIONS OF A MARITAL PARTNERSHIP

A special provision is needed to establish a new right to outline by marriage contract the responsibilities and duties between spouses regarding the management of the assets of the marital partnership and, also, the obligations and duties that each should assume in controlling and sharing family life.[8] However, the enforcement section should provide for enforcing only the specified contract provisions and the laws that concern property matters. Criminal law could, as before, punish failure to financially support the family or care for the children. But civil law should not attempt to require specific behavior within the marriage. Law is not a workable tool for regulating social behavior in a relationship as fundamental and personal as marriage. Therefore, the legal model should not attempt the futile task of compelling the performance of obligations to perform certain roles in the family. Family law should not interfere with the social structure of the family but should be restricted in its application to the area in which it is most effective—that is, in enforcement of the contractual property rights of husband and wife.[9]

A legislative provision insuring the freedom of marital contracts could be worded somewhat as follows: *The legal rights and obligations of husband and wife in the management and property of the family are subject to alteration by contract. When parties to a marriage recognized by the laws of this state enter into a marriage contract, they may define their rights and obligations in the family and in relation to the family property as they see fit, subject only to the rights of creditors and the obligation of each parent to serve the best interests of his or her children.*

CONCLUSION

Analysis of marital law dealing with household management, duties to render services and support, and separation of assets reveals that it is ineffective to further family stability. The result of an unequal legal status between husband and wife is unnecessary and destructive. The unequal status serves no purpose other than to encourage a largely outmoded model of family life. For a model that may increase family loyalty and the equality of both the marriage partners, we should enact in the law of every state the partnership model. The legislation recommended would (1) create an equal obligation of each partner to the family, (2) allow modification of obligations by contract between husband and wife, and (3) grant equal control of assets of the partners during cohabitation.

NOTES

1. The community property jurisdictions are Arizona, California New Mexico, Texas, Nevada, Idaho, Washington, Louisiana.

2. Rhonda Thomas and I first made this proposal in an article (1974) titled "Partnership Marriage: The Solution to an Ineffective and Inequitable Law of Support." Further research and thought since that time have reinforced the basic conclusions that we drew in 1974. Consequently, portions of the research and the concepts, including the proposal, which are presented in this chapter were previously presented in that article. I am grateful to Rhonda Thomas for the research, insights, and determined good humor with which she influenced my thoughts on this subject.

3. The situation at the time of divorce is analyzed by Margaret Gates in Chapter 9; consequently, it is not discussed in this chapter. However, I wish to remark that I do not recommend a law that requires a 50-50 division of marital assets at the time of divorce. Although I propose equal sharing during marriage, I believe that at the time of the divorce the economically dependent spouse (if there is one) might justifiably be given more than half the marital property. See Krauskopf (1976).

4. It is ironic that the move to ratify the Equal Rights Amendment has been stalled largely because of the unfounded beliefs that the wife has an enforceable right of support against her husband and that the ERA would terminate it. Many of the court decisions cited to substantiate those erroneous conclusions are decisions under the necessaries theory or family expense statutes, neither of which provide a cause of action for the wife. Incredibly, the leader of the Stop ERA movement often cites cases such as *Carson Pirie Scott* v. *Stanwood* (1923) to prove her point (Schlafly, 1973). The decision applies the Illinois family expense statute. She chooses to ignore the fact that that statute specifically places the obligation on *both* husband and wife and, therefore, would be valid under the Equal Rights Amendment.

5. This is a major theme of the respected sociologist, Jessie Bernard, in her book, *The Future of Marriage* (1972). Clare Booth Luce (1973:28) briefly, but forcefully, declared, "The awareness, conscious or unconscious, of women today that their traditionally full-time roles of wife and mother are in a state of decline, and that no other roles are open to them that promise them the same gratifications, is at the root of most of the restlessness, discontent, and psychological hang-ups they are experiencing."

6. Texas and Washington have recently given the wife substantially more equality (Kulzer, 1973). Further exposition of the situation in community property states can be found in Younger (1973) and DeFuniak and Vaughn (1971).

7. Each of the statutory provisions proposed in this section is intended merely to suggest a basic structure and not model legislation. Specific state legislation needs to be more carefully drafted and tailored especially for the enacting state.

8. Weitzman (1974) has presented a valuable discussion and collection of contracts both for the married and those who prefer not to enter formal marriage.

9. Karowe (1974:75) has recommended a contractual agreement for presentation of disputes to a mediator or arbitrator. This seems an excellent method of avoiding the expensive and reluctant court system. The law should certainly permit such means of dispute resolution.

REFERENCES

American Law Reports (1925). "Extent or character of support contemplated by statute making nonsupport of wife or child offense" (Annotation). Vol. 36, p. 866.

Attebury v. Attebury (1974). 507 S.W.2nd 87 (K.C. Ct. App.).

BERNARD, J. (1972). The future of marriage. New York: World.

Bradwell v. Illinois (1872). 83 U.S. 130.

California, Civil Code, §5101 (West, 1970).

Carson, Pirie, Scott Co. v. Stanwood (1923). 288 Ill. App. 281.

Citizen's Advisory Council on the Status of Women (1972). The Equal Rights Amendment and alimony and child support laws. Washington, D.C.: U.S. Department of Labor.

CLARK, H. (1968). The law of domestic relations in the United States. St. Paul: West Publishing.

Clouston v. Remlinger (1970). 22 Ohio St. 2d 65, 258 N.E.2d 230.

Committee on Civil and Political Rights of the President's Commission on the Status of Women (1963). Report. Washington, D.C.: U.S. Government Printing Office.

Commonwealth v. George (1948). 358 Pa. 118, 56 A.2d 228.

CROZIER, B. (1935). "Marital support." Boston University Law Review, 15:28-58.

DAGGETT, H. (1939). "Division of property upon dissolution of the marriage." Law and Contemporary Problems, 6:225-235.

De BEAUVOIR, S. (1953). The second sex. New York: Knopf. (Quotations in the text are from the Bantam paperback edition, 1970.)

DeFUNIAK, W., and VAUGHN, M. (1971). Principles of community property (2nd ed.). Tucson: University of Arizona Press.

DiFlorida v. DiFlorida (1975). 331 A.2d 174 (Pa.).

EAST, M. (1974). Statement presented to the American Home Economics Association, March 19.

Ewell v. State (1955). 207 Md. 288, 114 A.2d 66.

Fischer v. Wirth (1971). 38 App. Div. 2d 611, 326 N.Y.S. 2d 308.

FOSTER, H., and FREED, D. (1974). "Marital property reform in New York." Family Law Quarterly, 8:169-205.

Garlock v. Garlock (1939). 279 N.Y. 337, 18 N.E. 2d 521.

GLENDON, M. (1975). "Power and authority in the family: New legal patterns as reflections of changing ideologies." American Journal of Comparative Law, 23:1-33.

Graves v. Graves (1873). 36 Iowa 310, 14 Am. Rep. 525.

Haggett v. Hurley (1898). 40 A. 561 (Me.).

Hoyt v. Florida (1961). 368 U.S. 57.

Illinois Revised Statutes (Smith Hurd, 1959). Ch. 68, 15.

JOHNSTON, J. (1972). "Sex and property: The common law tradition, the law school curriculum and developments toward equality." New York University Law Review, 48:1033-1092.

JONES, S. (1959). "The problem of family support: Criminal sanctions for the enforcement of support." North Carolina Law Review, 38:1-61.

KAROWE, M. (1974). "Marital property: A new look at old inequities." Albany Law Review, 39:52-86.

KAY, H. (1972). "Making marriage and divorce safe for women." California Law Review, 60:1683-1700.

KRAUSKOPF, J. (1972). "Sex discrimination—Another shibboleth legally shattered." Missouri Law Review, 37:377-408.

——— (1975). "The Equal Rights Amendment: Its political and practical contexts." California State Bar Journal, 50:78-84, 136-141.

——— (1976). "A theory for a 'just' division of marital property." Missouri Law Review, 41:165-178.

KRAUSKOPF, J., and THOMAS, R. (1974). "Partnership marriage: The solution to an ineffective and inequitable law of support." Ohio State Law Journal, 35:558-600.

KREPS, J. (1971). "Sex in the marketplace: American women at work " Johns Hopkins Policy Studies in Employment and Welfare, 18(11).

KULZER, B. (1973). "Property and the family: Spousal protection." Rutgers-Camden Law Journal, 4:195-236.

LEVY, R. (1968). Uniform marriage and divorce legislation: A preliminary analysis. Chicago:

LUCE, C.B. (1973). "Women: A technological castaway." Britannica Book of the Year, p. 24-29.

Maynard v. Hill (1888). 125 U.S. 190.

McGuire v. McGuire (1953). 157 Neb. 226, 59 N.W. 2d 336.

Missouri Commission on the Status of Women (1973). Report. Columbia, Mo.: Author.

Norris v. Norris (1974). 16 Ill. App. 3rd 181, 307 N.E.2d 181.

Ohio, Revised Code, §3103.03 (Page 1972).

——— §3103.6 (Page 1972).

PAPANEK, H. (1973). "Men, women and work: Reflections on the two-person career." American Journal of Sociology, 78:852-872.

PAULSEN, M. (1956). "Support rights and duties between husband and wife." Vanderbilt Law Review, 9:709.

Phillips v. Graves (1870). 20 Ohio St. 371.

Popper v. Popper (1975). N.Y. Sup. Ct., New York City.

POWELL, R. (1936). "Community property—A critique of its regulation of intrafamily relations." Washington Law Review, 11:12-38.

RHEINSTEIN, M. (1972). Marriage stability, divorce and the law. Chicago: University of Chicago Press.

Rucci v. Rucci (1962). 23 Conn. Supp. 221, 181 A.2d 125 (Super. Ct.).

SAYRE, P. (1943). "A reconsideration of the husband's duty to support and wife's duty to render services." Virginia Law Review, 29:857-875.

SCHAFLY, P. (1973). "ERA: Loss of protection." Trial, 9(November-December):18.

SEDLER, R. (1972). "The legal dimensions of women's liberation: An overview." Indiana Law Journal, 47:419.

State ex rel George v. Mitchell (1950). 230 S.W.2d 117 (Sp. Ct. App.).

Tryon v. Casey (1967). 416 S.W.2d 252 (K.C. Ct. App.).

Uniform Partnership Act (1969). Uniform laws annotated: Master edition.

U.S. Commission on Civil Rights (1974). Women and poverty. Washington, D.C.: U.S. Government Printing Office.

U.S. Department of Labor, Women's Bureau (1970). Women workers today. Washington, D.C.: Author.

U.S. Senate (1972). Report 92-689, 92nd Cong., 2d Sess. 12.

Wallis v. City of Westport (1900). 82 Mo. App. 522.

WARREN, J. (1925). "Husband's right to wife's services." Harvard Law Review, 38:421.

Washington, Revised Code Annual, §26.16.030 (1961).

WEITZMAN, L. (1974). "Legal regulation of marriage: Tradition and change. California Law Review, 62:1169.

YOUNGER, J. (1973). "Community property, women and the law school curriculum." New York University Law Review, 48:211.

5

HEALTH AND FERTILITY ISSUES AND
THE DEPENDENCY OF WIVES

MARY E. KING
JUDITH ANN LIPSHUTZ
AUDREY MOORE

The overwhelming majority of women are married at some point in their lives, and 57% of all women are currently married with the husband present. There is evidence that a woman's marital status (and resulting life-style) can have a significant influence on her health, and health related issues can assuredly reinforce a woman's dependency on her husband.

There is some difficulty in addressing health problems of married women separately from those who are unmarried, and, in turn, it is difficult to determine the differences between the health statuses of wives. Neither accurate statistical data nor significant psychological inquiries are available with breakdowns by sex *and* marital status. Nevertheless, there is some indication that certain health issues probably affect married women as much as, or more than, other women and influence other aspects of their life, such as economic status. It is important to bear in mind that even if women are not separately categorized as married and single, marriage is often the presumed status, as in the case of fertility statistics, which include mostly married women, or in the case of a stereotyped image like the "pill-popping middle-class housewife." Thus in discussing the dependency of wives, we must bear in mind that the broader context in which we are working deals with women generally and that wives are a natural subcategory. To address the health status of married women, one must first understand that of women at large.

Increasingly critical voices have been raised by feminists concerning the quality of care, access to services, the responsiveness of professionals, and the financing of health services as these elements of health care systems and policies affect women. A growing body of literature has charged outright discrimination and insensitivity and a pernicious male dominance, said to occur in virtually all areas of health, including research, policy setting, and services delivery (Bart, 1973; Cherniak, 1972; Chesler, 1972; Cowan, 1974; Ehrenreich and English, 1972; Ehrenreich and Ehrenreich, 1973; Frankfort, 1972; Haire, 1972; Seaman, 1970, 1972).

As both users and providers of health services, women are numerically evident. In 1972 women made 5.6 physician visits for every 4.3 made by men, a figure which would be significantly higher if pediatric visits were counted (U.S. Congress, House Committee on Ways and Means, 1974). Roughly 75% of employed persons in the health services industry are women (Pennell and Showell, 1975), yet they are virtually absent from the ranks of physicians, medical school faculties and administration, and hospital trustees and directors and from the tiers of health and pharmaceutical executives.

However, there are some positive aspects of these issues that have become increasingly more evident in the past few years concerning women and health. The health of women in the United States has steadily improved. The availability of health services and of professional health care personnel, as well as the most advanced technology in the world, offers American women living in metropolitan areas considerable advantage over women in most other nations. Communicable diseases have almost been conquered.

Maternal and infant mortality and morbidity, traditionally a measure of the potency and effectiveness of a nation's health care system, have steadily decreased. Maternity mortality, where wives in particular are effected, has dramatically decreased over past decades. In the early 1920s, the death rate was 689.5 per 100,000 live births and in 1973, the rate fell to 15.2 per 100,000 live births, more than a 250% change (U.S. Bureau of the Census, 1976).

The World Plan of Action, which emerged from the United Nations World Conference of Women in Mexico City, and the U.S. National Women's Agenda, which was developed by nongovernmental women's organizations, both emphasize health as a major concern of women worldwide. Part of this interest is attributable to the fact that women are frequently the primary care providers for their families, and the principal teachers of hygiene, sanitation, and nutrition to families, as well as the users of services.

Obviously the role of women and, in turn, the role of wives in the health care system are significant. In this chapter, the married woman in this system will be explored via four major areas: mental health, fertility, alcoholism and drug abuse, and institutional policies.

MARRIAGE AND MENTAL HEALTH

Mental illness among women has often been measured against marital status. Most studies have traditionally held that women have higher rates of mental illness than men and that the rate is highest among the never married and formerly married women. However, this thesis has been discredited by Jessie Bernard (1972) in her finding that married women are more likely to have mental hazards than any other category of women, while married men, as well as single women, have the least amount of mental strife.

Gove (1972) concurs with these findings, noting that married women experience higher rates of mental illness reported among all women. Gove believes that it is the marital role played, rather than any biological differences, that causes psychological malaise. He outlines five major reasons for the handicaps placed on women as a result of being married:

(1) ... The married woman's "structural base" is typically more fragile than is the man's. Women have often occupied only one major social role, that of housewife, whereas men generally occupy two major roles, household head and worker.

(2) A large number of married women ... find that their major instrumental role, keeping house, is frustrating.

(3) The role of housewife is relatively unstructured and invisible.... She can put things off and let things slide.

(4) Even when a married woman works, she is typically in a less satisfactory position than the married male.

(5) Expectations confronting women are unclear and diffuse.... This lack of specificity in their role creates problems for women.

Marriage has come to be viewed as more psychologically strenuous for women than for men. When the household is a major source of gratification in her life, a wife automatically has a narrower source of fulfillment of her basic needs. Women have been found to be less happy with their marriages than are men and tend to be more introspective than their spouses (Gove, 1972). Introspection may tend to magnify their problems.

More and more married women are entering the labor force (58% of women wage earners are married with husbands present, U.S. Department of Labor, 1975b). What does this mean for marriage and mental health?

Stereotypes of the working wife of years past are quickly becoming a thing of the past. Indeed, one researcher, Elwood Carlson (1976), finds that instability in marriages occurs more often among nonworking wives than among those who are working. Although there is a growing increase in divorce, such breaks tend to occur more often among marriages with nonworking wives than those with working wives. The difference in the number of broken marriages between working and nonworking wives has been decreasing in the past two decades as has the notion that working wives are "deviant." There are more stable marriages among the working young, according to Carlson, while more nonworking middle-aged women have intact marriages than working middle-aged women. Carlson's findings show that, increasingly, the working wife cannot be considered a "home wrecker" and that work is not the culprit behind broken marriages. In fact, it now tentatively appears that presumptions about the instability of marriages with working wives will soon be completely reversed from what they were perhaps 25 years ago.

Furthermore, Gove (1972) contends that single working women are as satisfied with their jobs as single men and perhaps are less likely to worry about their work. Single women, unlike those who are married, have wider options for roles.

One conflict confronting the married working woman is fulfillment of a "masculine (professional) role" while still fitting into the role of "wife." One woman physician (Shapiro, 1971:402) was reported as being

> underprepared ... so that if she succeeded, it was "through luck" not through seeking the masculine type of success. She felt that perhaps this sense of being a deficient woman had led her to choose a husband who felt himself to be an inadequate man.

This physician wanted to be both a woman who was attractive to men and a woman who practiced medicine. This particular physician found these roles to be in conflict. The married man does not have to face this conflict since a duality of roles as both husband and father has long been acceptable (Shapiro, 1971).

Feelings of inadequacy on the part of women who are wives and mothers are described by one psychiatric social worker as follows:

> The roles of wife and mother deprive a woman of her identity in a still more basic way. These roles are intrinsically passive. They require the subjugation of oneself to the needs of others—a husband and children. But the concept of identity requires the assertion of the identity. No one self can survive for long if it never stands up, if it never occupies space. And the mere act of occupying space necessarily invites conflict with others who want that space or want to move through it. The myth of woman as a passive-dependent creature who cannot and should not stand up and assert herself has restricted humanity to the male sex. [Stevens, 1971:13]

Motherhood and wifehood, Stevens points out, can serve as enriching aspects of a woman's life, but cannot give her an identity that relates to something outside her home. She may thus feel insignificant and impotent.

Mental stability in married women is difficult to examine from the perspective of suicide. There is a preponderance of female over male attempters in all countries and time periods, but the actual suicide rate is higher among men than among women. The National Center for Health Statistics found that there were 18.1 suicidal deaths per 100,000 men as opposed to 6.5 per 100,000 for women (NCHS, 1976b). This has generally been explained by "the fact that men use more violent and effective methods, and consequently, become part of the successful suicide figures" (Weissman, 1974:740).

The NCHS does not divide figures according to marital status since coroners' and medical examiners' records from which government data are compiled are not usually maintained with marital information. However, several studies speculate that rates are lowest among the married, next lowest among the single, and highest among the divorced and widowed (Kramer, 1972).

Another study highlights an excess of separated and divorced persons of both sexes among suicide attempters. Between 1962 and 1967, there was an increase among married women in attempted suicides (Aitken et al., 1969).

Since data are not clearly defined, conclusions on suicide among married women are speculative. Many assume, and with good reason, that the majority of the married women who commit suicide are separated. Unfortunately, the category "married women" includes "separated women" as well, and there is usually no category for only "divorced women." To verify this assumption would require use of different data collection methods than are now in operation.

According to Bernard (1972:28):

> Although marriage protects both marital partners against suicide as compared with single men and women, it protects husbands more than wives. Only about half as many white married as single men commit suicide, almost three-fourths as many married as single women do. And although women in general live longer than men, marriage is relatively better for men than it is for women in terms of sheer survival, quite aside from suicide. That is, the difference in death rates between married and unmarried women is less than that between married and unmarried men (30 percent as compared to 48 percent).

The evidence is strong that women do in fact utilize psychiatric services of every kind—public and private, outpatient and institutional—far more than men do. In 1970, for example, there were 69 men for every 100 women in private mental hospitals and in the psychiatric wards of general hospitals. (The total ratio of men to women shifts to 104 men for every 100 women if Veterans Administration psychiatric admissions are included.)

Some believe that the higher utilization of private mental health services among women is not necessarily due to sex difference but to "men's great reluctance to admit to certain unpleasurable feelings and sensations since they are aware of cultural expectations regarding expressive control" (Phillips and Segal, 1969:69). Women may discuss inner feelings more readily and frequently than men; therefore, comparison of rates of mental problems must be approached cautiously. "Mental illness" is normally measured by treatment, but the figures reported do not include those who do not report psychological difficulties.

Although it cannot be shown that the health status of married women is substantially different in the aggregate from that of the unmarried woman, both mental-illness and suicide rates suggest a relationship between marriage for women and ill health.

FERTILITY

One of the primary issues that most married women confront is that of childbearing and its relationship to her education and employment.

Mednick and Tangri (1972) have noted that the more work experience that a woman has, the fewer children that she wants and has. They logically reason that if women worked only because of reproductive difficulties, or because they cannot bear children, then an increase in employment opportunities would not reduce fertility by much. They conclude (1972:9):

> Although attitudes about working may not be accurately reflected in actual employment at any given time, they do shape fertility behavior over time.

Whatever the reason, according to a 1970 census subject report (U.S. Bureau of the Census, 1975a) on Childspacing and Fertility Histories of Women, there are more than twice as many children born to married, nonworking women as to married working women.

Three times as many women newly entered the labor force last year than men (Raskin, 1976). If these trends continue, it is not unthinkable that by 1980 there could be half men and half women in the labor force. The Bureau of Labor Statistics projects an estimated 40 million women earning wages by the late 1980s.

Provisional data for 1975 from the National Center for Health Statistics indicate that the rate of births and number of children born continued to decrease for the fifth consecutive year despite the fact that between 1974 and 1975 there were slightly more women of childbearing age. For 1975, the fertility rate, which implies the number of children that the average woman has at family completion, was 66.7 births per 1,000 women in the childbearing years (15-44).

Epstein maintains that the lower fertility rate is both a consequence and a cause of altered lifestyles of families. She maintains that couples now are trying to postpone having their first child so that wives can establish a commitment to a career before dropping out of the labor force to bear children. The popular desire for large families documented in the 1950s has changed to a near majority preference for two-child families (Epstein, 1975). Indeed the level of fertility is now approximately 1.9 children per woman (National Center for Health Statistics, 1976).

Morse and Ralph (1973) found that governmental policies substantially favor the traditional family lifestyle associated with childbearing. In the traditional family of the upper economic classes, it is assumed that the wife does not work, while those wives of the traditional family in the lower economic classes do normally work. If the family has a child, there is a substantial differential expenditure benefit (expenditures proportionately less) in income taxes with a rise in family income. Without a child, the family loses benefits. If the wife does not work, tax policies are more favorable.

It has been speculated that there is some correlation between the rise in abortions and the reduction of fertility. According to the 1975 and 1976 Abortion Surveillance reports of the U.S. Center for Disease Control, the number of abortions performed has increased dramatically. However, the vast majority are among unmarried women. Among the married, abortions decreased from 1971 to 1974 by more than 5 percentage points (in 1974 abortions to married women were 18 times lower than abortions to unmarried women). There appears to be little direct evidence that liberalized abortion laws have influenced lowered fertility rates.

ALCOHOLISM AND DRUG ABUSE

If the public health areas of alcoholism and drug abuse are closely examined, it can be seen that there is a relationship between a woman's status as a wife and the treatment that she will receive for alcoholism and drug abuse in the health care delivery system. Unfortunately, as will be discussed later, the methodological problem of inadequate data collection arises, since few studies categorize married and unmarried abusers with any consistency and reliability. Although neither alcoholism nor drug abuse are presently considered "mainstream" health concerns, they constitute major health problems that are essentially preventable. In addition, alcoholism is a leading cause of death. Curiously, alcoholism and drug abuse have traditionally scarcely been addressed in medical education.

Reliance by women on such habits as drug and alcohol abuse is unquestionably more extensive and more tragic than either studies or statistics indicate. Women addicted to substances of drugs or alcohol are often "closet" cases in that very few are recognized as addicts and therefore treated for their condition, and treatment programs have only lately begun to realize that there may be need for special emphasis.

Interest in alcoholism has accelerated in the past decade, and, as a result, a wealth of information has accumulated. However, information specifically relating to women's abuse of alcohol is still comparatively nonexistent. In fact, between 1929 and 1970, only 29 studies published in English dealt with women alcoholics (Christenson and Swanson, 1974). Until recently, women alcoholics were either ignored in treatment or assumed to be identical to men in their manifestation of alcoholism as well as their needs for treatment. Most studies were carried out in institutional settings. Where women were discussed in the scientific literature, it was predominantly as the wives of men who were alcoholics.

There are no accurate figures available on the number of women alcoholics in this country. For that matter there are no accurate data on the overall number of alcoholics, both men and women. In a recent special report to Congress, one task force of the Department of Health, Education, and Welfare estimated the number of persons in the United States who drink at 95 million. Of this number, 10 million, or one in 10, is thought to be alcoholic. Conservative estimates figure the number of women alcoholics to be two million or 20% of the alcoholic population (Noble, 1976; Efron et al., 1974).

A 1975 publication of the Public Affairs Committee (Lindbeck) suggested that 90 million people drink in the United States and that 81 million of these are social drinkers. Nine million are alcoholics, and one-third of those are female, according to that source.

Some find these figures to be highly suspect, claiming that methodologies of gathering data are biased and thus not completely reliable. Since many women alcoholics are "hidden" and go undetected, they are often not counted in statistics. Also, women who are alcoholics are often treated within more traditional health or mental health facilities where alcoholism may perhaps be recognized but not treated as a disease in and of itself (National Institute of Alcohol Abuse and Alcoholism, n.d.). In her frequent public speaking engagements, Marty Mann, founder of the National Council on Alcoholism, "guesses" that the ratio of men to women alcoholics is 50 : 50.

While it is difficult enough to accurately assess the number of women alcoholics, it is virtually impossible to number those who are married. In summarizing 21 studies on alcoholics, Marc Schuckit

(1972) found that most data dealt specifically with male alcoholic populations. However, some findings point to significant patterns among women and specifically among housewives, which comprise the segment of married women that is normally addressed in these studies.

Women tend to begin alcohol abuse four to eight years later than men, but, on the average, they begin treatment at approximately the same time—in the late 30s or early 40s. Some say that women begin treatment at an earlier age than men, but whether earlier or at the same time, it appears that women, once started, lose control of their drinking more quickly than men (Curlee, 1970; Efron et al., 1974; Glatt, 1961).

Many studies suggest a strong familial history of alcoholism among women alcoholics. Alcoholic fathers of women alcoholics are found in 28 to 51% (depending on the study) of the cases followed (Winokur and Clayton, 1968; Wood and Duffy, 1970; Wall, 1937). Furthermore, female alcoholics tended to have had more parents, siblings, or spouses with drinking problems than did male alcoholics (Lisansky, 1957; Shefey, 1955).

Lisansky (1957) found that 35% of middle-class women alcoholics and 56% of lower-class women had spouses who were or became alcoholics, whereas only 9% of male alcoholics fit into this category.

Many professionals in the field of alcoholism and recovered alcoholics believe that women alcoholics are more prone to drinking for reasons related to life stress than are men and that very often this stress is related to a marriage or past marriage. One survey of clientele at the Eaglesville Treatment Center in Philadelphia (1976) found that of the women treated, 43% were divorced, separated, or widowed. Only 20% of the men alcoholics fell into this category. At the time of the survey, 17% of the women were married, while 22% of the men were married.

Studies that attempt to measure backgrounds of alcoholics through marital instability, psychiatric treatment, or suicidal gestures have often concluded that women alcoholics are indeed more likely to be admitted to hospitals for psychiatric problems and are also more likely to be divorced than are men (Curlee, 1970; Rathod and Thomson, 1971; James, 1975; Johnson, 1965).

There are no data that allow one to absolutely conclude that life stress is the main or only cause of alcoholism. There is some indication, however, that a combination of biological phenomena and depression from an environmental situation may precipitate a drinking problem (Lollie, 1953; Sclare, 1970). Lisansky (1957) concurs with these findings and believes them to be even more prevalent among women than among men.

Suicide attempts appear more frequently among women alcoholics (as they do among the general population) than among men. Women alcoholics also report more broken marriages than are reported by men either as a reason for their habit or as a result of it (Curlee, 1970; Wall, 1937; Pemberton, 1967).

Much of the problem involving the woman alcoholic, especially the nonworking housewife, lies in not recognizing alcoholism as a real public health problem confronting great numbers of women who stay home. The most obvious explanation is that, as a housewife, the married nonworker may resort to alcohol out of boredom. However, this commonly held presumption of the woman alcoholic as an "isolated, secret, lonely housewife" is perhaps the greatest poison of its own disease. In other words, the housewife may believe in her own stereotype, thus further reinforcing an alcoholism problem (Homiller, 1976).

Women are rarely seen drunk in public because it is not "socially acceptable," and thus, when a woman is drunk, she may be affected not only by her alcoholic state but also by feelings of nonacceptability. She may perceive herself to be "deviant" because she herself labels her "habit" as psychologically unstable and damaging. Some analysts believe that, compared to men, women in general believe they are sicker, are told that they are sicker, are treated as if they are sicker, and thus score higher on scales measuring psychopathology (Homiller, 1976; Chesler, 1972; Broverman et al., 1970). Many who are involved in the treatment of women alcoholics believe that this pattern is important in the treatment of women alcoholics.

Another aspect of this problem is what might be called conscious femininity as it relates to alcoholism. Some researchers have speculated that the married woman becomes dependent not only on a habit but also on proving her femininity through dependency on a man. It has been hypothesized that some women begin excessive drinking when they realize that their romantic dreams may not be fulfilled (Blane, 1968). It has also been theorized that women alcoholics have strong ambivalence and feelings of inadequancy toward their "womanliness" and that drinking can decrease those feelings for them (Wilsnack, 1973).

Married women alcoholics have been found to have more obstetric and gynecological problems than nonalcoholics who are married. One government study (Wilsnack, 1973) found that only 22% of their subjects reported no obstetric or gynecological problems, while 65% of a control group of nonalcoholics reported no problems.

Alcoholic women are said to have more difficulties in conceiving, repeated miscarriages, and permanent infertility (Wilsnack, 1973). Many alcoholic women place great value on the maternal role, and very few were not disappointed in their reproductive incapabilities, according to Wilsnack. Gynecological clinicians have long believed that reproductive incapabilities may be linked to psychological states, thus linking the alcoholic habits of some women to reproductive capabilities.

The woman who is a "hidden" drinker and is colloquially referred to as the secret drinker or lonely housewife may constitute as high as 51% of female problem drinkers or alcoholics. In both governmental and nongovernmental treatment programs, these women have heretofore been ignored as a group requiring special efforts for identification and services. When these women do seek help, they often seek out a private physician, such as a psychiatrist. Such a clinician is likely to be expensive and may often treat their alcoholism as if it were symptomatic of an "underlying problem" rather than as a disease or health problem. Such physicians are often untrained in understanding and treating the addictions. They may even offer medication which exaggerates the alcoholism. A woman in this group is rarely seen drunk in public and does not come to the attention of the law. Her family, friends, and employer try to protect her and shield her from stigma to "save face," only becoming accomplices in her illness.

Closely related to problems of alcoholism as they affect women are problems of drug abuse, which are, if anything, even more ignored in both research and treatment. Part of this is due to the fact that there is no solidly organized constituency capable of obtaining public visibility as there is with alcoholism. In addition, public recognition of drug abuse has been largely spurred by concern for crime associated with illicit opiate addiction. This has tended to obscure the daily misuse of amphetamines, barbiturates, and tranquilizers, which have been called the polydrugs.

Since women use more health services than men and since physicians tend to terminate medical encounters by prescribing medication, it follows that women will receive more prescriptions than men and that they therefore probably consume more drugs than do men. Gillenkirk (1973) found that physicians wrote 230 million prescriptions for psychotropic or mind-altering drugs in 1971. In the past year, 29% of American women received at least one such drug, while 13% of American men were prescribed such drugs. Among younger people aged 13 to 29, 25% of the women had used psychotropic drugs while only 6% of the men had. Men, on the other hand, had a greater tendency to use marijuana and alcohol as psychoactive remedies than did women. Again, although accurate documentation is virtually nonexistent, it is highly likely that housewives make up a high percentage of these drug takers (Gillenkirk, 1973).

Contrary to popular belief, one survey (Parry et al., 1973) found that the "pill-popping middle class suburban housewife" is an inaccurate stereotype, with "pill-poppers" instead found to be among the poor and undereducated. Parry rationalizes that the poorer the woman, the fewer alternative diversions she can afford. Rationalizes one clinician at a mental health clinic:

> The lower-class woman cannot consult a physician on a regular basis, so her ills are usually well advanced by the time she gets here. Under these conditions, the period of treatment will usually be longer. . . . And her educational limitations preclude verbal psychotherapy, so the lower-class woman is left with drug therapy and possibly group psychotherapy. [Gillenkirk, 1973:93]

Chambers and Schultz (1971) conducted a survey of 4,000 women to discover trends of drug use and abuse. Unlike Parry's work, their findings reinforce the stereotype. Housewives, they found, make up about 36% of the habitual diet-pill users but represent only 25% of the U.S. adult population. Among this group of diet pill-taking housewives, 99% were high school graduates and 14% had gone to college.

The use of multiple psychotropic drugs is not an uncommon phenomenon among housewives. Chambers and Schultz found that many of these women are often taking antidepressants, tranquilizers, sedatives, and other mind-affecting drugs along with amphetamines. In fact, more than three-fourths of the housewives habitually taking amphetamines also habitually take barbiturates, they found.

Women are involved with psychoactive drug use, but, unlike men, who are the major users of such illegal drugs as opiates and hallucinogens, virtually all studies show that women are more involved with drugs that are originally legally prescribed—barbiturates, relaxants, major and minor tranquilizers, diet pills, amphetamines, and so on (King and Trotter, 1974). While many, if not most, housewives who take these mind altering chemicals may think they are used for medical reasons, there is growing evidence that the users become all too often dependent on their use so that "use" becomes "abuse."

Some believe that physician-prescribing patterns for women and wives are responsible for a great deal of the overuse and abuse of drugs. According to psychologist Linda Fidell (1973), housewives, by virtue of stereotyped roles, are often prescribed more tranquilizing drugs. Fidell claims that this is because physicians conclude that housewives have time to take a nap and have little reason to be mentally alert. Thus the overall impact of tranquilizers on the married housewife is of less concern to physicians than it would be on men. Fidell asserts that women receive 67% of the prescriptions for psychoactive drugs. Although it is not surprising to find the sex with the greater number of visits receiving the greater number of prescriptions, Fidell maintains that the problem is that the numbers are disproportionate: women get more drugs than they make visits. Therefore, Fidell continues, a relationship that appears straightforward has, in fact, a heavy overlay of sex-role stereotyping.

Another study (Linn and Davis, 1971) found that 87% of the physicians questioned judged daily use of the tranquilizer Librium as legitimate for housewives. However, when it came to students, only 53% felt that it was legitimate. The physician may assume that the woman has few worries or intellectual demands and that, in addition, the physician can believe that the medical obligation as prescriber of medication to cure an illness has been fulfilled.

Thus it can be seen that the application of unbiased methods of identification, diagnosis, and treatment coupled with sensitivity to women would affect substance abuse among women, particularly wives. Unlike other diseases of advanced civilizations, these two self-afflicted conditions are theoretically preventable.

INSTITUTIONAL POLICIES

Of the 36 million women in the labor force in 1975, 58% of them were married with the husband present (U.S. Bureau of the Census,

1976). Most of that 58% can be presumed to obtain health insurance coverage through their husband's policy because of more generous benefits customarily accorded women as dependents as opposed to individual insurees. This means that, as wives, they are crucially dependent on their husband's insurance and therefore on his employment for health care. Furthermore, soaring costs of individual policies have increasingly placed individual health insurance out of reach of many Americans, so that it is the rule rather than the exception that most individuals obtain health coverage as a fringe benefit of their employment.

Some neglected groups in our population have received special attention and coverage under public assistance plans. For the past decade the health needs of the elderly have been covered under Medicare, and the poor have received coverage for health care under Medicaid. This has meant that two of the most vulnerable groups of women in our society have not been barred from essential health care by lack of money. This is not to say, however, that all elderly and poor women get adequate health care.

Old patterns of institutional discrimination still exist affecting women and health directly and indirectly. What happens to a woman who has no health insurance coverage in her own name, such as the married woman? Or what happens to the woman not covered by Medicare or Medicaid and who has to depend on private insurance? The unavoidable dependency of the married woman on the husband's insurance can lead to unpredictable and uncontrollable consequences. In the event of his death or a divorce, she will in all likelihood lose that coverage. If, as is increasingly common, she faces divorce or widowhood around the age of 55, which is prior to eligibility for Social Security old-age benefits, it is unlikely that she will be able to purchase health insurance. If she was dependent on her husband for support and is not employed, she will face severe barriers of cost and access in attempting to buy an individual policy. If she is employed or finds employment for the first time, it is highly likely that the very condition for which she may most need risk coverage will be excluded by her new enrollment even if she enrolls in her employer's group rather than in an outside plan.

Institutional policies of the health insurance industry not only tend to reinforce out-of-date stereotypes but are often flagrantly discriminatory toward women, and married women are a widely effected subgroup of this treatment. For example, one of the most obvious discriminatory policies, the lack of maternity benefits, largely affects women who are married. Again, it must be understood that, while discussing the effect of insurance policies on married women, the effect on women in general must first be understood: marriage is a variable which can increase or decrease benefits depending on the circumstances.

Since 1973, reports on insurance practices and their effect on women have been offered to state insurance commissions in Pennsylvania, New York, Iowa, Michigan, California, Arkansas, and Maryland. Hearings before the Joint Economic Committee of Congress on "Economic Problems of Women" in July 1973 addressed insurance problems of women and spurred the recent studies. Testimony by Herbert Denenberg, then insurance commissioner for Pennsylvania, stated,

> Denial of equal access to insurance, at fair rates, affects the economic status of women. It touches employment discrimination, opportunities to hold a job, ability to maintain a family in the face of personal catastrophe, and economic security. Other economic disadvantages of women can be magnified by discriminatory, inadequate or prohibitively costly insurance. [U.S. Congress, Joint Economic Committee, 1973:153]

As a result of this growing body of testimony and reports to insurance commissions, it has been established that the following occurs:

- Women have been denied the same insurance coverage available to men.

- Women pay more for the same or less coverage than men.

- Widows and divorced wives with dependent children have been denied policies previously held by their husbands.

- The older widow is often declared ineligible for a new policy because of a preexisting medical condition.

- Husbands of women employees may be excluded, whereas wives of men employees are included without restriction.

- Maternity coverage through commercial carriers is usually unavailable to single women.

- Maternity coverage is not available to dependent female children, whereas all other policy coverages are.

- Commercial and service carriers sometimes apply arbitrary waiting periods to maternity coverage in such a way as to exclude coverage for premature births.

- Complications of pregnancy are treated by commercial and service carriers differently than other conditions requiring medical and hospital treatment.

- Most maternity coverage from commercial and service carriers excludes routine and nonroutine pre- and postnatal care.

- Contracts with a set dollar maternity benefit cover a lower percentage of the costs associated with other conditions requiring medical attention.

- Under major medical policies, commercial and service carriers frequently exclude from coverage those costs not covered by a basic policy which are associated with normal pregnancy, with both normal pregnancy and complications of pregnancy are covered under the basic policy.

- Contracts seldom provide contraceptive services.

- Prescription drug riders frequently exclude from coverage oral contraceptives, whereas other prescription drugs are covered.

- Commercial and service policies seldom provide adequate coverage for voluntary sterilization.

- Commercial carriers frequently exclude from coverage costs associated with voluntary abortions.

- Health insurance contracts seldom cover preventive services which are essential to women's health.

- Limited benefit policies frequently exclude from coverage illnesses common to women, when no other exclusion is sex related.

- Commercial carriers under some policies apply special waiting periods to "diseases of female reproduction organs" before costs are covered. [Michigan, Department of Commerce, 1974]

One New York report contends, "Fertility-related services constitute 90 percent of all services women of child-bearing age require and this area of health and disability service has always been inadequate and subject to stronger controls and qualifying rules" (New York State, 1974b). Until 1972, when it was challenged in court by a women's organization, the California insurance code included a provision allowing insurance companies to refuse disability payments for injuries resulting from such calamities as "war, suicide, hallucinatory drugs, and organs peculiar to females." The insurance industry is not alone in the approach that "female disorders" are not within the realm of normal human experience. Negative attitudes about women's reproductive functions as institutionalized in the health insurance industry exert a serious influence on health care and the available coverage for women (Auchincloss, 1973).

Attitudes of the insurance industry toward women workers are most clearly expressed in confidential, carefully guarded underwriting manuals. Examples were obtained from manuals subpoenaed by the Senate Anti-Trust and Monopoly Subcommittee hearings held in May and June, 1972, and these also appear in later reports to a New York State commission.

The underwriting manual of the North American Reassurance Company asserts the following:

> Women's role in the commercial world is a provisional one. . . . They work not from financial need but from personal convenience. The subjective circumstances which create "convenience" tend to change; and if a woman has disability coverage, the temptation exists to replace her earnings with an insurance income once work loses its attractiveness.

The recent Metropolitan Life Insurance Company manual, under the heading "A Guide to Effective Administration of Group Health Insurance Plans (for Employers)" suggests that personnel departments consider the following:

> Hiring procedures for female employees deserve special attention. . . . Some employees, who must arrange for the care of their children during working hours, may actually be better off financially if they can collect insurance benefits. Some married women are willing to accept a loss of income periodically rather than face up to the hardships of working full time and caring for their homes and families.

The Metropolitan Life "Guide" recommends that some sick leave be handled as personal leave:

> This is particularly true of claims submitted from married females where the diagnosis is of extremely vague or indeterminate nature. Very often the reason underlying such claims is the fact that the employee has become tired or rundown from the dual responsibilities of working and taking care of her home and family. This is illustrative of a situation in which the employee may well require a leave of absence for rest and relaxation but still not be wholly and continuously disabled as required in order to qualify for benefits under the Weekly Indemnity policy.

Barbara Shack, Assistant Director of the New York Civil Liberties Union, testifying before the Joint Economic Committee of Congress in 1973, stated that Metropolitan Life increases the premiums on group health policies "if the benefits on females represent 11 percent or more of the total benefit" (p. 169). A 1975 copy of the "Underwriting Rules" of Bankers Life and Casualty Company contains this statement in the section titled *Unacceptable Groups:*

"If the female content is greater than 50%, the prospect must be submitted to the Home Office for prior approval to quote." Job discrimination toward women is sometimes encouraged as a result of policies mandated by health insurers. Said Shack, "Most insurance companies as mentioned [in the manuals subpoenaed for the hearings] load their premiums rates. The advice to employers and the extra premium is a clear warning that hiring women is both hazardous and expensive. The probable impact on hiring practices is obvious and contributes to the continuing vicious cycle that deprives them of equal opportunity" (U.S. Congress, Joint Economic Committee, 1973).

Two-thirds of the population in the United States is covered by health and disability insurance purchased by labor unions and employers. The employee in most cases does not shop around for health insurance. The extent of coverage and the cost of the benefits package are worked out through the careful cooperation of the insurance company and the labor union or employer. If the cost is too high, the package will be trimmed. It is this trimming that adversely affects women and their families, since maternity and fertility-related benefits are those most subject to limitation in health insurance.

Of the 32 million women who comprise 38% of the work force, 41% are single, widowed, divorced, or separated and therefore highly dependent on a single salary or income. Another 21% have husbands whose annual income is less than $7,000. In 1975, the number of women who were heads of households and the sole support of dependent children was more than 6.6 million. It can hardly be said that these women are working for mere "convenience." Women work for the same reasons that men work—because they need money. But, for more than 20 million women who are single, widowed, divorced, or separated and for their families, health care costs and loss of earnings could mean disaster (U.S. Congress, Joint Economic Committee, 1973). Without health insurance as a fringe benefit of employment, many women would be unable to afford any coverage, and thus they are dependent on the employer's choice of benefits. Many working women have no fringe benefits. These are employees who work in small businesses or part-time and who therefore are not eligible for fringe benefits. Others are working in jobs that have traditionally been low-paying, such as jobs as waitresses, and that have not been affected by unionization. A woman who works in her husband's or relative's business usually cannot get health and disability insurance. This is also true of women working in their homes.

In disability insurance, a woman must pay a price for becoming pregnant (Hollinger, 1974). Again the costs attached to bringing a child into the world are more often than not accompanied by marriage. It is common for disability income policies to exclude (along with self-inflicted injury) acts of war, nervous or mental disease or disorder, alcoholism and drug addiction, pregnancy, childbirth, miscarriage, abortion, or resulting complications. The rationale for excluding pregnancy is that it can be planned or controlled, whereas traditional insurance is for unforeseen losses. This is not always true for pregnancy and certainly is not true for complications resulting from pregnancy. Coupled with the health insurance industry's widespread lack of support for complete contraceptive coverage, these complimentary policies only serve to lessen control for women facing the possibility of pregnancy (California, Commission on the Status of Women, 1975). In addition, policies of covering unplanned medical expenses are not consistently followed in disability insurance, since coverage for cosmetic surgery is often available, whereas maternity benefits are not.

In health coverage, the second greatest need of women following maternity and fertility-related services is ambulatory preventive care. It has been demonstrated that the high toll taken by breast and uterine cancer can be reduced by early detection and treatment. Inexpensive, life-saving routine services, such as an office visit to a physician for a Pap smear, are not covered. Health insurers have traditionally covered acute hospital-based care, which is expensive, and have often excluded from coverage less expensive outpatient preventive care, which is offered in other than a hospital setting. Although this might appear to be a neutral exclusion, one that applies to both sexes, the effect on women is more severe than on men and therefore discriminatory.

This can be readily seen when considering maternal and infant mortality and morbidity. Prenatal and postnatal care is normally delivered on an outpatient basis and has been shown to be directly related to lessening death, defects, and dysfunction for both mothers and infants. Yet such care is frequently discouraged by health insurance policies. Exclusions, limited coverage, and higher rates are all barriers impeding women's access to health services at an affordable price. These barriers are set in the actuarial tables. Hollinger (1974) addressed the effect and validity of using sex-based statistics in setting premium rates for insurance coverage and in providing insurance plans with sex as a factor. Premium rates are computed by actuaries who expertly apply principles of mathematics to pricing factors of insurance. The fundamental technique is to estimate future losses based on past loss experience. Companies may rely on their own statistical experience, on statistics of risk compiled by the Society of Actuaries, or on a combination of these. Based on these figures, insurance companies justify higher rates and plan differences for women.

Until recently, insurance companies were not questioned on their choice of statistical bases or the conclusions drawn. Neither were they asked to justify classifications and rates with regard to sex. In studying the insurance industry's approach to rate setting for disability coverage and rates for women, Hollinger found that the industry's own statistics threw doubt on a premium structure that requires women to pay disability insurance premiums that average 66% greater than premiums paid by men.

The public disability protection system under Social Security shows that, by awards records, the rate of disablement of females in 1971 was 29% less than the male rate. In 1969 it was 24% less. The insurance industry has a screening program to eliminate deviant risks, yet Social Security accepts most workers. Social Security also shows remarkably similar work-loss patterns for men and women.

Public Health Service reports regarding work time lost because of illness or injury showed that in 1972 females lost an average of 5.6 days (including pregnancy) and males lost an average of 5.2 days. In 1967, comparable figures were 5.6 and 5.3. Men were more prone to be absent because of chronic conditions such as heart trouble, arthritis, and orthopedic impairment. Women's illnesses keep them away from work for shorter durations. Two additional factors may further narrow that slight difference by 1976. The birth rate has dropped, but, when women leave work because of childbirth, fewer are being required to leave at a specified time by employers. Some personnel policies forced a pregnant employee to leave as soon as she became pregnant, others no later than the fifth month. Some even specified how long she must remain out after childbirth. These patterns are changing.

The Equal Employment Opportunity Commission's revised

"Guidelines on Discrimination Because of Sex" of March 31, 1972, make it unlawful to discriminate between men and women with respect to fringe benefits. The commission held that it was a violation of Title VII of the Civil Rights Act to have an employment policy which excluded from employment pregnant employees or applicants. The EEOC guidelines state that all employment policies and practices must treat disability from pregnancy, childbirth, or abortion in the same manner as other temporary disabilities. It is the EEOC position that any pregnancy becomes a disability when the employee can no longer perform her job.

Employers and insurance companies have taken the position that the EEOC guidelines do not have the force of law, and some employers have contested them in court. In several cases, the courts have cited their reliance on the EEOC guidelines in making important sex discrimination decisions. Recent cases involving maternity leave policies are being watched closely by the insurance industry. The end result may be mandatory pregnancy inclusion in all group and individual policies.

To protect itself against excessive loss, an insurance company attempts to distribute the potential losses of policyholders among its insurees. Policyholders do not all pay the same premiums for the same coverage. They are grouped into classifications selected by the insurer according to comparable degrees of risk in an attempt to assess each group its fair share of losses (Iowa, Commission on the Status of Women, 1975).

Whatever classification system best reflects losses is acceptable to the industry. Denenberg maintains that, "Traditionally, sex has been used as a distinguishing factor or classification in insurance. It is a convenient, simple, and efficient way to divide people into risk categories that produce different loss potentials. Today, we have to ask, is this fair?" One writer asserts, "Insurance by its very nature is selective and discriminatory. Every possible consideration—personal, moral, statistical, and even whimsical—is taken into account in order to minimize the insurance risk" (U.S. Congress, Joint Economic Committee, 1973).

The insurance industry has traditionally established higher rates for one sex rather than the other whenever sex classifications produce significant loss or cost differentials. In some coverage, such as automobile insurance, the woman actually gets a lower rate. In others, such as basic health, major medical, and income disability, the woman pays more. Women also pay more for annuities and some other lines of coverage. There are other convenient bases for classification which the insurance industry does not now use. One is race. Although blacks have a shorter life expectancy than whites, no classification based on race is used. Such a classification is considered to be unacceptable from a public policy standpoint, and sex classifications have become suspect. Denenberg testified:

> Pennsylvania like some other states, has an amendment to its constitution guaranteeing equal rights to women. Hopefully we will have a similar amendment to the Federal Constitution in the near future. With changes in the economic, social and legal position of women, the once homogeneous classification of women has become less meaningful. It is clearly time to force the insurance industry to reevaluate all sex classifications of the insurance business. [U.S. Congress, Joint Economic Committee, 1973:159]

The Pennsylvania Insurance Department sent letters to insurance companies in 1973 citing the state equal-rights provision on sex discrimination and notifying them that the policies and rates filed with the Bureau of Regulation of Rates and Policies were insufficient since they contained different rates and premiums for men as opposed to women. The companies had to show the statistical variations or compelling rationale for discrimination by sex.

Maryland also has an equal-rights amendment to its state constitution. In the suit of *Voith* v. *Union Mutual Life Insurance Company* a complaint is pending with the insurance commissioners. Although this complaint challenges the denial to females of individual disability plans comparable to "male only" plans, a decision on this complaint would affect all underwriting policies based on sex for arbitrary, capricious, or unfairly discriminatory reasons. The Maryland Insurance Commission, through the Department of Licensing and Regulation, is closely scrutinizing the policies of nine insurance companies operating in Maryland.

CONCLUSION

Some facts concerning the married woman are clear: more women are working than ever before; the marriage rate is dropping; the divorce rate is rising; women are having fewer children; most married women in the work force are dependent on their husband's insurance; single women and married women have significantly different options for health insurance, with greater or lesser benefits to women of each status depending on the circumstances. How much these factors affect a woman's health status remains a relatively unexplored query. Because the status of women's health—especially the more narrowly defined category of married women—has not been a high research priority, what has been discussed here is not sufficiently documented. As the largest percentage of health consumers and as their societal role changes, women, of whom 57% are married, deserve more careful attention to their specific needs from both consumer advocates and health care providers. Such problems as alcoholism, pregnancy, drug abuse, and an inability to afford insurance are health-related issues which tend to limit a married woman's horizons and tie her to a life of dependency. There is some evidence that the current runs in the other direction as well. Jessie Bernard's review of mental health literature reveals that being a wife may be one of the causes of poor mental health. It is possible to conclude from the preceding, however, that the flagrant discrimination in health care services only reinforces the dependent status of the married woman.

REFERENCES

AITKEN, E., BUGLASS, R., and KREITMAN, M. (1969). "The changing pattern of attempted suicide in Edinburgh, 1962-67." British Journal of Preventive and Social Medicine, 23:111-115.

ALLEN, N. (1974). Suicide in California, 1960-1970. Los Angeles: California, Department of Health.

AUCHINCLOSS, K. (1973). "Unemployment benefits." Women's Rights Law Reporter (spring).

BART, P. (1973). "Sexism and health issues." Hyde Parker (June).

BERNARD, J. (1972). The future of marriage. New York: World Publishing.

BROVERMAN, I.K., BROVERMAN, D.M., CLARKSON, F.E., ROSENCRANTZ, P.S., and VOGEL, S.R. (1970). "Sex role stereotypes of femininity and clinical judgements of mental health." Journal of Consulting and Clinical Psychology, 34(1):1-7.

California, Commission on the Status of Women (1975). Women and insurance. Sacramento, Calif.: Author.

CARLSON, E. (1976). "Working wives." Unpublished study, University of California, Berkeley.

CHAMBERS, C., and SCHULTZ, D. (1971). "Housewives and the drug habit." Ladies' Home Journal, 138(December):66-70.

CHERNIAK, D., and FEINGOLD, A. (n.d.). Birth control handbook. Montreal, Quebec: Handbook Collective.

CHESLER, P. (1972). Women and madness. New York: Doubleday.

CHRISTENSON, S.J., and SWANSON, A.Q. (1974). "Women and drug use: An annotated bibliography." Journal of Psychedelic Drugs, 6:371-412.

COWAN, B. (1974). "One out of three hysterectomies is unnecessary." Her-Self, 3(August):4.

CURLEE, J. (1970). "A comparison of male and female patients at an alcoholism treatment center." Journal of Psychology, 74:230-247.

Eaglesville Treatment Center (1976). Unpublished survey. Philadelphia: Author.

EFRON, V., KELLER, M., and GURIOLI, C. (1974). "Statistics on consumption of alcohol and on alcoholism." New Brunswick, N.J.: Rutgers Center on Alcohol Studies.

EHRENREICH, B., and EHRENREICH, J. (1973). "Hospital workers: A case study in the 'New Working Class.' " Monthly Review (January).

EHRENREICH, B., and ENGLISH, D. (1972). Witches and midwives, and nurses—A history of women healers. Old Westbury, N.Y.: Feminist Press.

EPSTEIN, C. (1975). Reflections of the women's movement. New York: Institute of Life Assurance.

FIDELL, L.S. (1973). "Put her down on drugs: Prescribed drug usage in women." Paper presented at the meeting of the Western Psychological Association, Anaheim, Calif.

FRANKFORT, E. (1972). Vaginal politics. New York: Quadrangle Books.

——— (1973). "Why should doctors govern themselves?" Village Voice, November 29, pp. 25-29.

GILLENKIRK, J. (1973). "Psychodrugs." Washingtonian, October, pp. 92-95 ff.

GILLOOLY, T. (1974). "The developing issue of sex discrimination in insurance—An overview." Paper presented to the Association of Life Assurance Counsel, May 6.

GLATT, M.M. (1961). "Drinking habits of English (middle class) alcoholics." Acta Psychiatrica Scandinavica, 37:88-113.

GOVE, W. (1972). "The relationship between sex roles, marital status and mental illness." Social Forces, 51(September):34-44.

HAIRE, D. (1972). "The cultural warping of childbirth." International Childbirth Education Association News (special issue).

HOLLINGER, J. (1974). "Sex discrimination in health insurance." University of Maryland Law Forum, 4(summer):4.

HOMILLER, J. (1976). "Women and alcoholism: A statement of the problem." Unpublished study for the Committee of State and Territorial Alcoholism Authorities, Washington, D.C.

Iowa, Commission on the Status of Women (1975). A study of insurance practices that affect women. Des Moines: Author.

JAMES, J.E. (1975). "Symptoms of alcoholism in women: A preliminary survey of A.A. members. Journal on the Studies of Alcoholism, 36:1564-1569.

JOHNSON, M.W. (1965). "Physician's views on alcoholism with special reference to alcoholism in women." Nebraska State Medical Journal, 50:378-384.

JOHNSON, M.W., DEVRIES, J.C., and HOUGHTON, M.I. (1966). "The female alcoholic." Nursing Residents of Philadelphia, 15:343-347.

KING, M., and TROTTER, S. (1974). "Why do more women than men think they're sick in the head?" Vogue, April, pp. 171 ff.

KRAMER, M. (1972). "Consumer's influence on health care." Nursing Outlook, 20(September):574-578.

LINDBECK, V. (1975). The woman alcoholic. New York: Public Affairs Committee.

LINN, L., and DAVIS, M. (1971). "The use of psychotherapeutic drugs by middle aged women." Journal of Health and Social Behavior, 12:331-340.

LIPMAN-BLUMEN, J. (1976). "Changing sex roles: Their implications for family structure." Paper presented at the meeting of the Pacific Sociological Association, San Diego, Calif., March.

LIEBERMAN, A. (1970). "A case for the small family." Population Reference Bulletin, April, pp. 2-3.

LISANSKY, R. (1957). "Alcoholism in women: Social and psychological concomitants." Quarterly Journal of Studies on Alcoholism, 18:588-623.

LOLLI, G. (1953). "Alcoholism in women." Connecticut Review on Alcoholism, 5:9011.

MEDNICK, M.S., and TANGRI, S.S. (1972). "New social psychological perspectives on women." Journal of Social Issues, 28:2.

Michigan, Department of Commerce, Insurance Bureau (1974). Women's task force report to the Michigan Commissioner of Insurance on sex discrimination in insurance. Lansing: Author.

MORSE, E., and RALPH, S. (1974). "Family life styles, the childbearing decision, and the influence of federal activities: A quantitative approach" (Research reports, II: Economic aspects of population change). Washington, D.C.: Commission on Population Growth and the American Future.

National Center for Health Statistics (1976a). "Births, marriages, divorces, and deaths for 1975." Monthly Vital Statistics Report, March 4.

——— (1976b). "Vital mortality statistics, 1974." Monthly Vital Statistics Report, February 3.

National Institute of Alcohol Abuse and Alcoholism (n.d.). Alcoholism treatment monitoring system. Rockville, Md.: Author.

New York State, Temporary State Commission on Living Costs and the Economy (1974a). The cost of health care in New York State. Albany: Author.

——— (1974b). Discrimination against women in health insurance policies. Albany: Author.

NOBLE, E. (1976). Testimony before the Oversight Hearings of the Senate Subcommittee on Alcohol and Narcotics, February 3.

PARRY, H., BALTER, M., MELLINGER, G., CISIN, I., and MANHEIMER, D. (1973). "National patterns of psychotherapeutic drug use." Archives of General Psychiatry, 28(June).

PEMBERTON, D.A. (1965). "A comparison of the outcome of treatment in female and male alcoholics." British Journal of Psychiatry, 13:544-551.

PENNELL, M., and SHOWELL, S. (1975). Women in health careers. Washington, D.C.: American Public Health Association.

PHILLIPS, D., and SEGAL, B. (1969). "Sexual status and psychiatric symptoms." American Sociological Review, 34(February).

RASKIN, A.H. (1976). "Changing face of the labor force." New York Times, February 15.

RATHOD, N.H., GREGORY, E., BLOWS, D., and THOMAS, G.H. (1966). "A two-year follow-up study of alcoholic patients." British Journal of Psychiatry, 112:683-692.

RATHOD, N.H., and THOMSON, A. (1971). "Women alcoholics: A clinical study." Journal of Studies on Alcoholism, 32:45-52.

SCHUCKIT, M. (1972). "Alcoholic women: A literature review." Psychiatry in Medicine, 3:37-43.

SCLARE, A.B. (1970). "The female alcoholic." British Journal of Addiction, 65:99-107.

SEAMAN, B. (1970). The doctors' case against the pill. New York: Peter H. Wyden.

——— (1972). Free and female. Greenwich, Conn.: Fawcett.

SHAPIRO, E. (1971). "Women who want to be women." Woman Physician, 26(August): 399-405.

SHEFEY, J.M. (1955). "Psychopathology and character structure in chronic alcoholism." In O. Diethelm (ed.), Etiology of chronic alcoholism. Springfield, Ill.: Thomas.

STEVENS, B. (1971). "The psychotherapist and women's liberation." Social Work, (July):12-18.

U.S. Bureau of the Census (1975a). Childspacing and fertility histories of women by demographic employment characteristics, 1970 (Census subject report). Washington, D.C.: Author.

——— (1975b). Current population reports, population characteristics–Fertility expectations of American women. Washington, D.C.: Author.

——— (1976). "A statistical portrait of women in the U.S., 1975." Current Population Reports, April.

U.S. Center for Disease Control (1975). Abortion surveillance, 1973 (Annual summary). Washington, D.C.: U.S. Department of Health, Education, and Welfare.

——— (1976). Abortion surveillance, 1974 (Annual summary). Washington, D.C.: U.S. Department of Health, Education, and Welfare.

U.S. Congress, House of Representatives, Committee on Ways and Means (1974). National health insurance resource book. Washington, D.C.: U.S. Government Printing Office.

U.S. Congress, Joint Economic Committee (1973). Hearings on the "Economic problems of women," July 10, 11, 12.

U.S. Department of Labor, Employment Standards Administration, Women's Bureau (1975a). Why women work. Washington, D.C.: U.S. Government Printing Office.

——— (1975b). Women workers today. Washington, D.C.: U.S. Government Printing Office.

WALL, J.H. (1937). "A study of alcoholism in women." American Journal of Psychiatry, 93:943-953.

WEISSMAN, M. (1974). "The epidemiology of suicide attempts, 1960-1971." Archives of General Psychiatry, 30(June):737-746.

WILSNACK, S. (1973). "The needs of the female drinker: Dependency, power, or what?" In Proceedings of the second annual Alcoholism Conference of the National Institute on Alcohol Abuse and Alcoholism.

WINOKUR, G., and CLAYTON, P.J. (1968). "Family history studies: Comparison of male and female alcoholics." Quarterly Journal of Studies on Alcoholism, 29:885-891.

WOOD, H.P., and DUFFY, E.L. (1970). "Psychological factors in alcoholic women." American Journal of Psychiatry, 23:107-111.

6

BLACK WOMEN
AND THE FAMILY

DIANN HOLLAND PAINTER

Black and white women share many common experiences in their roles as wives, mothers, and members of the paid labor force, but racism and the higher incidence of poverty in the black community create additional handicaps for black women which significantly affect their family life and nonfamily relationships. Because blacks fall into many income classes and exhibit varied patterns of behavior in their social relationships, it is difficult to generalize about "the black woman" or "the black family," but, to the extent that the probability is high that black girls born in America will encounter the effects of discrimination and poverty, it is valid to analyze the problems faced by the majority of black women, the poor and near poor, at the expense of omitting an analysis of the situation of more fortunate black women. Indeed, one of the by-products of racism in America is that all blacks live in a precarious and dependent state: no black is ever truly safe and secure from the hazards of arbitrary treatment, unemployment, and poverty. Sexist discrimination operates in the same manner; therefore, black women are doubly afflicted.

FAMILY LIFE

One of the most controversial conclusions reached in the Moynihan report, *The Negro Family: The Case for National Action*

(U.S. Department of Labor, Office of Policy Planning and Research, 1965:5), was that "At the heart of the deterioration of the fabric of Negro society is the deterioration of the Negro family." The report juxtaposed the white family (and the black middle-class family) with that of the so-called lower-class Negroes: the former "has achieved a high degree of stability," and the latter "is highly unstable and in many urban centers is approaching complete breakdown." Whatever else the report accomplished, it did encourage a great deal of research on the black family and black community relations. Black scholars (see Billingsley, 1966) and others subsequently have taken the position that in fact black family types do not constitute pathological deviations from the norm. On the contrary, the diversity of family structures and the flexibility of roles within these structures constitute strengths rather than weaknesses because the adaptive mechanisms developed by blacks have allowed family life to survive under extremely adverse circumstances.

Lee Rainwater (1967) has noted that lower income blacks are aware of what family life should be, but they are frustrated in their efforts to abide by their ideals because of the direct impact of the economic disabilities which ravage black communities. It is not uncommon for people whose life styles deviate from the norm to verbalize values which conform to what might be called middle-class standards. Although currently American attitudes may be in the process of change as more and more women enter paid employment, most people, black and white, still tend to conceptualize "good" family life to include

> the notion of a father-husband who functions as an adequate provider and interested member of the family, a hard working home-bound mother who is concerned about her children's welfare and her husband's needs, and children who look up to their parents and perform well in school and other outside places to reflect credit on their families. [Rainwater, 1967:170]

The harsh reality is that this type of family can only be maintained under favorable economic and social conditions and that racism and the consequences of discrimination—unemployment, low income, lack of skills, residential segregation, etc.—reduce the viability of the middle-class family type for most minority people. Whether or not conventional ideals concerning the family and women's roles are compatible with the goals of today's women who are in the process of redefining their places in society, these ideals represent the day-to-day objectives of many women who have not experienced the amenities of middle-class status.

Researchers involved in a Washington child-rearing study found a range of behavior or several modes or styles of family life among their low-income subjects (Lewis, 1967). Such findings underline the danger of assigning certain stereotypes to different economic classes. In the data given below, statistical generalizations should not overshadow the diversity which exists within subgroups in the black population. Different types of families are found across class lines, and within family prototypes various behavior patterns may predominate.

The majority of black families have both spouses present. In 1975, 61% of the 5.5 million black families were in this category, as compared to 87% of the 49.4 million white families (U.S. Bureau of the Census, 1975:106-107). In general, husband-wife families have a higher median income than families that have either a male or a female head, because husband-wife families are more likely to have at least two earners. However, between 1970 and 1974, the proportion of black families with two or more earners decreased as the number of families headed by women increased for blacks and the proportion of all black families with wives in the labor force declined, again as a result of the decline in proportion of families with both spouses present. In 1974, the ratio of black to white median income of families was 0.58 for all families, 0.74 for families headed by men (including single men), 0.77 for families headed by men with wives in the labor force, 0.63 for families headed by men with wives not in the labor force, and 0.61 for families headed by women (U.S. Bureau of the Census, 1975:33). For blacks, in 54% of the husband-wife families the wives were in the paid labor force in 1974; the comparable figure for whites was 42%.

Over the years, proportionately more black women with families than white women with families have entered the paid labor force in order to provide basic necessities for their families or to supplement their husbands' earnings. The factors explaining labor force participation rates are discussed in the next section. Historically, the proportion of black families with incomes below the poverty line has been higher than that of whites. In 1974, when the low-income threshold for a nonfarm family of four was $5,038 according to the Federal Interagency Committee's poverty index, the proportions of families below this level were as follows: 27.8% for all black families

(7% for all white families), 14.2% for families with a male head (4.9% white), and 52.8% for families headed by women (24.9% white) (U.S. Bureau of the Census, 1975:43). In addition, since the Korean War period, the ratio of the jobless rate for blacks to whites has remained at 2 : 1 (the ratio for married males with spouses present is slightly less, while the ratio for teenagers is slightly higher).

Discrimination in the areas of formal education, vocational training, and informal training has reinforced the processes of occupational and employment discrimination. Blacks who are poorly qualified naturally find themselves in those occupations that are the lowest paid and have little status. As Lester Thurow (1969) has pointed out, the best way for a dominant group to maintain its supremacy in the labor market is to prevent or limit investment in minority human capital. One of the reasons for the high rate of unemployment among all groups of blacks is that blacks tend to be overrepresented in those occupations that have the highest incidence of joblessness.

Since 1960, educational differentials between blacks and whites as measured by years of schooling completed have narrowed. In fact, the proportion of high school graduates rose faster for blacks than for whites between 1970 and 1974 (U.S. Bureau of the Census, 1975:96). What rising levels of educational attainment of blacks will mean in terms of closing the earnings gap between blacks and whites is not clear. Economists concerned with the relationship between education and earnings have found that black-white income differentials widen as the number of years worked increases. It appears that, once workers enter the labor force, occupational discrimination, which limits the exposure of minorities (and women) to learning experiences and prevents upward mobility, and human capital discrimination, which bars workers from training programs, cause blacks to fall increasingly behind whites in terms of earnings. It remains to be seen whether or not equal opportunity programs and affirmative action will eliminate covert forms of discrimination.

Recently, there has been a steady decline in the proportion of husband-wife families in the black population. At the same time the number of female-headed households has increased significantly. For example, between 1970 and 1975, the proportion of black families headed by a woman (no spouse present) rose from 28% to 35% compared to an increase of 9% to 11% for white women (U.S. Bureau of the Census, 1975:106-107). Female heads include widowed, separated, divorced, and single women and women whose husbands are away from home involuntarily. In part, the rise for blacks reflected two phenomena: blacks tend to marry later, and they tend to have less stable marriages than whites.

> Despite the widespread belief that divorce is a white upper-class phenomenon, the incidence of divorce is nearly half again higher among nonwhites than whites. Moreover, divorce rates are rising faster among nonwhite than white males, though this is not true for nonwhite females. . . . Once divorced or widowed, black women are less likely to remarry than whites. In 1970, 49 percent of black women age twenty-five to thirty-four who had been widowed or divorced had remarried compared with 69 percent of whites.

> Separation without divorce is also much more common among blacks than whites. In 1970, 17 percent of black married women were currently separated, compared with only 2 percent of white married women. [Levitan et al., 1975:112-113]

According to Kenneth Clark (1967), the relative imbalance of status between males and females in black marriages is due in part to society's emasculation of the black male. Racism and discrimination prevent the black man from functioning in terms of the values of white society. Often, he cannot command the respect of the black woman in terms of the standards which this society considers important. In poor communities and in bad times, the economic foundation of marriages disintegrates; therefore, partners must rely on their respect for each other's personal attributes to sustain unions. As Clark (1967:144) has noted, it is not easy to build a relationship on this basis under the most optimistic conditions. Inevitably, crises occur which weaken relationships beyond repair.

Some of the anthropological work on low-income families has revealed how black women feel about relationships within the family, given the constraints that poverty imposes on their lives (see Stack, 1974). As stated previously, there is a desire on the part of most black couples to establish a viable nuclear family unit. The problem for the poor is how to break out of poverty and obtain the necessary resources to support this type of family. The low-income black wife is well aware of the vagaries of the economic system and knows that the support of her children and herself may eventually become either partially or totally her concern. She therefore may assume a role within the marriage which is more egalitarian or even dominant than that of her counterparts in the black and white middle class or in the white lower class, because she provides the continuity for the family. Rainwater (1967:177) has contended that in lower-class husband-wife relationships there is a high degree of conjugal role segregation; i.e., both partners conceptualize themselves as having different kinds of instrumental functions. This segregation of roles leads to a higher degree of matrifocality among black low-income families than among black middle-class families because the wife "makes most of the decisions which keep the family going and has the greatest responsibility to the family" (Rainwater, 1967:178).

When a man can no longer support his family, two forces may cause him to leave his home: first, he cannot face the disillusionment and disappointment of his status, and, second, his wife and family can manage just as well or better (given welfare regulations) without him, and his presence is not encouraged. Often, black women cautiously guard their independence in both their formal and their informal relationships with men. Care is taken not to be fooled or taken advantage of by men. In many instances, even when long-term meaningful relationships are established, no attempt is made to enter into marriage. Perhaps this different attitude toward marriage is a result of a diminished need for low-income women to be married. The conditions faced by these women may lead them to question the value of marriage.

Economists look upon marriage as an institution that has been essential to women's economic welfare (see Moore and Sawhill, 1976). According to one group of economists (Levitan et al., 1975:105-106), in a society in which men have great financial advantage, marriage in the form of the husband-wife nuclear family is the most desirable economic position for women with children. However, among groups in which men do not have a financial advantage, the institution of marriage becomes less desirable and essential to women and their children. Temporary alliances between women and men, in this case, are not indicative of loose morals but are a recognition of the objective reality of poverty and satisfy the participants' basic needs for companionship and support without binding them to ideals which cannot be realized.

LABOR FORCE ACTIVITY

Work in the paid labor force allows women to achieve some degree of independence and control over their lives. However, for many women, including minority women, the low wages and salaries that they earn barely allow them to subsist let alone attain any of the qualitative goals expressed by activists in the women's movement. Although in recent years the labor force participation rate of white women has increased much faster than that of black women, black women continue to show a greater attachment to the labor force than white women. In 1974, the labor force participation rate of black women was 49.1%, while that of whites was 45.2% (U.S. Department of Labor, 1975:60). The differential between the black and white rates was 14.3% in 1950 but only 3.9% by 1974.

In 1973, at each age level, except in the 16-to-24-year-old groups, black women had higher participation rates than their white counterparts (U.S. Department of Labor, 1975:59). The lower rate for younger black women was related to such factors as the presence of more children and job-search difficulties caused by poor educational backgrounds. The only other classification in which the white labor force participation rate exceeded that of the black was for married women with husband absent. Here, the lower black rate is primarily due to the presence of more children in black homes than in white. According to the 1975 *Manpower Report of the President* (U.S. Department of Labor, 1975:70),

> 61 percent of female heads of poor families do not even seek outside employment—some through discouragement and others through a reluctance to surrender child-care responsibilities to others. Moreover, divorced and separated women are often ill-equipped for market occupations other than those requiring a minimum of education and skill.

For the total population of black women, the presence of young children affects work status to a lesser extent than it does for white women. Fifty-four percent of black women with children under 6 years of age were in the labor force in 1973 compared with 31% of white women with preschool children (U.S. Department of Labor, 1975:60).

Although economists such as Bowen and Finegan (1969) and Cain (1966) have analyzed the factors influencing the labor force participation rates of women, the differences in black-white behavior patterns still have not been entirely clarified. The primary difficulty in unraveling causes of black-white differences lies in the formulation of testable hypotheses. Are black-white differentials due to different personal and family characteristics, different historical experiences, different responses to economic and social factors, different evaluations and expectations of the future, or some combination of all of these possible explanations? Black social scientists such as Ladner (1972) and Billingsley (1966) have stressed the importance of such historical factors as slavery in shaping black institutions.

Duran Bell (1974) has used regression analysis and cross-tabulation from the 1967 Survey of Economic Opportunity to analyze the nature of black-white differences in the labor force participation rates of married women with respect to such independent variables as the presence of children under 4, the number of children under 18, the age and educational attainment of the wife, geographical and residential location, family income, and the number of weeks in 1966 that the husband did not work. Quantitative findings like those in the Bell study cannot be interpreted in isolation. Awareness of the historical and cultural background of the subjects aids in the understanding of significant statistical relationships. In Bell's work, the introduction of the independent variable, residential location, allowed him to see if the participation rates varied by neighborhood (inside poor areas of central city, nonpoor central city, or suburbs). It is clear from Bell's coefficients (1974:467) that there are factors operating in poverty areas which constrain the labor force activity of poor blacks, but these factors do not affect whites in a parallel manner. Bell (1974:472) also found that "BLACK FAMILIES IN WHICH THE WIFE WORKS FULL TIME ARE AMONG THE MORE STABLE AND BETTER EDUCATED BLACK FAMILIES, WHEREAS THE WHITE WORKING WIFE EMERGES FROM THE LESSER EDUCATED, POORER AND MORE UNSTABLE WHITE FAMILIES."

Several factors could account for the observations cited above, but the primary explanation has to do with the nature and structure of the black middle class. Traditionally, the lower expected earnings and the limited occupational access for black males has meant that even for the well educated the attainment of middle-class status and its material benefits has necessitated that black wives work. Attitudes toward the "working wife" are much more favorable and supportive in the black community than they are in comparable segments of the white community. Black men are more likely to have grown up in a home where their mothers worked and their fathers shared home responsibilities than are white men in the middle class. Consequently, the combination of necessity and receptive attitudes results in relatively high labor force participation rates for black middle-class women. In the white community, white males have been capable of earning salaries sufficient to support the American ideal, and their wives have not had to work in order to insure the upward mobility of their families.

The question of why white women are entering the labor market at increasing rates is one that currently is well discussed but cannot be pursued here except to note one of Bell's (1974:478) conclusions from his data. In the past, sexist barriers to occupational placement limited even well-educated women to low esteem jobs; therefore, the entry of educated women into the labor market was associated with a loss of status. As sexist barriers are eliminated and job opportunities for women improve, better-educated white women find, first of all, that wages and salaries are attractive enough to warrant entry into the labor market and, second, that the available jobs entail no loss in social status. We therefore can expect the effective implementation of equal opportunity measures to be associated with an increasing rate of entry of educated middle-class and upper-middle-class women into the labor market.

The options of low-income white women are fewer than their affluent white counterparts in that the poor bear the burden of class discrimination as well as sexist discrimination. However, as a group, low-income white women fare better than low-income blacks. Although differences in the occupational distribution of black and white women are narrowing, white women may find placement in a wider range of occupations and earn higher wages than black women from low-income families. In 1973, the median wage or salary income of minority race women (of which 90% are black) who worked year-round full-time jobs was $5,772, or 88% of that of white women ($6,544) (U.S. Department of Labor, Women's Bureau, 1975:135). The black-white income ratio was 64% in 1963.

In 1973, 42% of minority race women held white-collar jobs as compared with 63% of white women (U.S. Department of Labor, Women's Bureau, 1975:102). If the categories of secretaries and typists are examined, it can be seen that black women are more likely to be typists than secretaries. There is a rather consistent pattern of blacks falling into the lower-paying lesser-skilled jobs within each occupational class. According to 1970 census data (U.S. Bureau of the Census, 1974:93),

> black women comprised about 12 percent of all employed women; however, they represented only 8 percent of all women working in professional fields, 4 percent of the managers and administrators, and 7 percent of the women who were employed as clerical and kindred workers in 1970. In contrast, 18 percent of the women farm workers, 17 percent of the women service workers (excluding private household), and 53 percent of the women private household workers were black women.

The data show rather dramatically that, despite advances in many areas, black women are still underrepresented in many fields. The data also point out that black women are often confronted with a choice between a low-paying, menial, physically demanding job outside the home and productive home activities. When this is the case, the opportunity costs involved do not justify the acceptance of employment outside the home.

There are three other factors that might account for a lower labor force participation rate for black women in low-income neighborhoods. First, the presence of young children combined with the lack of proper child-care facilities ties women to their homes. Second, the welfare regulations in most states impose prohibitive taxes on recipients who work. Finally, poor black women are even less qualified for stable and rewarding jobs than their white counterparts.

Some social scientists (Clark, 1967) have remarked that society as a whole is more willing to accept the black woman than the black man. We all are aware of the sexual myths and fantasies that have served to justify racism in America. The fact that traditionally the proportion of black women reaching higher levels of education has been higher than the proportion of black men is cited as proof of the relative psychological advantage that black women have over black men from white society's point of view.

In general, for the total population, women are more likely than men to have graduated from high school, but less likely to have completed four years of college. Statistical data (U.S. Bureau of the Census, 1975:96-97) on the level of schooling completed by persons 20-24 years old between 1960 and 1974 indicate that, generally, the proportion of white males completing four years of high school *and* one year of college is higher than the proportion of white females; however, the figures for blacks are reversed. It does appear that black men have made more rapid gains in college attendance during the

1970s as a result of the introduction and expansion of special programs for minorities. Whether or not these new programs discriminate against women needs to be investigated. According to a report from the U.S. Bureau of the Census (1974:65),

> The proportion of black women (18-24 years) enrolled in college appears to have leveled off in the 1970's after a rise during the preceding period, 1965-1970. On the other hand, the college participation rate for black men the same age has tended to increase over the entire period. Thus, in 1973, a higher proportion of black men than women was enrolled in college (19 versus 14 percent). In 1965, the rate was the same for both men and women—10 percent.

Jacquelyne Jackson (1973:226-227) has offered an explanation for the male-female differential in black educational attainment levels. The utilitarian theory of black female education which Jackson has discussed holds that education for black women has been a means to an occupation to produce income needed for a living; therefore, the educational motivation of black women has been largely work-oriented. With regard to parental aspirations and motivations in the education of their daughters, Jackson (1973:230) has stated that

> A realistic historical assessment of Black preferences for more education for females, where preferences may have existed, should be functionally related to the greater educational requirements for obtaining an occupation as a public school teacher, with almost the only visible occupation for Black females then being that of domestic employment, whereas most educational requirements for occupations open to the male (generally at higher income levels) were not so stringent.

Societal preference for or greater tolerance of black women relative to black men supposedly carries over to the job market. Proportionately more black women than men have moved into semiskilled and white-collar jobs in this century (Clark, 1967:142). If the ratio of black men employed in a given occupation to all men in that occupation and the ratio of black women employed in a given occupation to all women in that occupation are analyzed (Garfinkle, 1975:31-33) for detailed occupational groups for the years 1962-1974, black women made more pervasive inroads into higher-paying occupations than did black men. One possible explanation for the advance made by women is that there has been a growth in the number of jobs available in clerical occupations that traditionally hire women. Although black and white women have made occupational gains over the past two decades, they continue to be concentrated in lower-paying teaching, nursing, and social work fields if they are in the professional groups, while men are in such higher-status and higher-paying professions as law, medicine, accounting, and engineering.

In summary, compared with white women, black women tend to have a stronger attachment to the labor market; however, they tend to earn less, suffer higher rates of unemployment, and have jobs of lower status. Yet, even if racial differentials were to disappear, they would still be second-class citizens vis-à-vis black and white men. Between 1967 and 1971, the median income ratio of year-round full-time workers, black women to black men, increased from 0.67 to 0.75, but the same ratio for white women to white men remained constant at a level of 0.58 (U.S. Bureau of the Census, 1974:100). The movements for equality for minorities and women must work together if all people are to participate fully in our economic system.

IMPACT ON DEPENDENCE

There is some evidence (Ross and Sawhill, 1975) that marital instability is positively related to women's increasing economic independence. If this is true, as opportunities open up that afford women the chance to earn decent wages and salaries in attractive jobs, we can expect that the institution of marriage and the structure of families will undergo radical changes among all economic classes. In the future, greater economic independence will allow women and men to experiment with different life-styles as they adapt to the pressures of home and market work. At present, a majority of the increasing number of women who head households cannot support themselves and their children, and public and private policies have not come to terms with the problems posed by this segment of the population.

In the black population, the higher incidence of households headed by women is an outgrowth of the vicious circle of poverty that engulfs the black community. Compared with white women, black women tend to experience higher separation rates, lower remarriage rates, and more out-of-wedlock births (see Ross and Sawhill, 1975:67-92). These factors are linked directly to conditions generated by poverty. In addition, not only is it difficult for low-income black women to establish relationships with men who have stable economic futures, but also the overall male-female sex ratio is unfavorable in the black population. For example, in 1970 (Levitan et al., 1975:123), the male-female ratio for the 20-24 age group was 0.86, and for the 25-35 age group it was 0.84. Thus, even in the best of circumstances, the marriage prospects for black women would be limited.

How do poor minority women manage to insure the survival of their families? Their dependence shifts from within the nuclear family to dependence on other types of structures; they become dependent on kinship ties and friendship networks and public assistance. According to Rae Lesser Blumberg (1976:15):

Female-headed families tend to be joined with close kin (especially on the female side) in a network of give and take. Household composition may shift, with adults and children—as well as money, goods, and services— moving around the network as circumstances dictate. Moreover, it has been demonstrated mathematically that sharing aids in the survival of the group by smoothing out fluctuations in its scarce, uncertain, and variable resource base.

Mutual assistance enables a large segment of the poor population to exist on a day-to-day basis. Carol Stack's study (1974) of ghetto life in a Midwestern city describes the operation of networks of exchange involving swapping, child care, and moral and economic support. Stack has implied that the desire of members of a network to maintain the network may create conditions that limit the upward mobility of individuals within the network. Cooperating kinsmen realize that an individual cannot "simultaneously meet kin expectations and the expectations of a spouse" (Stack, 1974:113-114); therefore, a key member of a network might find that kinsmen fearing the loss of her resources might discourage her attempts to break out of the circle. Marriage and employment are the primary ways in which women who head households may escape poverty, but either course may involve estrangement from the network because of the pressures of new responsibilities; and, given the chance of failing at marriage or losing a job, members of a group carefully weigh the risks involved in disrupting existing ties. The sharing of resources has another drawback because it prevents members of networks from accumulating assets that could be used to finance a move away from ghetto life.

Public assistance programs constitute another type of dependency relationship from which it is difficult to escape. Because blacks have lower remarriage rates than whites, longer separations before divorce, and longer periods between divorce and remarriage, they tend to remain on welfare rolls longer than whites (Ross and Sawhill, 1975:113). In fact, in most states, regulations set up to minimize the costs of welfare actually work to insure that the poor stay poor. First of all, in most states, poor families headed by men receive little or no assistance, though the children in these families may have needs as great as those children from families headed by women. However, the extent to which the failure of the system to aid families in which a man is present has caused an increase in households headed by women has not been established definitively (see Ross and Sawhill, 1975:98-126).

Second, the high marginal tax rate on the earnings of welfare recipients (i.e., the amount of loss in welfare benefits for each additional dollar earned) discourages recipients from seeking paid employment or may force them to engage in illicit activities or to take low-paying jobs in activities where the earnings cannot be traced. Third, in most instances, welfare recipients are not allowed to maintain personal property. To qualify for assistance, people are forced to dispose of most of their assets. Such policies have psychological as well as economic ramifications. Finally, although numerous manpower programs have been developed over the past 15 years, as yet the programs available to welfare recipients have not allowed substantial numbers of people to move into stable jobs.

Dual labor market theory (Gordon, 1972:43-52) provides one of the best explanations of the failure of recent manpower programs and is particularly applicable to the problems faced by women. Basically, low-income people were not trained and provided with the "work skills" needed to enter the primary labor market where the jobs are characterized by "high wages, good working conditions, employment stability and job security, equity and due process in the administration of work rules, and chances for advancement" (Piore, 1971:91). On the contrary, under the programs, people received qualifications that confined them to the secondary labor market where the job characteristics are the opposite of those outlined above; consequently, their economic futures remained unstable. In addition, racial, sexist, and statistical discrimination in the labor market combined to work against the disadvantaged workers whom the programs were designed to help. In the case of statistical discrimination (Piore, 1971:91), employers tend not to hire members of certain groups (minorities and women) because their superficial characteristics appear to be statistically associated with such undesirable traits as a high rate of turnover, absenteeism, or tardiness. Dual labor market theory points out that groups such as women cannot move into better jobs unless manpower programs are accompanied by reforms in other areas.

Dependency that has its origins outside marriage can be eliminated or at the very least minimized primarily in two ways: restructuring the labor market on both the demand and supply sides and reforming current public assistance programs, including those that provide in-kind benefits (food stamps, housing assistance, and Medicaid). It is crucial that policy makers identify the nature of the problems faced by different groups of women. Some women need training or retraining, others need child care, etc., and the solutions to their problems require specific approaches if programs designed to help women are to succeed. As more and more women either have to or want to work, public and private policy makers should recognize that, if the welfare of all members of the family is to be maximized, then adults must be assisted in the performance of their functions within the family as well as in the execution of their market activities. Child-care facilities and arrangements are obvious needs, but the other types of services provided within kinship networks point out other needs—transportation, access to credit, better housing, etc.

CONCLUSION

An examination of the range of options available to black women enhances understanding of their roles and relationships within the family. Middle-class women who choose or have to remain in the home are economically and socially dependent on their husbands, since the men's status and goodwill determine the nature of the women's existence. The low-income single or married woman may be less dependent on her mate than she is on kinship ties and on the social services set up by society to take care of those whom it otherwise neglects. Given the present-day status of women in and outside the home, it is highly likely that any woman who has to maintain a household alone will face economic hardship at one time or another. The plight of minority women highlights the problems created by discrimination and points to the need for reform of the basic institutions that affect the status of women.

REFERENCES

BELL, D. (1974). "Why participation rates of black and white wives differ." Journal of Human Resources, 9(fall):465-479.

BERNARD, J. (1966). Marriage and family among Negroes. Englewood Cliffs, N.J.: Prentice-Hall.

BILLINGSLEY, A. (1966). Black families in white America. Englewood Cliffs, N.J.: Prentice-Hall.

BLUMBERG, R.L. (1976). "Fairy tales and facts: Economy, family, fertility, and the female." Pp. 12-21 in I. Tinker and M.B. Bramsen (eds.), Women and world development. Washington, D.C.: Overseas Development Council.

BOWEN, W.G., and FINEGAN, T.A. (1969). The economics of labor force participation. Princeton, N.J.: Princeton University Press.

CAIN, G.G. (1966). Married women in the labor force: An economic analysis. Chicago: University of Chicago Press.

CLARK, K.B. (1967). "Sex, status, and underemployment of the Negro male." Pp. 138-148 in A.M. Ross and H. Hill (eds.), Employment, race, and poverty. New York: Harcourt, Brace and World.

GARFINKLE, S.A. (1975). "Occupations of women and black workers." Monthly Labor Review, 98(November):25-35.

GORDON, D. (1971). Problems in political economy: An urban perspective. Lexington, Mass.: D.C. Heath.

——— (1972). Theories of poverty and underemployment: Orthodox, radical, and dual labor market perspectives. Lexington, Mass.: D.C. Heath.

JACKSON, J.J. (1973). "Black women in a racist society." Pp. 185-268 in C.V. Willie, B.M. Kramer, and B.S. Brown (eds.), Racism and mental health. Pittsburgh: University of Pittsburgh Press.

KREPS, J.M. (ed., 1976). Women and the American economy: A look to the 1980's. Englewood Cliffs, N.J.: Prentice-Hall.

LADNER, J. (1972). Tomorrow's tomorrow: The black woman. Garden City, N.Y.: Anchor.

LEVITAN, S.A., JOHNSTON, W.B., and TAGGART, R. (1975). Still a dream: The changing status of blacks since 1960. Cambridge, Mass.: Harvard University Press.

LEWIS, H. (1967). "Culture, class, and family life among low-income urban Negroes." Pp. 149-174 in A.M. Ross and H. Hill (eds.), Employment, race, and poverty. New York: Harcourt, Brace and World.

MOORE, K.A., and SAWHILL, I.V. (1976). "Implications of women's employment for home and family life." Pp. 102-122 in J.M. Kreps (ed.), Women and the American economy: A look to the 1980's. Englewood Cliffs, N.J.: Prentice-Hall.

PARSONS, T., and CLARK, K.B. (eds., 1967). The Negro American. Boston: Beacon Press.

PIORE, M. (1971). "The dual labor market: Theory and implications." Pp. 90-94 in D. Gordon (ed.), Problems in political economy: An urban perspective. Lexington, Mass.: D.C. Heath.

RAINWATER, L. (1967). "Crucible of identity: The Negro lower-class family." Pp. 160-204 in T. Parsons and K.B. Clark (eds.), The Negro American. Boston: Beacon Press.

ROSS, A.M., and HILL, H. (eds., 1967). Employment, race, and poverty. New York: Harcourt, Brace and World.

ROSS, H.L., and SAWHILL, I.V. (1975). Time of transition: The growth of families headed by women. Washington, D.C.: Urban Institute.

STACK, C.B. (1974). All our kin: Strategies for survival in a black community. New York: Harper and Row.

THUROW, L. (1969). Poverty and discrimination. Washington, D.C.: Brookings Institution.

TINKER, I., and BRAMSEN, M.B. (eds., 1976). Women and world development. Washington, D.C.: Overseas Development Council.

U.S. Bureau of the Census (1974). Current population reports: Special studies (Series P-23, no. 48). Washington, D.C.: U.S. Government Printing Office.

— — — (1975). Current population reports: Special studies (Series P-23, no. 54). Washington, D.C.: U.S. Government Printing Office.

U.S. Department of Labor (1975). Manpower report of the President. Washington, D.C.: U.S. Government Printing Office.

U.S. Department of Labor, Office of Policy Planning and Research (1965). The Negro family: The case for national action. Washington, D.C.: U.S. Government Printing Office.

U.S. Department of Labor, Women's Bureau (1975). Handbook on women workers. Washington, D.C.: U.S. Government Printing Office.

WILLIE, C.V., KRAMER, B.M., and BROWN, B.S. (eds., 1973). Racism and mental health. Pittsburgh: University of Pittsburgh Press.

7

CHILD CARE FOR THE 1980s
Traditional Sex Roles or Androgyny?

MARY POTTER ROWE

A young father in Massachusetts recently watched his wife die of cancer, leaving him and their five young children. Responsible, caring, grief-stricken, he went to the Welfare Department, planning to quit his job, go on welfare, and stay at home until the youngest child was in kindergarten. "It is tasteless in our society for a man to stay home," he was told. "We will find foster homes for your children." The young father protested, unwilling to lose his children and unwilling for them to lose him, each other, and their home, as well as their mother. His feelings were finally heard, but not until our traditions about child care had been vividly dramatized: Responsibility for young children lies with women, and the primary role of women is to be with children (Pope Paul VI, 1976).

In this essay we discuss parenthood and child care from the point of view of *sex-roles* rather than of *institutions*. Many people use the words "traditional child-care" in a different way, to mean "care within the *institution* of a nuclear family." For these people, nontraditional care then means care in an institution different from the nuclear family—say, a commune or day-care center or a 24-hour state nursery or a household following death or divorce or a lesbian household. I, on the other hand, will use the words "traditional child care" to mean responsibility for children and care of young children by women, under circumstances where men would find it difficult to care for those children and where only women would be comfortable doing so in our society. Thus, day-care and 24-hour state centers, foster care, care by divorcees, and lesbian households might all be "traditional child care," in my sense, if the female child carers perceive themselves to be constrained by sex-role stereotypes so powerful that neither they nor would-be male child carers have the freedom to negotiate who will care for the children.

By the same token, *androgynous* child care, according to the definitions of this paper, might occur in families, centers, and other institutions and occurs wherever both men and women have equal options to negotiate with themselves and each other on who will care for children. (Of course there is a shading, from tradition toward androgyny, along a continuum where women and men experience different degrees of options, which may vary by age of child or family income or other individual circumstances.)

This paper discusses present-day child-care arrangements and some consequences of our present arrangements. The negative consequences of traditional arrangements are seen as part and parcel of the negative consequences of American sex-role stereotypes as a whole. The paper concludes with a discussion of further androgynous options for parents and what is needed to support those options in terms of laws and of human attitudes.

PRESENT-DAY CHILD CARE ARRANGEMENTS

About four-fifths of American households with children under 14 are in nuclear family form (Unco, 1976).[1] (I estimate, however, that about half the American children in the 1980s will live for some part of their childhood with a single parent or in some other nonnuclear family arrangement.) About 90% of all households with children under 14 now use some kind of care (other than the mother in her own home) at some time in a given week; more than half use care more than an hour per week; about a quarter use a child-care arrangement 10 or more hours per week; about an eighth use care 30 or more hours per week.

The main types of care are relatives in one's own or another home or a nonrelative in one's own home or another home. Day-care centers, cooperative programs, nurseries and preschools, and before- and after-school programs together comprise at most a 10th of all arrangements. About two-thirds of all households pay no cash for child care, but many arrangements are reimbursed in kind; only about a 10th of all arrangements are considered "free."

Multiple arrangements are very common, with over half of all care-using households reporting the father as a regular, supplementary caretaker, three-tenths regularly using an older sibling, and an eighth regularly leaving children alone, in addition to the relatives and nonrelatives and formal care reported above as "main types of care." Hours that children are in school after school are also an important "child-care arrangement" for two-ninths of all children under 14.

Of interest to the present discussion, we find fathers estimated as fewer than 10% of all "main types" of child carers, but they are clearly "helping out" significantly, as noted above. How much are men becoming involved in child care? There is scattered evidence of the importance of men as child carers in some specific groups of the population. For instance, among the families of professional psychologists, roughly a sixth to a quarter of the care of the children is reported to be by husbands—with nonspouse arrangements on the same order of magnitude, and mothers caring for children 60% to 70% of the time (Bryson et al., 1976). The Michigan Survey Research Center study of 5,000 American families is also reported to have found many men comparably engaged in child care. And about 8% of all children under 18 years who were reported living in nonnuclear families were in nonnuclear families headed by a male, in 1974 (U.S. Department of Labor, 1974).

On the other hand, time budget studies of several years ago showed that employed mothers spent seven to 10 hours more per week on total work and work-related activities (including commuting, homemaking, child care, and paid employment) than did employed fathers (Holmstrom, 1972; Walker, 1970; Szalai, 1973).[2] And the "extra" time devoted by employed mothers was predominantly in child care and homemaking. Moreover, there is some reason to believe that fathers, on the average, got more sleep and had more time in leisure activities than did mothers (L. Harris and Associates, 1970; Szalai, 1973). The mothers, in fact, appeared to get less than optimal sleep on a regular basis (Szalai, 1973).

Some evidence has indicated that the amount of time spent by employed fathers on child care and homemaking depended primarily on what these men were otherwise doing; it did not depend very much on whether the mother had a paid job or on the number of children in the family (Walker, 1970). On the other hand, some studies appear to indicate that husbands/fathers have performed a little more housework and child care when wives/mothers are employed, the increase usually expressed as an increase in the percent of total homemaking taken on by the husband (Hoffman and Nye, 1974). My own experience also indicates that many women *believe* this is the case. However, I now believe that the major shift that occurs when a wife/mother takes a paid job is that the total amount of family work time drops very sharply (by half to a third, according to Walker, 1970) and that because the husband's family work time stays nearly the same, he is doing a larger *proportion* of the homemaking.

On the basis of my clinical experience I believe there may also be a shift in the *type* of work performed by husbands (from less urgent to more urgent). Moreover, the standard deviation in amount of family work performed by all husbands may be rising. That is, I believe more husbands may be doing either *less* family work, because of moonlighting, or *more,* because of a shift toward androgyny by younger men, while the "average" amount of family work performed by "all husbands" has risen only a little in the 1970s.

Of course these statistics on child-care arrangements tell us nothing certain about the attitudes of the child carers and the extent to which they are or feel constrained by sex-role stereotyping. But we find fathers as primary care givers (as distinguished from being regular supplementary caretakers) for only a few percent of American children and mothers as the primary care givers for nearly half of all U.S. children. Moreover, most mothers retain basic responsibility for children most of the time, and seven-eighths of all households use nonmaternal care only 30 hours per week or less, out of the 168 hours in a week (Unco, 1976). It is easy, therefore, to hypothesize that serious sex-role stereotyping with respect to children is very important in the U.S.

Comparable statistics do not exist for other countries. We know that, in predominantly rural areas of the world, it is usually women who care for children, at home or at work and usually together with other women, or that older children care for younger children under the eye of a nearby adult. In other industrialized nations more like our own, sex-role differentiation appears to be as common as in the United States. In at least 18 other nations with time budget surveys, patterns are reported similar to those in the United States (Roby, 1975; Szalai, 1973).

In the Soviet Union, top government officials will say, "We believe women to be better suited to child care"; Soviet fathers are kept out of maternity hospitals and have no paternity leave the first year of their child's life, and practically no men are involved in the day-to-day formal care that affects perhaps 40% of Soviet urban preschoolers (Rowe, 1975). In China (Sidel, 1972) and in Israel (Gerson, 1971) comparable sex-role differentiation obtains. Thus even where widespread child-care systems are available, they are traditional according to my view and tend to maintain the women-with-children stereotype.

Only in the United States and Scandinavia do we find significant, if small, proportions of men involved in formal child care. And only in Scandinavia and Cuba have top government leaders systematically asserted equal rights for men in the home and with children and equal sharing with women of social responsibility for reproducing and socializing the human species. Nowhere does that equal sharing appear yet to have taken place.

Support for traditional practices and policies has generally rested on two grounds. First, it is asserted that women are biologically better able to care for children and that men are hormonally and morphologically better able to support a family.[3] Second, it is asserted that a whole socioeconomic system has been erected on the basis of the biological differences and that this system is a good thing, because sex-role differentiation has been effective and efficient in getting done the work of the world. It is my point of view that differences in child-rearing capabilities and requirements formerly *did* mean that women were better adapted to child care, but that biological differences with respect to parenting no longer have much meaning in this era of zero population growth, planned parenthood, and bottle feeding. Hormonal and morphologic differences in men may also have meant that males were in some societies better providers, in an age of hunting and frontier life. I believe that this is not generally true in our services-oriented economy, where cooperation and human organization are so exceptionally important. I believe that the traditional social and economic sex-role differentiation is no longer helpful to industrialized society and that androgyny offers a more effective and humane system for child care as well as for other employment.

WHAT IS THE EFFECT OF PRESENT-DAY
CHILD-CARE ARRANGEMENTS?

EFFECTS ON CHILDREN

Many experts in recent years have surveyed the evidence concerning the effect on children of different child-care arrangements. Extensive and exhaustive, these reviews regularly conclude that stable, responsive, consistent care is important, indeed critical, to young children. Recent studies also conclude that care of this nature can be delivered by a variety of different kinds of people, men and women, teenagers and grandparents, single and multiple attachment figures, in a variety of settings (Fein, 1974; Howell, 1973a, 1973b; Kotelchuck, 1972; Talbot, 1976). Although questions have been raised about the effect of 24-hour care on children in institutions (Bowlby, 1951), in kibbutzim (Bettelheim, 1970), or in 24-hour centers in the Soviet Union (Rowe, 1975) or about the effects of too much violent television, by and large it is very difficult to demonstrate long-term effects on children from any kind of nonabusive care and education arrangement (Rowe, 1974b; White et al., 1973). The public consensus in the United States also appears to be swinging toward a belief that child care may help socialize children, especially those in small families (Morgan, 1975; Unco, 1976) and that parental employment and child care may make children more independent. It seems reasonable to conclude that many types of arrangements are suitable for children, where the environment is safe and supportive and there are consistent, warm, responsive, stable attachment figures as caretakers (Talbot, 1976).

On the other hand, numerous observers believe that families need more support (Howell, 1976; Talbot, 1976), that children are happier when they see more of their fathers (Green, 1976), and that children might be happier with several different parental figures to turn to instead of depending exclusively on overworked, isolated mothers (Howell, 1976). And many people are deeply concerned by the number of children under the age of 10 who are now regularly left alone or who are in abusive care situations—numbers which may total 10% or more of our young children.

EFFECTS ON WOMEN AND MEN

Our traditions about women and children bring great joy and happiness to many men and women. Others have for decades ignored the traditions equally happily. Still others were brought up in different traditions, where women shared financial responsibility and/or men shared in all nurturance activities; many of these people and their families have also thrived.

There are many women and men, however, who are not happy either ignoring the modal tradition or living within it. And still others are happy for years with traditional sex roles and then feel constrained and confined and frustrated and bewildered. In this discussion we will concentrate on the difficulties with traditional roles with respect to child care since we are concerned mainly with providing options. (Androgyny includes people being free to behave traditionally, so options are more available than in a traditional setting, where only the ordinary sex roles are appropriate.) The ensuing discussion presents what I see as negative consequences of our present child-care arrangements. In a larger sense these consequences are due to the whole pattern of sex-role stereotyping rather than just to child care. And, as we noted above, there may be several reasons why sex-role differentiation occurred in the first place. At present, however, I believe that child-care arrangements have come to symbolize all the reasons for sex roles; they constitute perhaps the most powerful remaining institutionalization of our stereotypes. It is in this sense then that I present some consequences of sex-role differentiation in the context of consequences of child care arrangements.

The Sense of Separateness of Men and Women. The presumption that children and family were women's work has, I believe, led through our early socialization patterns to an extraordinary segregation of most men's lives from most women's lives, especially in industrialized societies. In my own work I am continually impressed by the extent to which men and women do not understand each other's experience.

More damaging yet is the frequent presumption that, at base, men and women *cannot* ultimately understand each other or live the same life-style. Liberal men will often support the entrance of women into, say, engineering. But, then, if someone asks about men in child care, this same liberal may ask, "But could men *really* take care of children as well as women?" The Soviet Union and China assert complete equality for women. These countries have, however, desegregated only lower- and middle-level "male" occupations, leaving child care and homemaking (and top-policy positions) as segregated as ever. Conservative—and radical—women also often speak as if only women could care for children. We are all accustomed to hearing very conservative women speak this way, but it is sometimes as true for radical women. Revolutionary feminists deplore the oppression of women which may result from women's traditional child-care responsibilities. But then some radical feminists turn to discussions of gestation in test tubes and of child care in 24-hour day care centers in a way which appears by exclusion to accept the notion that fathers and children might damage each other's lives. In other words, some feminists reject the oppression of individual women, but then turn to day-care (provided largely by women) as if it were an improvement. Some improvement may in fact occur; the caretakers are usually paid (at low rates) and sometimes have each other to talk with, but the traditional sex-role pattern obtains.

Another result of traditional thinking is that large numbers of men and women, including, sadly, some parents, have concluded that children and/or child care is too much for them (as distinguished from those who limit their families for idealistic reasons). For example, Ann Landers recently reported that 70% of 10,000 parents who wrote her about having children reported that they "would not do it again." And a recent Gallup Poll reported that one in 10 of all mothers randomly surveyed "regretted having children" (McCall's, 1975).

Loneliness. Present child-care arrangements are lonely for many parents. Isolated mothers and paid caretakers are often lonely; men who commute and moonlight and do not see their families are often lonely. Marriages in which one spouse is a homemaker, working 99 hours per week, and the other works overtime or moonlights up to 80-90 hours per week are hard on communications. The disproportionate numbers of depressed young mothers (Radloff, 1975) illuminate the sadness of spouses with not enough chance to be with those they love.

Moreover, in many of the shared parenting arrangements that now exist, the parents both work full time in paid jobs, with one or both (often the father) in charge of the children during hours when the parent(s) should be sleeping. (Of course the children may then also be sleeping.) Here the parents share care, sometimes at the price of sleep. However, since our society as a whole is set up for paid workers without child-care responsibilities (with fixed working hours and few half-time and three-quarter-time jobs), the parents may be able to earn two incomes only by staggering their work hours. This means that, in many two-job families, one parent is with the children primarily when the children are asleep and also that the parents have little waking or sleeping time together.

Loneliness exacts a high price. There can be a sense of desperation and resentment when a spouse alone must care for a sick child or a rebellious child; there can be a sense of desperation and resentment when a spouse alone must face a layoff or middle age without fulfillment. Sexual relationships suffer acutely when spouses are lonely.

Financial Difficulties. Families with one wage earner are less secure than those in which there are two. A single wage earner is under more pressure to succeed, to compete, to have to travel, to stay at a hated job in order to survive unemployment. A second wage earner provides a buffer, so his or her spouse may change jobs or train or retrain. A widowed or divorced spouse without labor force experience faces a very bleak world, financially and psychologically. So also do the homemaker parents whose children have grown and who have no further identity to turn to. Finally, at any given time we would have many millions more families on welfare, if both spouses were not in paid employment. Two wage earners obviously have a much better chance to provide a reasonable standard of living for themselves and their children.

Deprivation from Nurturance. Each parent faces a significant chance of widowhood or divorce. Most young men face single parenthood without enough training for the task and without equal rights to custody and child companionship and support.

Less often recognized is the gross deprivation of most men even where there is no widowhood or divorce. Occasionally, we deplore the specter of men governing our nation who have never taken care of a child or an aged parent or a pet or even a plant. Occasionally, if much too rarely, we take note of the fact that modern managers and modern foremen need to be nurturant, sensitive, and patient at least as much as they need to be aggressive, brave, and tough. We see this perhaps most clearly as we view with concern a generation of women who might become managers without being socialized to take care of other people.

It is extremely rare for us to discuss in public what it means for individual men to be cut off from children and other direct, personal, nurturant activities. The belief that men may reasonably spend their lives without the right or expectation of direct caretaking may lead to a variety of damage. One knows many men who do not physically or emotionally take care of *themselves,* who lose much of their joy in life by being cut off from their feelings, who suffer considerably in childhood, adolescence, and manhood by competing with other males, who have essentially lost the sense of meaning and continuity of life by being cut off from aged parents and children, by being sanitized at every turn from human emotion. The female experiences of separateness and loneliness, bad as they are, seem to me mild compared with the destruction of self involved in our cutting off many men from their nurturant selves and their caring potential.

Work Satisfaction and Leisure Satisfaction. Analyses of work satisfaction indicate that some people value work for the process of working, some for the product, some for the remuneration, some for work-group relations. Some value status, the chance for creativity, the sense of autonomy over one's work. Joy in leisure-time activities is similarly related.

In traditional families each parent has only one work arena in which to seek satisfaction, friends, status, a sense of identity, and a sense of challenge and growth. If the home environment or the paid-work environment happens to provide the right processes, products, remuneration, friends, status, creativity, and autonomy for the parents assigned to that environment, all is well. But for many people having only one work arena provides a severe sense of constraint. Leisure activities are often similarly constrained. Moreover, the inequity of work-status and leisure-activity status between husband and wife in traditional families means that it is hard for many to maintain the love and comradeship which flourish between equals.

Finally, just the presumption that each individual will conform to the requirements of a stereotyped and arbitrary role is felt by many to be very constricting. This feeling has probably become more pronounced in recent years. In a simple society, role differentiation still permitted a wide range of expression. In the specializations of industrialism, much of this range has been lost, so that role requirements have become for many people much more constraining and are felt by many to be destructive to individuals.

Economic and Educational Discrimination Against Women. Of all the difficulties caused by and symbolized by traditional child-care patterns, perhaps the best understood is economic discrimination against women. Discrimination against women is often alleged to occur with respect to education, job recruitment, promotion, benefits, work ambiance, and the wage gap (unequal pay). The index of sex inequality most frequently cited is the wage gap between men and women; women's wages on the average are less than 60% of men's wages. Because the wage gap between men and women is easily quantified, it is the most easily analyzed indicator of sex discrimination. Economists interested in discrimination often begin with some estimate of wage gaps and then seek to explain these gaps by controlling for education, years of experience, entrance into given occupations, and promotional patterns, thereafter assigning any residual gap to "pure" or direct discrimination. Many feminists look upon these studies as analyzing indirect discrimination in order to isolate direct discrimination.

How much of gross wage gaps can be attributed directly or indirectly to sex-role differentiation in *child care,* as distinguished from *sex-role differentiation in general*? Here again, as with the rest of the discussion above, we cannot be sure exactly what part of discrimination is caused by, and what is symbolized by, differentiation in roles with respect to child care. We do know that, on the average, single women and childfree women have done better with respect to education, labor force participation, promotions, and wages. And we know that these "success" patterns are in general reversed for men, who typically thrive better when married and with children. But we do not know enough about selection factors (what kind of women choose to remain childfree?) or about indirect discrimination (what kind of women do men prefer to promote and pay well, other things being equal?). And economists disagree on exactly how to analyze the gross wage gaps. Thus there is no exact one-to-one evidence on the discriminatory importance of sex roles in child care. On the other hand, we do know some of the broad outlines of the effect of child-care patterns and how they may affect economic discrimination.

To begin with, many economists believe that a large part of the wage gap between men and women can be explained by occupational segregation (Kahne, 1975). Women are in general found in certain occupations which pay rather low wages or none at all.

Systematically low wages in "women's" occupations are variously explained by "crowding," "tastes," and human capital theory. "Crowding" is thought to result in lower wages for women because women have unequal access to many jobs. This produces a crowding of women into a few occupations such that their average productivity in these few occupations is lower than that of men in other occupations (Bergmann, 1974). The "tastes" argument suggests that employers and consumers simply "don't like" women in certain jobs or "assume they are inferior" and therefore discriminate against them (Arrow, 1972; Phelps, 1972). Both of these arguments would suggest that there is a psychological reason for denying women access to well-paying positions. Human capital theory suggests that women are on the average paid less than men because they are less productive and that they are less productive primarily because they are less well educated and trained. All of these theories find justification in empirical studies.

In addition to wage gaps produced by occupational segregation, most economists agree that part of the gross wage gap can be explained by differences in real and expected labor force participation—hours per week, weeks per year, years per lifetime.[4] But most now agree that these differences are less important than those rooted in occupational segregation. And most also agree that straightforward unequal pay for equal work is of only minimal importance.

How do our traditional expectations about child care lead to wage gaps? One may raise hypotheses all along the line, with respect to each theory above. Some have suggested that crowding and "discriminatory tastes" arise in part from a desire by males to compensate for not being able to gestate or nurse babies. This theory suggests that men have more need than women to create and control outside the family and that they have a signal fear of competing directly with women because of a primitive fear that they *cannot* really compete, with respect to creation (Rowe, 1974a).

With respect to human capital theory, many have suggested that the reason that women ask for and are permitted less education and less valuable training is that they need less education because their chief role is to marry and have children. In the 19th century, prolonged study was widely believed to be too strenuous for female anatomy and also likely to weaken a woman's reproductive capabilities. Although higher education is no longer considered damaging to motherhood, it is still widely considered unnecessary for mothers. Child-care responsibilities and the presumption that women should have full responsibility for children still directly interfere with equal educational opportunities for women.

During the 1970s, in the course of my work in and around universities in New England, I remember many very direct statements on this subject. For example, there was the admissions committee professor at a professional school who would admit women only if they "promise to stay celibate here." Many educational institutions have only recently permitted pregnant women to continue to study. Many others still do not have reasonable provisions for part-time graduate work and residencies for young parents.

By the same token, we still find daily stories of women asked in recruitment interviews about their family plans and contraception or stories of women not offered jobs or promotions or raises because of presumptions about their family life.

To the (relatively minor) extent that hours per week, weeks per year, and years per lifetime *are* important in explaining the wage gap, it is easy to see a very direct connection between our traditional child-care arrangements and labor force participation. With mothers in the paid labor force typically working a much longer total work week than fathers, it is easy to understand the direct conflict between paid and unpaid work.

Another area of economic discrimination where the relationship between labor force participation and traditional child care is very direct has to do with benefits—health care, vacations, pensions, Social Security. Adequate benefits coverage does not yet exist for men, but for women the situation is much worse. Women produce nearly 30% of family incomes; gross national product would rise by another estimated 20% if the unpaid work of women were included in GNP. Yet millions of women are without adequate health care, without vacation time, without appropriate pensions. This happens partly because much part-time work carries no benefits, because unpaid work in the home carries no direct benefits, because women as mothers have been considered their husbands' dependents, and because of the wage gap discussed above, which means that women's benefits, where they exist, are often lower. All these facts follow quite directly from the traditional vision of women as child carers.

Another and similar economic problem concerns our inadequate income tax deductions for child care. Money paid for child care should be reckoned as a business expense, which means it should be subtracted before the estimation of taxable income. Instead, and probably partly because child care is traditionally not paid for, we have an inadequate deduction, which constitutes another economic discrimination.

Finally, as we consider economic discrimination, the *subtle* importance of traditional child care may be much greater than we know (Rowe, forthcoming). To the extent that women and men maintain the *image* of women as dependent child carers (despite the fact that women in paid and unpaid employment might actually account for about 50% of a properly reckoned GNP), it is easier for us all unconsciously to discriminate against women in paid work (and men in unpaid work).

In addition, the woman whose total work experience has been in unpaid work may herself have a poor idea what she is "worth." As she considers paid work, she may have a tendency to think in terms of her "next best" (or "fall back") occupation, which is to be paid nothing in direct wages. Such women, and men too, may think of her work as "not worth very much," and by extension the work of all women may seem not to be worth very much.[5] When "all women" are imagined to be restricted to "nurturance," it is easier to think of women as all alike; one need not then worry about rewards for individual productivity.

As we consider our own homemaking and child care, which usually have no direct price, some may consider these activities to be "worth" very little, and others may consider them "priceless." Many people in fact argue eloquently that no financial figure can approach the value of human care; they would hate to see all caretaking paid for. I find this feeling easily understandable. However, I believe that, if most nurturance is not to be cash paid, it should generally be shared equally between men and women. One can, in other words, believe in the value of child care and all nurturant activities without accepting systematic economic and educational discrimination against women. In fact, it is the premise of this article that one can believe in children and child care, without all of the separateness, loneliness, financial insecurity, deprivation from nurturance, work and leisure dissatisfactions, and discrimination which are at present part of our inheritance from traditional sex roles.

What About Day Care? We have argued that traditional child care may not now be ideal for children and parents and families. Many people, faced with these feelings, advocate universal child care external to the home, available 24 hours per day and subsidized by the government on a sliding fee scale.

Excellent child care would certainly speak to the needs of many children, especially those now left alone, the malnourished, the rat-bitten, the abused. Provision of better care for all children would directly improve the lives of a fourth of our population for a fifth of their lives. It would rescue at least 10% of our children from conditions that we ought to consider intolerable.

With respect to parents, the availability of excellent care would certainly alleviate some of the loneliness and much of the financial insecurity we discussed above. It is an absolute necessity for the 10th of all parents who are single, especially if they work outside the home. However, day-care delivered on a traditional, woman-oriented basis, as it is now, might not do much to alleviate the sense of separateness between men and women, the deprivation from nurturance, the work dissatisfactions, and economic discrimination. In fact, on balance, our present day-care arrangements probably contribute as much to traditional stereotypes as they provide options. In particular, the employment of women in paid as well as unpaid child-care arrangements probably substantiates the occupational segregation which is the strongest source of economic discrimination.

Full-time day-care, on the average about 8.5 hours a day, 42.5 hours per week, probably also causes some feelings of deprivation for some parents. It seems probable that, if they had optimal choices, many parents would prefer to be able to take somewhat more care of their children than is the case with full-time day-care.

In summary of sections above, we have reviewed paid and unpaid U.S. child-care arrangements, which suggest a strong sex-role differentiation of the work and joy involved in having children. This author believes that this differentiation is one major factor in maintaining all other attributes of sex roles. More options with respect to child care and new socialization patterns for both sexes toward caring for children and others might make a major difference in the quality of life for adults and children. This leads us to a discussion of androgyny.

ANDROGYNY AND CHILD CARE

Androgyny means that how people spend their time should be influenced primarily by skills and interests, not by gender. It would mean that men and women would equally share financial responsibility and child-care and homemaking responsibilities. Equal sharing of responsibilities would not necessarily mean that men and women would exactly divide the laundry and the diapers and the bills. Rather, there would be a social and legal presumption that performance of these duties would be negotiated between spouses, on a continuous lifetime basis, with equal moral rights and responsibilities.

The theoretical basis of androgyny is the proposition that both men and women have both "masculine" and "feminine" potential with regard to character development (where "masculine" is taken in the traditional sense of "instrumental" and "feminine" in the traditional sense of "nurturant"). There is no presumption that individuals should (or could) all be alike, but that everyone has some nurturant and some instrumental potential.

In individual instances, of course, an androgynous society would support responsible childlessness and full-time homemakers that were female, as well as male. But the society as a whole would be set up to support male and female parents as wage-earners and to support male and female wage-earners as parents, in whatever responsible patterns that spouses might choose.

Let us take the example of a young couple with the modal one or two children. In a society which supported young parents to work in half-time or three-quarter-time paid jobs, the family would receive one or one and a half salaries. Suppose both parents worked 30 hours a week in paid jobs. Suppose further that they used child care 10 to 20 hours per week, including evening baby-sitting, and that otherwise they split child-care responsibilities. They would each get to know the children and the skills of homemaking and they would have a chance to spend some time alone together.

With respect to our list of concerns in the section above about the effects of child-care arrangements, androgynous spouses would have a much keener sense of each other's lives. The "learned helplessness" of each sex toward the other's role might generally disappear. Spouses who intimately shared responsibilities might feel much less taken for granted and much less lonely. One can imagine women being very supportive of a spouse's need to relax after the office and men no longer dropping laundry on the floor.

Family financial security would grow, along with family incomes, since lifetime earnings and one's ability to find and keep a job depend much more on continuous years in the labor force than on hours per week. Promotions might come one to three years later for a typical worker who took a three-quarter-time job while the children were small. However, if the typical worker shared family responsibilities with a spouse who also worked three-quarter-time in a paid job throughout the years of young parenthood, each could expect much higher lifetime earnings than if he or she dropped out for family responsibilities. Thus the expected later promotions permit much higher (and more secure) family earnings. We would expect that the quality of life for many people would rise, as they gained another arena for friends, status, productivity, and self-image. Both spouses would have one work area at home where there would be considerable autonomy over one's work. Women might gain more sleep; men might gain more options for self-expression and a respite from competition.

Spouses left alone, through death or divorce, would be likely to survive in both paid work and family life. Men who equally cared for their children would have, in practice, more rights with respect to custody and visitation. One can imagine that retirement from child raising and paid work would be much more comfortable under circumstances in which both spouses had a wider range of skills and interests. Mid-life crises might also be less severe, with a wider range of options offered by two sets of skills and two incomes in the family.

With respect to discrimination, one may imagine that many of the direct sources of wage and promotional inequality might disappear in an androgynous society. Both men and women would have equal access to education, training, and jobs. Many couples might choose to share family responsibilities so completely that neither spouse ever dropped out of school or a job for family reasons. Other couples might choose to have one or the other spouse as full-time homemaker for a period of time. Nationally, however, we might expect androgynous socialization and work patterns to produce a random distribution of men and women as full-time homemakers. By the same token, sex-based wage differences now attributable to mobility, years of experience, and hours per week in the paid labor force would also disappear as men and women began to spend their time in similar ways.

The physiological bases for work differentiation seem already much muted. Some jobs requiring great strength might remain forever disproportionately male. These, however, seem unlikely to produce national wage gaps between men and women. If there are hormonal differences of significant importance to work aggressiveness, these may persist. But we will not know to what extent, if at all, they are important until we have offered boys and girls equal options in cooperation and assertiveness. One may guess from cross-cultural studies that culture is enormously important and may "wash out" whatever minor hormonal differences exist.

Motivational differences between men and women (whatever they are) might be expected to have less and less effect on sex-based wage and promotion gaps. Men who cared directly for children and others would find gestation and nursing much less important than lifetime nurturance. Such men might conceivably be somewhat less driven to create (and to destroy). Women, on the other hand, knowing they would share financial responsibility, might work harder to be recruited, paid, and promoted appropriately.

What would happen to the concentration and perseverance required for extraordinary intellectual, scientific, artistic achievement? One may guess that some people will always choose to stay single and/or childless. Others will find supportive spouses or communes or other families. Many will simply postpone achievement for a year or several years. In any case, the achievements will come to both men and women.

What of total social productivity? Is it true that one must be young to innovate? Would the total number of innovations drop? There is some reason to believe that extraordinary scientific achievements now occur within several years of taking on new intellectual problems; these are not necessarily limited to young people (Tobias, 1975). (In earlier times, with short life expectancies and little accumulated knowledge and no information retrieval, genius may have been associated with youth.) In modern times, genius often requires extensive teamwork, many building-block experiments, and then a new look. It is not at all clear that having men and women in part-time work for several years would jeopardize creative breakthroughs over a lifetime; indeed, many very innovative people have waxed and waned in creativity several times throughout a lifetime.

What probably *is* very important, from the point of view of social productivity, is that intellectual, artistic, and social genius find options to flower. If we imagine, for example, that scientific, artistic, and caring potentials are randomly distributed among males and females, then we could nearly double the incidence of scientific, artistic, and human achievements by opening all occupations to both sexes. Moreover, while some kinds of achievements seem to require a lifelong, even celibate concentration, other kinds of work seem to require some relief from concentration. Thus children keep some people sane for the laboratory or factory, and the factory or laboratory keeps them sane for the children.

Finally, from the point of view of social productivity, we may discover that androgyny provides us with a more caring world.[6] Suppose that more women, socialized to nurturance and cooperation, get into influential jobs? And suppose that we also socialize our young males to expect to care for children and others? Might we see a reordering of values for governance and management?

This article makes no pretense to the notion that sex-role differentiation causes all evil and that androgyny will iron out all pain. If sexism begins to disappear, perhaps we will become caring enough to eliminate racism and other forms of human violence as well, but it seems likely that we will move only slowly at best. Some androgynous couples will divorce, and some men and women will be as miserable with more options as they were with fewer. There may also be children who would flourish more if they saw their parents less. But on balance one may believe that freeing all humans to share in child care on a part-time basis may bring more happiness to children and adults. Children will have a greater chance to be with someone who wants to be with them; both children and adults will be free to explore their caring and inventive selves.

SOCIAL POLICIES IN SUPPORT OF ANDROGYNY

Present-day androgynous couples often find it difficult to combine paid work and family life in an equitable manner. One would therefore recommend changes in social policies which would make it easier for parents to share the responsibilities and advantages of home and paid work.

The first and most basic legal and social change should clearly be the Equal Rights Amendment to the U.S. Constitution. No other single change would be more likely to permit protection of males as nurturant parents as well as protection of women in public life.

With respect to the organization of paid work in our society, many changes are needed. First there should be a reconsideration of what is meant by "full-time work." At a time of structural as well as cyclical unemployment, it seems reasonable to ask whether full-time work should be redefined as 30 to 35 hours per week. This alone would permit young parents more time to share child care as well as spreading the work of the nation among more different people.

Part-time work (part-day, part-week, or part-year work) needs systematic support for both sexes. Discrimination against part-time workers, in terms of promotion and benefits, should be forbidden. Benefits should be prorated, including pensions. In general, we should take those steps that support "bumpy" career ladders, so that parents may work longer and shorter work weeks, depending on the stage in their life cycles. Mandated seniority and promotional patterns—in union contracts and tenure ladders, for instance—should take account of periods of part-time work. At least 10% of government jobs should be set aside for part-time workers.

Employers have not traditionally been enthusiastic about the extra expense of extra sets of paper work involved in hiring proportionately more (part-time) workers. However, I believe we need extensive research to see whether productivity per hour may not be higher for part-time workers. It may be that in many jobs part-time workers (more than) repay the extra expense involved in having proportionately more people.

We need many more flexible-time jobs. Some employers can adopt the system whereby all employees may choose (sometimes for set periods of time) to come in between 7 a.m. and 10 a.m. and to leave between 3 p.m. and 6 p.m. Others may wish to designate only certain jobs for flexible times of a standard type or for individually designed times.

Some jobs can be designated for people who need flexible, short-term leaves of absence. For instance we need more "undertime" jobs, whereby employees can agree to accept 2%, 4%, or 6% less salary, on a prorated basis, in return for 5, 10, or 15 days leave of absence on a planned, approved, and voluntary basis.

One important structure to support part-time and flexible-hour jobs is a well-run posting system within organizations. A posting system means that all job openings are widely advertised for a certain period of time within a given organization. Supervisors describe the job opening, including a description of whether a job can be part-time, shared-appointment, flexible-hours, or under-time job. Such posting systems also serve the purpose of supporting career development and perhaps should be mandated by law or fostered by tax incentives.

In times of economic prosperity, employers have been reluctant to institute work structures supportive of family life. However, with high turnover, worker discontent, and budget crunches, many employers are considering shortened work weeks and flexible hiring plans as ways to raise productivity and cut costs. Under-time and part-year jobs in particular offer a chance to plan leaves of absence during work lulls; well-run posting systems help to alleviate the pain of retrenchment while helping to protect long-term employees.

Parental leave needs further change in most American firms. We should consider the parental insurance systems of Sweden, whereby parents have a right to paid leave up to seven months after a birth (they can divide the time between them). We should further consider the Swedish system of parental sick leave for children's illnesses. At a minimum, maternity leave should be treated as a temporary disability (with the possibility of extended disability). This minimum improvement should also include unpaid leave for either parent (after maternity leave ends), up to six months postpartum, and the right to use some days of personal sick leave for children's illnesses, for children under 12.

Further changes should include reform of child-labor and insurance laws so that children can work (paid or unpaid) in nonexploitative apprenticeships. Our present segregation of children under age 16 from many workplaces has the effect of keeping age groups unnecessarily apart. We also need changes in Social Security so that people over 65 can legally continue to work and earn, so that more grandparents are available to more children.

The definition of work itself needs change. If unpaid homemaking and child care by full-time homemakers were reckoned into the GNP and defined as "work," we might pave the way for redefinitions of Social Security, welfare, pensions, and other benefits. If Social Security were vested individually in all responsible (paid and unpaid) workers, it would be easier for both men and women to consider full-time homemaking, without all the present risks to displaced (abandoned, divorced, and widowed) homemakers. If child rearing were seen as socially constructive work, Aid to Families of Dependent Children would become payment for child care, with attendant benefits and pensions, akin to military service, military benefits, and military retirement. Moreover if full-time homemakers were seen as responsible workers, socially as worthwhile as military employees, we would have a stronger theoretical reason for a universal health plan for all Americans.

Changes in the tax laws could also help family programs. Further tax write-offs for employers for family support structures (like the child-care center write-offs) are badly needed. Work- and training-related child-care expenses should be business expenses for income tax purposes and should also be allowed where payments are made to (nonspouse) relatives. Work- and training-related child-care allowances should be automatic for families earning incomes below the poverty level, continuing on a reduced basis to a level up to 1.5 times the poverty level.

Finally, we plainly need changes in marriage and divorce laws. In further support of displaced homemakers of either sex, we should consider government support for (re)training parents who have been full-time at home for, say, 10 or more years. And all the myriad laws surrounding custody, alimony, visitation, and child support should be changed toward equity between men and women.

How could we support further attitudinal change toward androgyny? First, we need much more national information and debate. Many ardent feminists of both sexes understand women in engineering without understanding men in nursing and child care. Yet it is obvious that women will never be equal in formerly male occupations without a mirror image change occurring for men. If this were not to occur—if men were not to have equal opportunity in formerly female occupations—women would wind up doing three-fourths of the nation's work. This fact and its attendant implications for socialization patterns and educational curricula need the widest possible discussion.

Fortunately, we may presume that androgyny itself may foster androgyny. Early generations of children raised by both men and women, who see caring men and self-reliant women, have androgynous role models to emulate. Today's parents, knowing that a daughter has one chance in two of becoming a chief wage-earner for at least part of her life, are beginning to support daughters in androgynous patterns. This in turn has inevitable consequences for the lives of men. Perhaps if we succeed in social policies that support androgyny, we will reap the benefits in terms of increased options for men and women and children. If we lag in supporting androgyny, we may see yet more anguish, in terms of personal bewilderment and of children left more and more alone.

I believe that many men are tired of being asked why they want to take care of children, of themselves, and of others. Many women would *like* to be asked. Many women are tired of being asked why they want a paid career. Many men would *like* to be asked. Androgyny offers some new options for child care and child carers in the 1980s.

NOTES

1. Unless otherwise indicated, the data in this section are from the Unco National Day Care Consumer Survey (1975).

2. In recent years there have been a number of household time budget studies, which, however, have varied greatly in methods and population sample. At least one early study attempted to measure the division of labor between husband and wife without including child care, an omission which seems extraordinary in its illumination of postwar sex-role stereotyping.

3. The "biological differences" hypotheses for origins of sex roles have generally been based on several ideas:

(a) Women need to be protected somewhat in pregnancy and while nursing.

(b) Originally only women could feed infants.

(c) Men are on the average a little more aggressive and stronger.

(d) Men perceive themselves as unable to "create" and "nurture" in the same ways as women and feel themselves "isolated" from the cosmic chain of generations. They therefore must find some alternative ways of feeling that their lives have cosmic meaning and therefore have a stronger urge to build monuments and/or destroy and kill, in order to feel important.

(e) Because men have external genitalia which change shape in one kind of creative and masterful activity (intercourse), men have a particular need for their creations to be visible and recognizable and for their work processes to provide the possibility for promotion, advancement, status, and dominance.

4. Absenteeism and high turnover of women used to be considered possible reasons for systematically paying women less. Most labor economists now agree, however, that absenteeism and turnover figures are very much more strongly affected by occupation and rank than by sex.

5. I believe this to be a leading reason why the high cost of excellent, formal day-care comes as such a shock to some people.

6. One notes with interest that Matina Horner of Radcliffe is finding men significantly less "cooperative" than women in an ongoing research study. Traditional sex roles, especially with respect to child care, may have made many men less nurturant and cooperative than women.

REFERENCES

ARROW, K. (1972). "Models of job discrimination." Pp. 83-102 in A.H. Pascal (ed.), Racial discrimination in economic life. Lexington, Mass.: D.C. Heath.

BERGMANN, B. (1974). "Toward more useful modes of research on discrimination in employment and pay." Sloan Management Review, 15(3):43-45.

BETTELHEIM, B. (1970). The children of the dream. New York: Avon.

BOWLBY, J. (1971). Maternal care and mental health. Geneva: World Health Organization.

BRYSON, R.B., BRYSON, J., LICHT, M.H., and LICHT, B.G. (1976). "The professional pair." American Psychologist, 3(1):10-17.

FEIN, R. (1974). "Men's experiences before and after the birth of a first child: Dependence, marital sharing and anxiety." Unpublished Ph.D. dissertation, Harvard University (University Microfilms no. 75-7383).

GERSON, M. (1971). "Women in the kibbutz." American Journal of Orthopsychiatry, 41(4):566-573.

GREEN, M. (1976). Goodbye father. London: Routledge and Kegan Paul.

Harris, L., and Associates (1971). The Harris survey yearbook of public opinion, 1970. New York: Author.

HOFFMAN, L., and NYE, F.I. (1974). Working mothers. San Francisco: Jossey-Bass.

HOLMSTROM, L.L. (1972). The two-career family. Cambridge, Mass.: Schenkman.

HOWELL, M. (1973a). "Effects of maternal employment on the child." Pediatrics, 52(3):327-343.

――― (1973b). "Employed mothers and their families." Pediatrics, 52(2):252-263.

――― (1976). Helping ourselves, families and the human network. Boston: Beacon.

KAHNE, H. (1975). "Economic perspectives on the roles of women in the American economy." Journal of Economic Literature, 13(4):1249-1292.

KAMERMAN, S.B. (1975). Child-care programs in nine countries. New York: Columbia University School of Social Work.

KOTELCHUCK, M. (1972). The nature of the child's tie to his father. Unpublished Ph.D. dissertation, Harvard University.

McCall's (1975). "Parents who wouldn't do it again." November, p. 37.

MORGAN, G. (1975). Personal communication. Cambridge, Mass.

PAUL VI, Pope (1976). Speech in Rome, January 31.

PHELPS, E.S. (1972). "The statistical theory of racism and sexism." American Economic Review, 62(4):659-661.

RADLOFF, L. (1975). "Sex differences in depression: The effects of occupation and marital status." Sex Roles, 1(3):249-266.

ROBY, P.A. (1975). "Shared parenting: Perspectives from other nations." School Review, May, pp. 415-431.

ROWE, M.P. (1974a). "Prospects and patterns for men and women at work." Pp. 91-118 in Child Care Reprints IV. Washington D.C.: Day Care and Child Development Council of America.

――― (1974b). "Should mothers mother, or should mothers work?" Pp. 30-52 in Child Care Reprints IV. Washington, D.C.: Day Care and Child Development Council of America.

――― (1975). Personal observations, Moscow.

――― (forthcoming). "The Saturn's rings phenomenon: Micro-inequities and unequal opportunity for women in the American Economy."

SIDEL, R. (1972). Women and child care in China. Baltimore: Penguin.

SZALAI, A. (ed., 1973). The use of time: Daily activities of urban and suburban populations in twelve countries. The Hague: Mouton.

TALBOT, N. (ed., 1976). Raising children in modern America. Boston: Little, Brown.

TOBIAS, S. (1975). Personal communication, Wesleyan University.

Unco (1976). Presentation of Initial Results from the National Day Care Consumer Survey (HEW Paper no. 105-74-1107, for the Office of Child Development). Arlington, Va.: Author.

U.S. Department of Labor, Bureau of Labor Statistics (1974). Children of working mothers. Washington, D.C.: Author.

WALKER, K. (1970). "Time spent by husbands in household work." Family Economics Review, June, pp. 8-11.

WHITE, S., et al. (1973). Federal programs for young children: Review and recommendations. Washington, D.C.: U.S. Department of Health, Education, and Welfare.

8

PUBLIC POLICY AND THE FAMILY
A New Strategy for Women as Wives and Mothers

SHEILA B. KAMERMAN

When one talks about United States public policy and the family, many people assume that there is an explicit, national policy on the family, that there is consensus on how the family is to be defined, that there is adequate knowledge and agreement about what is good for the family, and that there is ability to assess consequences of policies for the family as a whole as distinct from individual family members. In fact, there is neither coherence, consistency, clarity —nor even consciousness—in the ways that public policy takes account of the family or that government actions affect the family. Yet no one doubts that there are consequences of government actions for families. The question is, therefore, *How can we think about the effects of public policies on the American family? And, more specifically, how can we analyze the consequences of such policies for women as family members, as wives, and as mothers?*

There is no explicit or single public policy regarding or affecting the family in this country. Instead, there are multiple and inconsistent policies. For example, some policies provide incentives for marriage, and others provide disincentives; some policies implicitly encourage family breakup, and others discourage it. Moreover, it is clear that the term "family" covers a wide variety of structures and forms, ranging from the traditional two parent/one son/one daughter family of the television commercials and magazine ads, to the increasingly prevalent one parent/one child (or more) family. The Census Bureau defines a family as any two related people living together. Public policy toward families may focus on or show preference for one or another family member or family structure in a variety of different or even conflicting ways. Thus, it sometimes favors old people rather than children (social security benefit levels in contrast to the benefit levels of Aid to Families of Dependent Children), or it stresses concern with children's rather than parents' rights (protective services for children[1]), or it addresses household units regardless of whether or not the members are related (supplemental security income benefits), or it rewards married couples with children (income tax policy).

From another perspective, public policy may favor men over women (income tax laws permitting deduction of a wide range of business-related expenses but not the costs of child care to an employed mother), or it may confirm women's dependent status (the absence of social security coverage for the full-time housewife-mother), or it may penalize women for fulfilling their traditional role (the unavailability of unemployment insurance benefits for women who leave employment because of child birth and maternity), or it may penalize men (only now is there beginning acceptance of the husband's entitlement to benefits as a dependent under social security).

HOW TO THINK ABOUT THE AFFECTS OF PUBLIC POLICY ON THE FAMILY: THE CONCEPT OF FAMILY POLICY

Recent efforts at systematic analysis of public policy as it affects the family have suggested the concept of "family policy" as a useful framework for organizing thinking (Kamerman and Kahn, 1976b). Clearly, public policy toward the family can be directed at a variety of objectives. Goals could range from the reenforcement of traditional family structures and family roles, in which the dependent status of women would be even more strongly confirmed, to the goal of equality of the sexes, neutrality toward family forms, and support of all basic primary relationships. The concept of family policy permits analysis of policies affecting families in such a way as to highlight inequities and differential consequences wherever they occur. This chapter will illustrate how the concept could be employed to facilitate thinking about the status of women as family members. The essay will conclude with some discussion of the relationship between family policy and women policy.

The basic definition of family policy is everything that government does to or for the family. Preliminary thinking suggests three distinctions within family policy:

—Explicit family policy: (a) specific programs and policies designed to achieve specified explicit goals regarding the family; (b) programs and policies which do things to and for the family, but for which there are no agreed upon, overall goals regarding the family.

—Implicit family policy: governmental actions and policies not specifically or primarily addressed to the family, but which have indirect consequences.

More specifically, some actions involve things done deliberately, such as day-care, child welfare and family counseling, income maintenance, family planning, some tax benefits, and some housing policies. The family is clearly the object of such governmental policies. These may be thought of as *explicit family policy.* Other actions may be addressed to quite different targets, but they also affect families, often as an accidental by-product. For example, industrial location decisions, road building, trade and tariff regulations, immigration policy. These are elements of *implicit family policy.*

The purposes of family policy may be *manifest* (to provide for optimum child development) or *latent* (to encourage women to enter the labor force). Consequences may be *intended* or *unintended, direct* or *indirect, consistent* or *inconsistent.* Family policy includes both the affects on the family of all types of activities and the efforts to use "family well-being" as an objective or goal or standard in developing public policy. *Family* policy, then, is both a field of activity and a perspective.

In addition to these distinctions, it is essential in family policy analysis to differentiate the interests of the family as a unit from those of particular roles and statuses within the family. It is quite possible, for example, that programs will have a differential impact within the family, affecting some members more than others, even perhaps advancing the interests of some and impeding those of others. Policy on behalf of the family unit may not necessarily always be constructive for every member and vice versa. Family policy must learn to cope with these tensions.

I have already mentioned the possibility of conflict between parents and children when children are inadequately cared for. Some of the debate about social security raises similar questions regarding the potential for tension between adult workers and the retired aged, when one considers social security benefits and contributions. To continue, expanding job opportunities may offer greater options for women and raise the standard of living for the family unit. Yet, as a consequence, tensions may arise in families in which men still define the male role as that of family breadwinner. Efforts at enhancing certain basic family functions must be evaluated in the context of the consequences for all family members. Thus, an important question to raise is whether the traditional female roles will be assumed to continue or, on the contrary, equitable role sharing will be the assumption.

BACKGROUND AND ALTERNATIVE APPROACHES

Family policy is hardly a new concept. It was employed, first, in Europe in the context of income redistribution policies favoring large families (e.g., family allowances or demogrants, income tax policies) and, second, in the context of population policy and concerns about long term demographic projections.[2] A third use has been to describe public policies providing supportive and substitute care for dependent and/or inadequate family members (e.g., orphans, the handicapped, the aged, the poor, and the homeless). An extension of this is the broader use of the concept in recent years to cover the concern of industrialized societies with preventing dependency and other social problems generally and with providing supportive and helping services to average, ordinary families faced with the growing complexities and stresses of daily living (Kahn and Kamerman, 1975).

More recently, the concept of family policy has been employed in two other contexts. Some experts in the field of child development, recognizing that helping the family may be the most effective way to improve the conditions of children's lives, have begun to use the concept as a way to think about public policies affecting children.[3] Finally, in some countries and among some people, the whole field of social policy for women has come to be defined as a major component of family policy.[4] This field encompasses, among others, such issues as social insurance benefits for working mothers and housewives, child-care programs, and social welfare benefits for child care; a wide range of supportive services for working mothers; changes in income tax and social security treatment of women generally; part-time and flex-time employment. Clearly, these matters are central to family policy. (Whether there needs to be a distinction between "women" policy and "family" policy will be discussed subsequently.)

Traditionally, then, family policy as a *field* has parameters which include population policy and family planning, cash and "in kind" transfer payments and, in more recent years, employment, housing, nutrition, health policies. Personal social services,[5] child care, child development, and the whole field of social policy for women have all been defined by some analysts, at least, as part of the family policy field.

If one employs family well-being as a criterion of social policy, thus using family policy as a *perspective* as well as a field, the relevant policy areas are even more extensive. Tax policy, military policy, transportation, land use, environmental policy—all have consequences for the family, major consequences. In fact, employing the family as a criterion could affect every policy arena. Family policy has rarely been conceptualized this way, but Uri Bronfenbrenner in the United States and the Swedish leadership in the equality movement have, by implication, argued the desirability of doing so (Bronfenbrenner, 1974; Sandberg, 1975; Myrdal, 1971). They would relocate industry, change working hours, and do much more, on the assumption that social relations and the quality of family life should dominate labor market considerations. The general, but not unanimous, response elsewhere has been skepticism about the family as a perspective, as a criterion for policies in many other fields of family life. Few debate the extent to which the family is victim or object, however, of tax policy, road building, land use, and even policies for recruiting and maintaining the armed forces—to limit the list. The skeptics wonder whether society is willing to have family interests predominate. Or they note that, when family policy merges with all of "people policy," it is all social policy and no longer a useful subcategory.

If family policy, in a more constricted sense, is a field and a perspective, it is also an *instrument*. Government sometimes has used the family as a vehicle for achieving objectives vital to other institutions or policies. There is no doubt that over the long run most countries have seen the family as a significant vehicle for achieving broader political or social goals ranging from political indoctrination to labor market behavior. The most important, long-standing, and familiar illustration is in the field of labor market policy. (See, for example, Webb and Webb, 1927; Piven and Cloward, 1971.) Women have been recruited into the labor force in Eastern Europe, Cuba, and China through the establishment of child-care facilities, maternity allowances, child-care leaves. But the more subtle and indigenous incentives and disincentives are not as readily acknowledged, and the debate continues as to whether the desire of women to work or the decision to make work feasible and attractive come first in a given country at a given time.

Of particular interest in this category are recent discussions about supporting the family in its social service role—to work in conjunction with (or as an alternate to further costly expansion of) formally organized social services that may be less satisfactory.[6] After all, in a sense, the family has always absorbed and cared for the aged, the handicapped, and the deviant and has been the major child welfare institution. It still is. Yet the changing role of women raises questions as to how and where responsibility for this function will fall. Future projections for the social services depend on some assumptions about the validity, effectiveness, and costs of policies directed toward these family functions. Trends in community care of the aged and child care alone identify these as major questions.

While there is certainly no conscious or coherent family policy in the United States, issues arise daily and actions are proposed or taken by the government which have obvious—if often unarticulated and unexplored—consequences for family life. Employing the concept of family policy makes it possible to identify those actions and to facilitate thinking about them and their implications for the family and for family members. In effect, use of the concept can highlight family-related issues, make consequences for families more visible, expose inconsistencies and contradictions in the context of the family, and clarify policy options and policy debate.

EMPLOYING A FAMILY POLICY PERSPECTIVE ON WOMEN: HIGHLIGHTING INEQUITIES AND INADEQUACIES

How, then, can the concept of family policy facilitate analysis of policy consequences for women as wives and mothers?[7] Will a "family" focus necessarily confirm traditional perspectives on women's roles and reinforce the dependent status of married women? Or, in contrast, can it provide a broader perspective in which to view the inequities, inadequacies, and inconsistencies of public policy affecting women?

Among the policy domains central to women as wives and mothers are income maintenance (including social security), income tax, family law, employment, health insurance and services, personal social services (including family support services generally), and child care. A detailed analysis of each of these fields, employing family policy as an analytic framework, would require a volume by itself. Instead, what follows will illustrate selectively and briefly how the use of a family policy perspective offers the possibility of a deeper and more fruitful formulation of issues that are important to women.

INCOME MAINTENANCE

Social Security. Analysts agree that women are treated inequitably under our current social security program. (See also Chapter 3 in this volume.) Many working women receive no retirement benefit from social security beyond what they would have received anyway as the wife of an insured working man. Social security, in fact, is predicated on the one-earner, male-breadwinner family, a family form that is no longer dominant. Social security taxes are paid in on an individual basis, but benefits are allotted on a family basis. As a consequence, two-earner families are penalized. In 1973, the average couple paid about $200 more in social security taxes than a couple with the same income but only one earner. Thus, even though most wives are working—or will work for most of their adult lives—only if the wife's entitlement is more than one-half her husband's will she receive a benefit larger than she would receive as a wife who had never worked.

Marital instability has increased sharply in recent years, yet a divorced woman who has been married fewer than 20 years cannot draw on her former husband's record and may lose coverage entirely unless she remarries or establishes her own credits as a worker. In contrast, a widow receiving full widow's benefits would lose half her benefit if she remarried even though her husband might have full entitlement himself. As a result there is a growing phenomenon of elderly couples living together out of wedlock, rather than marrying and forfeiting a portion of their badly needed income.

The "housewife" role—child rearing, household management,

housework—is viewed as indispensable to the functioning of the family and society and presumed by many to be women's responsibility regardless of whether such a presumption is appropriate or not. If one applies a family policy perspective it becomes clear that defining these basic functions as "nonproductive" or "noneconomic" work when done by a wife and mother but productive work when done by a stranger can only demean and diminish this core family role. Moreover, a mother's incapacity because of illness or accident may impose severe financial and social hardships on the entire family. A critical inequity in current public policy is leaving this key family role uncovered by sickness benefits, disability benefits, and social security old-age and retirement entitlement.[8]

Public Assistance. A family policy perspective would underscore the fact that one consequence of a public policy whereby the government provides a cash benefit to low-income women living alone with dependent children, but provides no such benefit to low-income intact families, may be to undermine the family and support family disorganization. In fact, current research indicates how public policy provides a disincentive for marriage and remarriage and encourages a trend toward one-parent, female-headed families (Ross and Sawhill, 1975; Bernstein and Meezan, 1975). Certainly, concern with enhancing the family would indicate the need for providing income support for low-income families regardless or whether they are intact or broken. Cognizance must be taken of the disincentives for women to remarry inherent in public policy and the need to develop a more neutral policy stance if there is real concern for the family.

CHILD CARE AND CHILD REARING

Child development experts worry about the absence from home of the mother when infants are very young. Women—and researchers generally—may note that the evidence for concern is mixed. The quality of parental care may be far more important than the quantity of care. There is some evidence that indicates that women who work (in paid employment outside the home) spend more time with their children than women who do not work. Moreover, as intrafamily roles change, we have yet to learn about the effects of increased participation of fathers in child rearing. (See Chapter 7 in this volume for a discussion of androgynous child care.) Regardless, the real issue is that, if there is such concern, why does public policy not support maternal care as a viable option?

Clearly, as expectations regarding standards of living rise and as decent living conditions come to require two incomes, more and more mothers of young children work because of economic pressures. At present almost one-third of the mothers of children under age 3 are gainfully employed. If there is real concern about young children, a family policy focus would suggest design and implementation of policies that would permit a parent the *option* of staying home and caring for very young children, if he or she wished to, without economic hardship. As yet, no public policy in this country takes account of this. In fact, on the contrary, not only is there a policy "gap" here, but there is also inconsistency and inequity. Those women who do leave the labor force—who stop working and stay home to care for their children in the early years—are penalized doubly. They not only lose the income from their jobs but also lose out on social security basic retirement benefits, when they are computed subsequently.[9]

Different policy options are available: a paid maternity or parental benefit, a child-care benefit, and alternative work patterns are among them.[10] These should be explored for women (and men), for children, for families as a whole, for employment and industry —rather than offering one model only.

Second, if there is real concern that children should have a parent at home to care for them, why should mothers receiving Aid to Families of Dependent Children be coerced to go out and work? Congress has been pressuring such mothers to work and place their children in day-care although such care costs almost as much for one child as an unskilled worker can earn, and even more for two children. Such a policy is inequitable, inconsistent, and, at present, even uneconomic! Surely poor mothers should have the right to stay home and care for young children if nonpoor mothers have such options? If the concern is really for optimum care of children, what might be more helpful, instead, would be to debate alternative policy instruments to achieve this, including their costs and consequences (e.g., demogrants for all children, income supplements for intact as well as broken poor and working class families, higher minimum wages, child-care allowances).

Expansion of child-care programs is high on the list of unmet needs relating to the status and independence of women. Yet legislation providing extensive child-care programs was vetoed in 1971 because it would commit the federal government to supporting "communal approaches to child rearing over against the family centered approach."[11] When one-third of all children under age 6 have mothers who work (50% of the women with children that age) and when most work full time, organized child care clearly does not undermine the family but rather supports the family in fulfilling its role, given existing realities. Moreover, inadequacies in the quantity and quality of existing programs not only affect women but also penalize those children who may be inadequately cared for as a result—and have negative consequences for society generally, because of the loss of productive female employment and the potential problems of poorly cared-for children.[12]

It is a very shortsighted policy that would deny care to children whose mothers are in the labor force, on the obviously foolish and clearly false premise that this would harm families. Furthermore, all evidence indicates that when available, all mothers—not just working mothers—want and will use child-care programs for children aged 3 and older. In short, such programs are increasingly being viewed as important for all children, everywhere.

Public expenditures for delinquency programs and children's institutions are enormous. Public concern is extensive. Women rarely define this issue as part of the women policy arena, yet a family policy perspective would suggest perhaps that we should. For example, it is well known that, before and after school hours and during school vacations, delinquent behavior is more likely to occur. More than one-half of all mothers of school-aged children work, and most work full time. Yet there are no systematic data about what the school-aged children of working mothers do before and after school and on vacations—and certainly no extensive program coverage for such children.[13]

There is a miscellany of other issues related to child care that emerge from a family policy perspective. Among these are such questions as: Does it make sense for government to pay strangers but not relatives to provide foster care for children? Or to pay more to unrelated foster parents than what public assistance provides for a mother to care for her own child? Or to permit tax deductions for child-care expenses only when paid to a stranger although sometimes a loving grandparent could provide the best quality care, at a lower cost? Or to permit tax deductions for work-related travel and entertainment expenses but not (except to a very limited degree) permit child-care expenses—which may be even more essential if mothers are to be able to work—to be deducted as a business-related expense?

PERSONAL SOCIAL SERVICES

Abuses occur in nursing homes, and costs are horrendous. Women generally live longer than men and are more likely to be poor and alone and resident in a nursing home at some point in their lives. Women, appropriately, struggle to redress the inequities that leave them financially impoverished when they are old. Yet a family perspective would suggest additional policy options. For example, if the government pays for institutionalizing an elderly parent, why should it not also provide funds (or tax credits) for long-term care in the person's own home or in the home of adult children who want to keep the aged person with them though they work during the day? Such care may be less expensive.[14]

Everywhere there are new preventive programs and pilot projects addressed to the "rehabilitation" of one-parent, female-headed households. Yet there is evidence that would indicate that such a family form is not necessarily symptomatic of social pathology but occurs as a consequence of changing norms and expectations regarding marriage and realistic assessment of changing opportunities. Moreover, it seems increasingly apparent that many such families are transitional in nature and may be reformed as two-parent families after a few years.[15] A family perspective would suggest that instead of public policy defining this family form as deviant and "disorganized," requiring intervention to stop the process and a therapeutic posture toward mothers and children, investment should turn toward exploration of new ways to support these families so that they become viable and sound child-rearing environments (with meal and baby-sitting arrangements, after-school homework centers, access to male role models, etc.).

INCOME TAX POLICY

Finally, income tax policy is illustrative of another field in which a family perspective provides insights on how public policy has negative consequences for families and tends to penalize working wives and mothers.[16] For example, married couples with a single earner receive more favorable treatment than unmarried individuals, who in turn are better off than married couples with two incomes. Additional inequities in the treatment of two-earner families mean for example, that a man with a $20,000 income and a nonworking wife pays no more taxes than a husband and wife who each earn $10,000 in spite of the fact that the latter may have less leisure or may have to purchase many of the services provided by a full-time wife.

Clearly, the issues discussed above are of great concern to women. Merely a sample has been touched upon, but they serve to illustrate the position taken in this article. Employing family policy as an analytic framework can help identify dilemmas, gaps, and outright contradictions that might not be addressed otherwise.

PUBLIC POLICY AND THE WORKING MOTHER: A FAMILY POLICY STRATEGY AND PROGRAM

The previous section provided illustrations of how a family policy perspective—looking at government policies in which the family is the object of the policy or in which family well-being is the primary outcome criterion—can raise questions and identify issues of major import to women as wives and mothers. This section focuses on a major policy gap or policy inadequacy regarding women as mothers and suggests how a family policy strategy and program could be developed to address this.

DEFINING THE ISSUE

Working women in the United States, as in all other industrialized countries, face the problem of reconciling home and family roles with labor force participation. When family responsibilities, particularly motherhood, are added, the two roles become even more burdensome. This situation is faced by growing numbers of women. In effect, the burden is doubled. The potentially grave consequences of such overload for the women themselves, for job performance, and for family life generally require public policy intervention. The object of such intervention is the development of a social infrastructure supporting these dual responsibilities. The infrastructure would, in fact, make shared home and parenting responsibilities more possible. Such a support system would be needed even when occupational roles and familial and home responsibilities are more equitably shared by men and women. Among the suggested components of a family support system are the following:

- Expanded high-quality child-care services and programs (for infants, preschool and school-aged children).
- Social welfare benefits related to child care (and/or care of other needy family members, either aged or handicapped).
- Improved technology for household tasks, including arrangements for some of these tasks to be completed outside the family.
- Expanded provision of services facilitating housework and household management (e.g., restaurants, workshops, recreational facilities).

THE IMPORTANCE OF THE ISSUE FOR PUBLIC POLICY

Child rearing and housework are generally agreed to be indispensable to the functioning of the family and society and are presumed by virtually every society to be the women's responsibility. As women move increasingly out of the home and into the labor force, these responsibilities are not relinquished. Indeed, they continue to be defined as presumptive minima for adequate fulfillment of the female role. On occasion, as elderly parents live longer, they incur additional home responsibilities, but these, too, are borne primarily by women. The result is that most working women hold two jobs, one as paid worker and the other as unpaid housewife.

While it is true that in recent years men have begun to participate in home and family tasks more than previously, all available research evidence indicates that the employed wife and mother in the United States spends at least three times as much time on home and family tasks as does her husband. In fact, in addition to the time spent on the job, married women workers with children usually devote six to eight hours a day to household tasks.

Such a schedule creates concern about the long-term effects on the quality of family life and child development. Moreover, this double burden has immediate impact on women's earnings, occupational status, and career development and indeed on her inclination to seek paid employment in the first place. Obviously, most working women have neither the time nor the energy to invest themselves in their jobs the way men can; they cannot work overtime for pay or job advancement. They may lose pay or opportunity for advancement because of time lost when a child is ill or because of late arrival or early leaving when there is a household emergency. They often cannot take advantage of special courses or training programs available outside regular working hours.

Yet despite these obstacles, the number of women workers has more than doubled since the period immediately preceding World War II, and the number of working mothers has increased eightfold. In March 1974, 55% of the mothers of children aged 6-17 were in the labor force as were 39% of those with children under age 6 and 34% of those with children under age 3.[17] Nor is the phenomenon confined to the mother of the poor or broken family. More than half of all wives living in households with their husbands and with children between ages 6 and 17, 37% of those with children under age 6, and 33% of those with children under age 3 worked in March 1974. Two-thirds of these mothers worked full time.

There are more and more one-parent, female-headed families than ever before, and such mothers have still higher labor force participation rates: 67% of the mothers of children aged 6-17, 55% of the mothers of children under age 6, and 50% of the mothers of children under age 3 worked during the March 1974 survey. And over 80% of these mothers worked full time.

It is quite characteristic in the United States to develop social services around problem categories and age groups. However, working women—in particular, working mothers—have never been identified as a special category to be served except in the limited instance of day-care for low-income or welfare mothers (as a public policy incentive developed by those who want to get these women into the labor force) and some tax benefits related to child-care expenses for middle-income working mothers. Public policy has simply not addressed the special problems and needs of working mothers. In fact, the reverse may be true: some schools refuse to participate in school lunch programs, unrealistically insisting that children should have lunch at home. For school-aged children, systematic provision for before and after school hours or for school vacations does not exist. Some 50% of the children aged 3-6 are in some form of preschool program, but most are half-day, a substantial portion are under private auspices, and many charge high fees. There is great scarcity of provision for children under age 3, and much of what exists is informal, unregulated, and of unknown quality. Neither paid maternity benefits nor special leaves are mandated by law.

Although some women work because they want to, the vast majority apparently work because they have to—because of economic need. The trend is clear. Yet public policy in the United States thus far has not responded to the implications of this development. A frequently held position assumes that the problems faced by working mothers affect only a small group and should be coped with on an individual basis. The reality is very different, given the prevalence of these problems and the large numbers of women so affected. These are urgent and immediate questions of broad social policy cutting across several fields (social security, income tax policy, social services, education, housing), governmental and nongovernmental agencies, the public sector and the private market.

A POLICY AGENDA

The development of supportive systems for working mothers—or a general family support system—involves change, reform, and innovation in policy and in program development. More specifically, a social infrastructure supporting family and employment responsibilities of married women with children would involve such things as the following:

—Social security benefits (e.g., special maternity benefits and child-care benefits, as well as reforms to eliminate current inequities).

—Employee wage contracts and the components of fringe benefit packages, to include family support measures (e.g., vacation facilities, housing programs, flextime, paid sick leave for a parent to care for an ill child).

—Federal legislation setting a shorter work day for parents of young children.

—Federal, state, and local legislation and program development for preschools and child health.

—Implementation of programs to create universal general social services (such as Title XX, Social Security Act) which emphasize measures in support of normal family development.

—Housing development design and construction.

—Local school board planning (regarding the use of school facilities for other than school activities).

—Community agencies and youth programs.

THE RELATIONSHIP OF FAMILY POLICY TO WOMEN POLICY: CAVEATS AND RISKS IN THE USE OF FAMILY POLICY

Family policy as a field—be it population policy, income mainte-nance, personal social services, women policy—is a somewhat familiar concept, known to and accepted by many people. Family policy as an instrument—be it labor market policy or child development policy—may be more controversial, but its usage is becoming more familiar over time. Family policy as a perspective—as a criterion of choice along with social justice and equality—is a much newer component of family policy and employed far less frequently. Many people continue to be skeptical of such usage, seeing it primarily as rationale for other motives.

Yet there are stirrings. Concern with policy outcomes is growing. People are beginning to search for ways to make policy choice more conscious and deliberate and to make consequences more explicit. There is some acceptance of the idea that family forms are changing and that a variety of types of families (one-parent, two-parent, married, and contractual, with and without children) may warrant concern and buttressing. There is discussion of the desirability of developing a family impact review process and a family impact statement to assess potential affects on families of proposed legislation or regulations.[18]

However, there are dangers and risks, and these are not to be minimized. Family policy could be applied in conservative or regressive ways. "Family" could be defined in narrow, traditional terms to mean a married couple with at least one child, ignoring the growing numbers of one-parent families or other emerging family forms. What is "good" or "bad" for the family might be perceived in rigid, moralistic fashion, ignoring the lack of consensus—and the large gaps in knowledge—regarding many areas of family functioning and child and human development.[19] Family roles could be seen in traditional perspectives only, and policy consequences could be assessed in the context of reinforcing such roles (e.g., the woman as homemaker, housewife, mother; the man as breadwinner, protector).

Differential consequences of policies for family members may be denied—or ignored—because of the complexities surrounding such an assessment.[20] Alternative approaches will be necessary. Among the possibilities are: developing a single measure for assessing conse-quences of policies on the family as a totality or organic whole;

assessing consequences for individual family members and weighting these differently, based on some exercise of judgment; assessing the consequences for individuals, making them explicit and assuming that the choice of the primary member (or of weighting) will be done on an individual policy decision basis in the context of public debate and value preferences. Clearly, recognition of—and assessment of—differential consequences of policies for family members is essential even though discussion may reveal tensions and conflicts that some would prefer to deny. Inevitably, there will be differences, sometimes between parents and children, sometimes between husbands and wives. Choices will have to be made, but such choices require making consequences explicit and visible.

There are those who would urge support of "women policy" or "social policy for women" to avoid such risks. A contrary position is taken here. Indeed, it is here held that, if those women who are concerned with public policy consequences for themselves as wives and mothers employ the concept of women policy as a yardstick for social policy rather than the broader perspective of family policy, they will lose the opportunity for fundamental policy innovation as well as the opportunity to mobilize a large constituency in support of their desired goals.

The women's movements in several European countries are increasingly taking the family policy position. Initiated by the Swedish leadership, this position has grown in Scandinavia generally and is now being discussed by women in other countries, representing different classes, ideologies, organizations, and women's groups. The argument is that, just as concern for family well-being requires addressing issues of inadequacies and inequities in public policy affecting women, concern for women's equality requires that some attention be paid to the structure of society generally and to that of the family in particular. Major reforms are needed, and changes must be implemented in the ways that work is structured for all people, in the workplace and in the physical and social environment in which we live. Moreover, there is growing recognition that, although a family focus may precipitate and stimulate tensions related to differential effects, a family focus can provide new insights into the larger consequence of inequitable burdens and treatment and offer a new basis for informed choice about alternative policies.

There is no question that a women policy perspective is not only appropriate but essential in certain domains—in particular in those areas where the concern is with women regardless of family status. A women policy perspective is the only effective stance when addressing the condition of women outside family roles—in particular, in employment, in trade unions, and in education. In contrast, however, where the concern is with women as wives and mothers, a narrowly conceived women policy could suggest that, where women are concerned, the potential results of a family perspective must be to penalize women who are family members. In fact, it is up to women to insist that the contrary be true—that a family policy in which the criterion is family well-being may, in fact, be the only perspective that will enhance all family roles and encourage the participation of men in family responsibilities. If it fails to do so, it cannot be adequate as a "family policy."

Current public policies in the United States that affect the family and family members are fragmented, inconsistent, and contradictory. Some are benign, some are adverse, and some are mixed in the results that they have for the family. As indicated earlier in this chapter and elsewhere in this volume, there are clearly many policies that reinforce women's dependency on her husband, or that limit women's choice and options regarding major roles, or that treat women inequitably or inadequately. Employing the concept of family policy can serve to underscore these issues in the context of the family, an institution central to society and to family members, be they women as wives and mothers, men as husbands and fathers, children as sons and daughters, sisters and brothers.

The validity of this argument for conceptualizing women policy in the context of family policy obviously holds only if family policy is broadly and dynamically defined. What is needed is a flexible perspective on social change as well as on family structure. The true objective of family policy, in this sense, is to maximize both male and female participation in both public and private life, not to play off the one against the other.

NOTES

1. An even stronger illustration of this point can be found in Goldstein et al. (1973). The position taken in this monograph is that in matters of custody or placement the child's needs should be paramount and take precedence over all else.

2. There is an extensive and valuable tradition of research and writing in these fields. See, for example, Beveridge, 1942; Finer, 1974; Friis, 1969; Hunt, 1973; Laroque, 1958; Myrdal, 1968; Wynn, 1970.

3. Some of the testimony reported in U.S. Senate Subcommittee on Children and Youth—dealing with *American Families: Trends and Issues* (U.S. Congress, 1974)—reflects this approach. See, in particular, the testimony of Uri Bronfenbrenner and Edward Zigler.

4. This has been discussed most eloquently by some of the leadership in the Swedish movement for women's equality.

5. "Personal social services" is an increasingly popular term, which describes those individual and family services concerned with direct help, social care, counseling, and access: it includes family welfare, child welfare, etc.

6. The subject has been explored with reference to the frail elderly and the mentally retarded in England by Robert Moroney (forthcoming).

7. The *politics* of a family policy perspective requires extensive analysis and is only touched upon in this article.

8. In contrast, in Sweden housewives receive sickness benefits and entitlements to old-age pensions under social insurance (social security). This benefit is described in greater detail in Kahn and Kamerman, *Not for the Poor Alone* (1975).

9. The so-called primary insurance amounts are related to monthly earnings averaged over one's working life and include those years when an individual may have been out of the labor force. This clearly penalizes those women who move in and out of the labor force because of childbirth and child care in the early years.

In contrast, there are some countries that assign a double credit for each year that a woman is out of the labor force caring for children, when calculating entitlements to an old-age pension.

10. Several European countries support this concern for early child rearing years by providing a paid maternity benefit for 6 months to a year at a proportion of the mother's salary. Some countries also have a child caring allowance for mothers who stay home after their maternity leave ends, and care for a child up to age 2 or 3.

11. This comment occurred in President Richard M. Nixon's veto message concerning the Child Development Bill, December 10, 1971.

12. In contrast to the United States, France, a country with an explicit family policy, emphasizes the value of child-care programs to maximize child development and support of the family. Even with fewer women in the labor force and greater stress on supporting a family-centered approach to child rearing, close to 90% of the children aged 3-6 are in preschool programs. For a picture of how other countries view child-care programs see Kamerman, 1975. For a discussion of child care in the United States (issues, policies, and programs), see Kamerman and Kahn, 1976a.

13. The problem of the "latch key" child is international, with little attention paid to provision anywhere.

14. Sweden, the Netherlands, and the United Kingdom have extensive provision of home helps to care for the elderly in their own home at very low or no cost. Moreover, in Sweden relatives may receive a cash benefit for providing such care to aged or handicapped family members. For a discussion of this benefit see Kahn and Kamerman (1975).

15. There is evidence also that public policy plays a role in discouraging such reformation, in some instances. See the earlier discussion.

16. See Harvey E. Brazer's statement as reported in U.S. Congress, 1974.

17. In fact, 61% of the mothers of children aged 6-17, 50% of those with children under 6, and 46% of those with children under 3 worked at some time during 1974—even though they may not have worked at the time of the census.

18. See, for example, Kamerman, 1976. A. Sidney Johnson III is directing a Family Impact Seminar; the principal focus of his project is to study the political and administrative feasibility of developing a family impact statement.

19. For example, some experts testifying at the U.S. Senate hearing on American Families seemed to assume far more knowledge regarding what is "good" for the family than does in fact exist (U.S. Congress, 1974).

20. This is a critical issue that has been completely ignored in discussions of family policy and family impact thus far. Development of procedures for assessing family impact, however, would be incomplete and in fact, meaningless, if they did not take account of this issue.

REFERENCES

BERNSTEIN, B., and MEEZAN, W. (1975). A preliminary report: The impact of welfare on family stability. New York: Center for New York City Affairs for the State Board of Social Welfare.

BEVERIDGE, W.H. (1942). Social insurance and allied services. London: His Majesty's Stationery Office.

BRONFENBRENNER, U. (1974). "The origins of alienation." Scientific American, 231(2):53-61.

FINER, M. (1974). The report of the Committee on One Parent Families (Cmnd. 5629, 2 vols.). London: Her Majesty's Stationery Office.

FRIIS, H. (1969). "Issues in social security policy in Denmark." In S. Jenkins (ed.), Social security in international perspective. New York: Columbia University Press.

GOLDSTEIN, J., FREUD, A., and SOLNIT, A.J. (1973). Beyond the best interests of the child. New York: Free Press.

HUNT, A. (1973). Families and their needs. London: Her Majesty's Stationery Office.

KAHN, A.J., and KAMERMAN, S.B. (1975). Not for the poor alone. Philadelphia: Temple University Press.

KAMERMAN, S.B. (1975). Child care programs in nine countries. Washington, D.C.: Office of Child Development, Department of Health, Education, and Welfare.

——— (1976). Developing a family impact statement. New York: Foundation for Child Development.

KAMERMAN, S.B., and KAHN, A.J. (1976a). "Child care." In Social services in the U.S. Philadelphia: Temple University Press.

——— (1976b). "Explorations in family policy." Social Work, 21(3):181-186.

LAROQUE, P. (1958). Réflexions sur les prestations familiales. Paris: Union Nationale de Caisses d'Allocations Familiales.

MORONEY, R. (forthcoming). The family and the state: Considerations for social policy.

MYRDAL, A. (1968). Nation and family. Cambridge: Massachusetts Institute of Technology Press. Originally published in 1941.

——— (1971). Towards equality. Stockholm: Prisma.

PIVEN, F.F., and CLOWARD, R.A. (1971). Regulating the poor. New York: Pantheon.

ROSS, H., and SAWHILL, I.V. (1975). Time of transition. Washington, D.C.: Urban Institute.

SANDBERG, E. (1975). Equality is the goal. Stockholm: Swedish Institute.

U.S. Congress, Senate, Committee on Labor and Welfare, Subcommittee on Children and Youth (1974). American families: Trends and issues, 1973. Washington, D.C.: U.S. Government Printing Office.

WEBB, S., and WEBB, B. (1927). English Poor Law history (part I in English local government). London: Longmans, Green.

WYNN, M. (1970). Family policy. London: Michael Joseph.

9

HOMEMAKERS INTO WIDOWS AND DIVORCEES
Can the Law Provide Economic Protection?

MARGARET GATES

The dissolution of marriage, whether by death or divorce, is almost inevitably a highly traumatic event for the dependent wife. Not only is it a psychological and social crisis (see Chapter 10 in this volume), but it can give rise to financial and legal problems which will cloud her life and those of her children for years to come.

Needless to say, the ending of a marriage can be an unhappy experience for either spouse whether or not he or she was financially dependent upon the other. But my purpose here is to point out how much more damaging divorce and widowhood can be for the homemaker who has no preparation or experience in work outside the home, especially if she has children in her care.

The information upon which this chapter is based is drawn from papers on how state and federal laws affect homemakers during marriage, in widowhood, and in divorce. They were written by experts in each state, as well as the District of Columbia, and were published and distributed in the relevant state by the Committee on the Homemaker, which is a committee of the National Commission on Observance of International Women's Year (IWY).[1] The purpose of the project was to focus attention on those laws and judicial precedents that fail to give proper recognition to the value of the homemaker's role and to the welfare of children.

The most pervasive and unfair of these legal practices will also be highlighted here. However, no attempt will be made to name or number all the states that subscribe to each practice or to create a matrix that would offer such detailed information. Instead, principles embodied in statutes and judicial decisions will be discussed and compared with an eye to developing more equitable family law policy.

The focus of this chapter is on the plight of the person who undertakes to provide services in the home in exchange for financial support and then loses that source of income through death or divorce. Since most such persons are still women, despite the fact that more and more couples are alternating roles, I refer to them as women, although often the effect on financially dependent men would be the same. However, many states have domestic relations laws which treat men and women differently—that is, they apply to persons of one sex or the other without regard to the role that the persons actually play in the marriage. Laws which provide that alimony be paid only by men to women are an example. Although I am opposed to such laws and support the Equal Rights Amendment which would abolish them, the purpose of this paper is to examine the problems of a dependent spouse, not to make the case against sex discrimination in the law.

The information that follows will demonstrate that although marriage is commonly referred to as a "partnership" and is actually conducted as though it were a partnership by many happily married couples, marital unions that end in death or divorce are often revealed to have been a poor investment for the women involved. Restructuring marriage legally so that it more closely resembles a partnership (as suggested by Joan Krauskopf in this volume) is certainly a step in the right direction. The question which will be considered in the conclusion to this chapter is whether revising the marriage, divorce, and probate laws, improving the enforcement of support laws, and educating the judiciary with respect to the problems of divorced women will be sufficient to guarantee that the role of full-time homemaker is one that future generations of American women can afford to assume.

WIDOWHOOD

In most cultures throughout the ages, the widow has been the object of pity and charity. The first public assistance programs provided for the woman deprived of income through the death of her husband. Today 85% of wives outlive their husbands, and many spend their final years in poverty. Some 13% of women over 65 have no income whatsoever, compared with only 2% of men over 65.

Some husbands provide for their surviving wives through life insurance and by willing them property or other assets. Others are too poor, ignorant, or careless to do so. Some men actually take steps to leave their wives penniless. Contrary to popular belief, men who are well able to provide for the needs of their surviving dependents are not required by law to do so in every state.

INHERITANCE WHEN THERE IS NO WILL: INTESTATE SUCCESSION

Every state has a law that provides for the distribution of the property of a deceased person who leaves no will. In Arizona, for example, the spouse of a married person receives the whole estate. But in most states, a widow or widower does not fare so well.

In the first place, Arizona is one of eight states known as community property states, which derive their property law from that of Spain or France, rather than from that of England as do the so-called common-law property states. In those eight states, each spouse is presumed to own one-half of all property accumulated by either spouse during the marriage, with the general exception of gifts and inheritances. (The property owned by both is referred to as marital property.) Therefore, in the community property states, a woman who never earned a penny while she was married would, nevertheless, be considered to own one-half of all the money that her husband earned and one-half the property that he bought with it. In some community property states she would have difficulty controlling these assets while her husband is alive, but, once he is dead, she clearly owns and controls one-half the marital property.

When there is no will, the widow in a community property state may have to share her husband's half of the marital property in varying proportions with their children (or his children by a previous marriage), his parents, and his siblings. When the entire estate consists of the family home or farm, the widow may have to sell the property and divide the proceeds with the other heirs because she has no other resources with which to buy out their interests.

Despite such cases of hardship, it is generally considered that having the wife own half the marital property and inherit part of the rest is equitable (if perhaps not as desirable as the Arizona law which would give her her deceased husband's entire estate). It appears especially fair when compared with the distribution of property under similar circumstances in most common-law property states. There, wives who cannot prove that they have contributed money to the accumulation of marital property are presumed to own none of it. Therefore, a homemaker who has raised a family, improved the value of the house through her own labor, or even worked in her husband's business or assisted him professionally without pay may be considered to have no ownership rights in either property or profits earned from her labor.

Although most states have now altered or abolished it, some maintain the common-law principle of tenancy-by-the-entirety. Under this form of property ownership, a man can choose to make a gift of a one-half interest in a piece of property to his wife. When one spouse dies, the other automatically becomes the owner of all the property without the need for probate court action. Another advantage of the tenancy-by-the-entirety not present in other forms of joint ownership is that property owned in this way cannot be taken to satisfy the separate debts of either spouse. Of course, the law does not require a person to share ownership in this way with his or her marriage partner. If a man chooses to hold all marital property in his own name and does not write a will, his widow in a common-law property state will have to share all the property with his surviving relatives, whereas if she had owned it jointly with him, she would share only his half.

The IWY commission criticized the provisions of the Uniform Probate Code, a model law proposed by the National Conference of Commissions on Uniform State Laws, approved by the American Bar Association, and widely used as a source for states when considering revision of their laws. The IWY commission agreed with the model law provision that the spouse inherit the entire estate when there are no living parents or issue (children or grandchildren) of the deceased. It also approved of having the spouse receive one-half of the estate when there were children of her husband by another marriage. However, in the case where the children were the widow's, whether they were minors or adults, the IWY commission was of the opinion that their mother should receive the entire estate. There was no recommendation as to what should be the disposition when there were surviving parents.

DISINHERITANCE BY WILL

It has always been a tenet of public policy in this country that people should be able to will their property to whomever they wish. Running counter to this freedom is another which would prohibit a person from leaving dependents to become wards of the state. A third principle has been introduced when states have questioned the equity of permitting an individual to disinherit a marriage partner who has provided personal services in return for financial support.

The latter two principles are the reasons why in all states some provision is made in the law for part of the deceased spouse's property to go to the surviving spouse. These allowances differ in value and kind from state to state, but most have the advantage of being protected from the deceased's creditors. It may be a percentage of the estate, a fixed dollar amount, or the actual cost of family support for one year. In Georgia, what is called a "year's support" can include title to real property which does not have to be disposed of in one year. Some statutes provide that the wife receive certain implements such as the sewing machine or kitchen utensils in apparent belief that these more than other things are essential to the survivor.

What is called a "forced share" or "widow's election" is also available in all but three states. By this means a widow can require that her husband's will be set aside, at least in part, so that she may inherit a statutory share of his estate—usually one-third to one-half. Even if he has not completely disinherited her, she may benefit by electing to take her share against the will, because by doing so in many states, she can protect that much of the estate against his creditors.

When one marriage partner earns the family income, he not only can will it all to persons other than his spouse but can conceal or waste it so that there is nothing to be transferred to his wife when he dies. Women who do not participate in the management of family income cannot know how it is spent or invested. When they are widowed, they may not even know what their husbands owned in order to claim it.

Hopefully, women will no longer choose to enter into dependency relationships which do not permit them to know what their financial situation will be if the breadwinner should die. Presumably, as women's opportunity to earn a living becomes equal to that of men, their power position in the family will improve, so that their leaving the work force to raise children can be conditioned upon equal control with their spouses of his earnings. In any event, it is arguable that such a bargain is a matter of personal, rather than public, policy.

The question of the distribution of marital property upon the death of a spouse, especially if the survivor is financially dependent, is more clearly a social policy issue. Although the IWY commission made no recommendation with respect to how "forced share" statutes should be revised, it recommended "further study" of the provision contained in the Uniform Probate Code. The Committee was concerned about the fact that it is extremely difficult, if not impossible, to devise any formula which will be equitable when applied to all fact situations. For example, it is plain that a dutiful wife of 30 years is more deserving to receive the full estate than is a woman who recently married the deceased man and contributed little or nothing to his life or to the accumulation of his property. That is why legal authorities advise that, outside community property states, wives should insist on joint ownership of marital property at the time of its purchase.

INHERITANCE TAXES

The federal government levies an inheritance tax on the value over $60,000 of all estates unless they are left to a government agency or charity. The principal purpose of the law is to limit the wealth which can be passed from generation to generation within a family. Many people, including the Committee on the Homemaker of the IWY commission, feel that spouses should be permitted to transfer property between themselves without being taxed, since to do so would not be contrary to the basic purpose of the law and would be advantageous to the widowed homemaker.

In community property states the federal inheritance tax, at least, is sex-neutral in its impact, affecting husbands and wives equally. A greater injustice occurs in the common-law states, where the wife's share of property owned jointly by a married couple is inherited tax-free by him when she dies, because he is presumed to have paid for it. The wife, on the other hand, must pay taxes on one-half of her husband's share, subject to a $60,000 exemption, unless she can prove she contributed money toward the purchase or improvement of the property. Particularly hard hit by this policy are farm wives who inherit large tracts of land which they may have co-owned and worked for many years. If the market value of the land is high, they frequently must sell at least part of the property to meet estate taxes.

PENSIONS AND SOCIAL SECURITY

It has come as a cruel shock to many a widow to learn that her husband's pension ceased upon his death. This happened when he did not notify his employer before retirement that he wanted his wife to receive survivor's benefits. Many husbands did not wish to provide for their wives in this way because it meant that the benefits paid during their own lifetimes would be smaller. Other husbands simply never realized that they had the option of choosing such a plan.

In 1974 the federal law governing pension rights was amended so that, for employees retiring after 1976, a surviving spouse will receive 50% of the reduced benefit unless the worker affirmatively requests that there be no survivor's benefits. The new provision protects the dependent homemaker from losing this source of income through the ignorance or oversight of her deceased husband, but it still permits him to deliberately leave her without a share of his pension.

Under social security, on the other hand, not the worker but the federal government decides who receives survivor's benefits. The law now provides that the dependent wife of an eligible worker will be covered only if she either is at least 62 years of age, is permanently disabled, or has children under 18 who are living with her. This means that women in their 40s and 50s who have never worked outside the home and whose children are grown must learn to support themselves unless they have substantial sources of income from property, trust funds, or other assets. Most such women are able to make a living, albeit a greatly reduced one. For some, doing so may even be a very positive experience. But for others who are ill or emotionally unable, the prospects for training and entrance into the labor market at middle age are poor.

DIVORCE

The divorce rate continues to rise. In 1975 in the United States there was almost one divorce for every two marriages, for a grand total of over a million marriages ending in the courts. The actual number was twice as great as in 1966 and three times that registered in 1950.

If marriages were typically unions of two economically self-sufficient people for the purpose of sharing the management of a home and the rearing of children, there would be no need to write this chapter. Since, instead, matrimony usually ascribes sex-based roles to the husband and wife, and they become a mutually dependent team, certain inequities almost inevitably arise when the marriage is dissolved by divorce. First, if she has been the primary parent, she will almost always be awarded the custody of young children; and, second, if he has been the primary "breadwinner," he will have greater earning power than she does.

The long-range solution may well be the one that we seem to be moving toward in which husbands and wives share market labor, household work, and parenting—a model which appears to be better for children as well as mothers and fathers. (See Chapter 7 in this volume.) But the fact remains that millions of American men and women have already entered into and invested their lives in more traditional marriages. Those husbands and wives would argue that, when they entered into a marriage contract, they had certain expectations which should be recognized and respected by the law and the courts.

One of the most serious legal transgressions against the bargain struck by those marriage partners has been the increased availability of divorce and, particularly, the so-called "no-fault" divorce. Some states have abolished all the old grounds for divorce and have adopted the model of marriage "dissolution" when the court finds upon the allegation of either spouse that an "irretrievable breakdown" of the marriage has occurred. Other states have a no-fault provision but retain the traditional grounds for divorce so that a person can sue for divorce on the basis of adultery, insanity, cruelty, desertion, and other such reasons in order to obtain a better settlement from the guilty spouse. They may also permit a couple to separate for a prescribed number of months and then obtain a divorce "by mutual consent."

When the Commission on Uniform State Laws wrote and rewrote the Uniform Marriage and Divorce Act, they incorporated the no-fault concept, but they also imposed criteria to be used by courts in ordering support and property settlements. Their idea was to protect the interests of blameless wives who, under the old system of fault, could have bargained fair settlements from their husbands in exchange for their freedom. Unfortunately, many of the states which have adopted the no-fault concept have not incorporated the criteria for settlements into the law. And even where the law includes the criteria, they are frequently ignored by judges who are supposed to be guided by them.

Another problem which faces every dependent spouse in a divorce action is that of obtaining legal representation. The laws of many states provide that the court may award attorney's fees to the spouse who is not able to pay. Unfortunately, lawyers will often not accept a case without a retainer to cover the minimum amount of time which they will have to invest. This is especially so when there are substantial disputes between the parties. Moreover, when the extent of the husband's property and earnings is not known, it may be necessary to take depositions (transcribed answers to questions under oath). The cost of these transcripts is substantial and are out-of-pocket expenses which the attorney will not want to undertake without a retainer to cover them. When a court does order the wife's attorney's fees paid, a middle- to low-income earner may be permitted to pay in installments. These awards often become entirely unenforceable because they are too small to warrant another trip to court to collect them.

The following is a brief and generalized discussion of the major pitfalls for the dependent wife whose marriage is being dissolved in the courts, along with suggestions for law reform to make the process more equitable.

PROPERTY DIVISION

As was explained in the previous section, in the eight community property states, one-half the marital property belongs to each spouse regardless of the monetary contribution that each person might have made toward its purchase. Other states, by enacting legislation similar to the Uniform Marriage and Divorce Act, have achieved he same result with respect to the equal division of property at divorce.

In 14 common-law states, the courts have no authority to distribute marital property at divorce. In those states, the property goes to the spouse who holds title to it. If the husband has not seen fit to put the home in joint ownership, for example, he will have no difficulty retaining it when he divorces his wife.

But in most common-law states, who holds title to the property is not the governing factor. On the one hand, property owned jointly may be presumed to belong to the husband unless the wife can prove that she contributed money toward its purchase. On the other hand, the property may be distributed without regard to title but taking into consideration such factors as the length of the marriage, the number of children, the relative age and financial status of the parties, and—in some states—who is at fault in the breakdown of the marriage.

In only a few states is the wife likely to get more than half the property—in the South, where courts are apt to be chivalrous in their awards, and in Arizona, where property is divided "equitably" rather than equally. It is considered equitable to award more property to the wife than to the husband for two reasons. First, he usually has developed his earning power over the life of the marriage, while she has not, because she has assumed the care of their children. Second, if she is still rearing children, she is more in need of the home. Some judges recognize that a good property settlement is more valuable to a wife than alimony or child support, which may never be collected.

Pensions and social security retirement benefits are another form of property which can be of particular importance to the older couple in divorce. A dependent wife who has been married less than 20 years has no right to share her husband's social security benefits after divorce. Many commentators feel that the law should be changed to permit dependents to collect an amount proportionate to the number of years of marriage. Similarly, a homemaker usually has a weak claim on her former husband's pension despite the fact that contributions were paid on it during the life of the marriage. A pension is usually not treated as property until it vests, and so it cannot figure in many divorce settlements.

ALIMONY

Contrary to popular belief, most divorced women do not receive alimony. A poll of 1,522 women conducted in September 1975, at the request of the IWY commission, indicated that only 14% of divorced wives are entitled to alimony by award of the courts or through a voluntary settlement approved by the courts. Of those women, fewer than half collected it regularly. Surprisingly, the situation was much the same in 1922, the last year in which the U.S. Government collected such national data; then, alimony was awarded or agreed to in 14.7% of divorces.

In the states that have revised their laws to resemble the Uniform Marriage and Divorce Act, "rehabilitative alimony" may be awarded to enable a woman to prepare to support herself. In some cases it is designed to permit her to finish a degree or take a training course, and in others it is simply an amount that diminishes over time. The Uniform Act refers to the purpose of allowing the wife to find "suitable employment," but it is not clear what kind of work is suitable. For example, is selling hosiery in a department store suitable work for a middle-aged homemaker who was married to a business executive? Is she expected to develop a business career for herself? Perhaps the only really suitable work for her is being a homemaker for another successful man.

Under the Uniform Marriage and Divorce Act and its progeny, judges, when awarding alimony, are directed to consider a number of factors such as the length of the marriage, the age of the spouses, their relative financial situations, and the number of children. In some states with no-fault divorce, the question of fault emerges in setting the amount of alimony, thereby completely undermining the purpose of no-fault law. Divorce attorneys in all systems are appalled at the variety of outcomes in similar cases even when decided by the same judge.

Women with children in their custody often prefer to receive larger child-support payments, which are tax-free to them, in lieu of alimony. They may also prefer a "lump sum" in cash or property rather than periodic payments despite the tax consequences, because of the difficulty of collecting alimony and child support from an angry or irresponsible former spouse.

CHILD CUSTODY

The woman who dedicates herself to home and family is still almost certain to obtain custody of her children in divorce despite specific language in some state statutes that neither parent is presumed to be the more suitable custodian. In all but two states (Georgia and Louisiana), the governing factor is "the best interest of the child," but most often it is clear that the mother has the best understanding of and closest relationship to the children simply because their care has been her primary responsibility.

Of course, some mothers are electing to relinquish custody of all or some of their children. It is also true that courts occasionally find a father a more appropriate custodian for an older boy. Once a father has remarried and has a wife at home, his chances of obtaining custody by proving his former wife an unfit mother are enhanced. However, many courts have refused to find a woman unfit to have custody of her children, despite her conduct, if her acts do not affect the child.

Obtaining custody of children in divorce is the problem mentioned earlier as the inequity suffered by husbands who play the role of breadwinner to the exclusion of that of parent. The correlative problem of the wife who is given custody of her children is how to support them in light of often inadequate awards and the difficulties of enforcing them.

CHILD SUPPORT

The 1975 IWY commission poll cited earlier showed that only 44% of divorced mothers were awarded child support and that only 47% of those were collecting it regularly. A similar picture emerges from a review of a sample of cases of recipients of Aid to Families of Dependent Children (AFDC)—a review in seven states conducted by the Government Accounting Office at the request of the Honorable Martha Griffiths when she was Chairwoman of the Subcommittee on Fiscal Policy of the Joint Economic Committee of the U.S. Congress. It shows that many fathers were not bound by court order or voluntary agreement to pay child support, that the accounts supposed to be paid had little relationship to the father's ability to pay, and that less than one-half of the amounts due were being collected.

The relationship of these facts to the burgeoning welfare rolls can be surmised. What is less obvious is the hardship endured by those women and their children who do not qualify for or do not desire public support. Many of these female-headed households cannot be expected to survive on the child support that they are awarded, assuming that they can collect it. The usual amounts per child when cumulated frequently fall below the poverty line for a family of that size. If the mother attempts to supplement this income by working, she may find that the low wages which even a well-educated woman who has been out of the labor force can expect to earn are gobbled up by the cost of child care.

Since low- to middle-income families claim that it is increasingly necessary for both parents to work to sustain one home, it should be clear that, however these incomes are divided at divorce, they will be insufficient to maintain two households. Welfare may be the only answer for the parent with custody of the children. But in many middle-class cases, when the custodial parent is the mother, the father enjoys a much higher standard of living after the divorce than do his former wife and his children. This follows naturally from the fact that judges will rarely require a man to give up as much as half his income for fear he will decline to work altogether.

There are two elements to the question of how to assure that children of divorced parents are supported in an equitable way by both parents—the appropriateness of the award and the means of enforcement.

Awards. The overwhelming majority of divorcing parents agree between them to the amount of child support which will be paid. A court determines the amount only when this issue is litigated. However, many women are forced to bargain about child support under threat that their husbands will contest their custody of the children. If an obviously inadequate sum is agreed upon, the courts usually have the authority to protect the child by ordering a reasonable amount of support, if they choose to do so.

Unlike alimony, child support obligations do not terminate in most states when the mother remarries. However, if the father remarries and undertakes a new family or if he loses his job or other financial resources, he may apply to the court to reduce his obligation. Support usually ends when the child reaches maturity, the age for which varies from state to state but which under a recent Supreme Court decision must be the same for males and females. However, in some states it may be ordered continued until the child's education is completed.

Several states, including Washington and Michigan, have guidelines which may be used by the courts in setting the amount of an award. The guidelines are based on the earnings, after taxes, of the person ordered to pay—only, however, up to $15,000 per year maximum. Apparently, it is believed that the financial affairs of persons with incomes above that level may be too complex to be susceptible to a formula of this kind. These guidelines or schedules were designed for use during separations pending divorce, but they have begun to influence permanent awards by some judges in the few jurisdictions where they exist. They have the advantage of standardizing awards which can otherwise vary dramatically from judge to judge, but they are faulted by attorneys because they are not updated often enough to keep pace with inflation. Of course, awards themselves are also not adjusted to the cost of living and, therefore, become more and more inadequate over the years while the child's needs increase with age.

Enforcement. For many reasons fathers decide not to pay child support. Some are furious with the mother and leave the jurisdiction, although this means never seeing the children. Others meet their obligations regularly for a few years and then pay less often or less money before stopping altogether. A woman who has a court order for child support can enforce it, but doing so can be more trouble than it is worth for the following reasons.

First, in most states she will have to hire a lawyer. Few attorneys are willing to take such cases because frequently the only way to be paid for such work is on a contingency basis—that is, by receiving a percentage of the amount collected. If it is not clear where the father is or whether he can pay a judgment against him, or if the amount in question is small, it will be difficult to obtain legal counsel. Even women who qualify for free legal services may find that these services do not include domestic relations work.

Assuming that a lawyer takes the case and gets a judgment against the man, it will be for a sum already past due. The process of accumulating a worthwhile debt, suing, and collecting could absorb many months during which the mother and children would be without the income. It is not uncommon for judges to reduce the amount that the father owes or permit him to pay in installments if he shows he does not have the means to pay the full amount. Then, should the money be collected, part would be owed for legal services.

A private attorney will often not take a child-support collection case until the debt is great enough to make the legal action worthwhile. By that time, the mother and children could be in dire circumstances. Even if a judgment for the money owed is obtained, the judge may order it paid in installments because the husband has spent what should have been paid to his wife. These installments are likely to be as difficult to collect as the past debt.

Once a judgment has been obtained, a wife may levy against her husband's property in the same way as any other creditor; but, in many states, her claim does not get priority. Some states have provisions for the garnishment of wages to meet such obligations, but courts are loathe to use this power. The salaries of federal government employees, including military personnel, which were once immune from garnishment, can now be reached under a relatively recent amendment to the Social Security Act.

In some states, such as Washington, the father may be ordered to pay child support to the clerk of the court, who then forwards it to the mother. This process produces a delay in the mother's receipt of the money, but it can speed up the collection procedure if the payment is not made promptly. Typically, a delinquent father can be given notice and an opportunity to appear to explain the nonpayment within 30 days. If he does not appear and refuses to pay, he can be held in contempt of court and jailed until he does so.

A similar means of collection has been set up in social service agencies of some states. Their primary purpose is to collect child support owed to welfare recipients who are required to assign their rights to the payments to the state in return for AFDC payments. But a few such agencies will also collect for non-welfare parents for a reasonable fee which is deducted from the support payment if it is collected. For the low- to middle-class woman, this is both a faster and less expensive method of collection than hiring a lawyer and suing for arrearages.

This form of collection will become available to women in all states as amendments to the Social Security Act popularly known as the "IV (d) Program" are fully implemented. This legislation conditions the receipt of federal welfare funds upon the operation of such a child-support collection effort in each state and also provides for a federal Parent Locator System to help track down persons who have left the jurisdiction of the award.

When a woman knows the whereabouts of her former husband, she can utilize a procedure established under the Uniform Reciprocal Enforcement of Support Act (URESA) to collect in another state. Before this law became effective in all but one state, it was necessary for a woman to go to court in her own state and get a judgment for the amount of money owed her. The reason for this lies in the U.S. Constitution, which requires only that each state enforce the final judgments of other states' courts. A support order in most states is not final in the legal sense because it can be modified both prospectively and retroactively. Under URESA this step is eliminated, as is the need to hire a lawyer in the foreign jurisdiction, where under the law she will be represented by its state attorney.

Nevertheless, URESA has not been an effective enforcement tool for several reasons. First, it requires that a woman know where her ex-spouse is. Second, court delays range from six months to a year. Most importantly, it changes procedural law but leaves untouched such substantitive problems as the possibility of a modification of the order with respect to money already due. In only several states does the right to payments vest in the obligee when they are due so that the debt is established when the obligor fails to pay.

CONCLUSIONS

Too many women are unprepared for the financial reverses that they suffer when they are divorced or widowed. The law of the state in which they live usually influences how well they will fare relative to the wealth of their husbands and the worth of the property that the two have accumulated during the marriage. The principles set forth in the Uniform Marriage and Divorce Act and the Uniform Probate Code when incorporated into state law are advantageous to wives and can be used as a legislative agenda for women's advocates. The recommendations of the International Women's Year Commission can serve the same function with respect to federal laws.

Women's groups must also pressure for quick and inexpensive means of enforcing the child-support laws for low- and middle-income families as well as for welfare mothers. In addition, programs must be mounted to train women who have lost their source of income to support themselves and their children. All these measures are needed to help women who became homemakers rather than wage earners in the expectation that their husbands would support them for the rest of their lives or at least during their childbearing and childrearing years.

What such laws and programs cannot be expected to accomplish, however, is to equalize the financial future of a man who has developed considerable earning power during many years in the work force and the financial future of his wife who has not. It is simply not possible to force someone to give over half his income for the rest of his life (or his former wife's, if she predeceases him) irrespective of their ages or other family obligations that he may create or undertake in the future. This is especially true when his salary is barely adequate to support one household. It can certainly be argued that award of such long-term periodic alimony is fair, but it should be recognized that as a practical matter it would be extremely difficult to collect.

A better solution to this problem is to reduce the economic dependency of women upon men—not because it is easier to accomplish, but because doing so would have a number of additional beneficial side effects for many women, not the least of which would be an improved self-image. The value to society of homemaking and especially parenting is not diminished by acknowledging this. Housework and child-rearing are no less important or dignified than labor market work, but they normally do not result in wages when performed by a woman for her husband and children. In a sense the homemaker barters her services for a share of her husband's salary. Unfortunately, however, he is usually the only person in the world who is willing to compensate her for nurturing her own children and maintaining a happy, healthy home. This fact is not an anomaly in our culture. Artists are another example of people whose work is highly esteemed but poorly paid in most quarters. We accept that all but a few of our painters, musicians, dancers, actors, and sculptors will be poor unless they have a patron or some other way of earning money.

Having acknowledged that women should be prepared to earn their own living, one must recognize that there are many obstacles to their doing so, especially if they have children. Aside from the numerous forms of sex discrimination in the job market, they lack the supportive services and programs that they need to enable them to leave their homes. Among these is child-care for preschoolers, after-school programs for older children, and the availability of more part-time and flex-time jobs.

Furthermore, if women are to compete with men for careers, they should not in fairness be expected to shoulder what has come to be called the "double burden" of market employment and housework. Of course, many wage-earning women do nevertheless perform both roles either because there is no male breadwinner in the family or because he does not take over a significant part of the housekeeping and child-rearing. A large proportion of minority and low-income families fall into this category. Ironically, the goal of many of these women is to be able to be a full-time homemaker in the fashion of the stereotypical white, middle-class mother at a time when the latter has begun to question her satisfaction with this role.

Currently a young woman approaching marriage has considerable latitude in defining a role for herself in that relationship. She might be well advised to make certain agreements with her future spouse and commit them to paper before the marriage. Even though such a document might not constitute an enforceable contract, it would provide some guidelines by which the couple could develop a mutually dependent relationship that does not include a division of labor that is bound to economically cripple one partner. It might also cause her to plan how she would support herself if she were on her own again, since her chances of divorcing or outliving her husband are extremely good.

As we have seen, the law of divorce in practice does not protect the financial interests of the homemaker adequately. Although it can and should be improved, it is doubtful that it can ever guarantee long-term financial equity between spouses and former spouses who adopt the traditional division of labor patterns in marriage. The law can intrude itself only so far into family matters without jeopardizing freedoms that we prize. The remainder of the change that is needed must be accomplished through the educated decisions of young women to plan self-sufficient lives.

NOTE

1. The Center for Women Policy Studies commissioned and edited these papers under a contract with the Committee on the Homemaker. However the opinions and conclusions expressed in this chapter are those of the author and do not necessarily reflect the thinking of the Committee, the IWY Commission or the writers of the papers on state law. It should be noted that federal inheritance tax law was revised after this chapter was in print.

10

A CRISIS PERSPECTIVE ON
DIVORCE AND ROLE CHANGE

JEAN LIPMAN-BLUMEN

A woman confronts a major role transformation when (as Jessie Bernard reminds us in the "Introduction" to this volume) she "dwindles into a wife." She faces an even greater and less prepared-for trauma when divorce dwindles her further into an ex-wife. This second dwindling into a former wife may be seen as a major crisis, one which anthropologists rarely have bothered to include among the recognized "life crises" that mark the way-stations of the human life cycle.

Despite the conceptual neglect of divorce as a recognized and increasingly expected life crisis,[1] the demographic evidence about the prevalence of divorce sharply commands our attention. As a worldwide phenomenon, divorce is steadily growing. While divorce has always been a well-documented aspect of less-developed societies, divorce is becoming more and more widespread in the developed societies as well.

A major increase in both American divorce and remarriage rates began around 1960 and during the following decade rose dramatically. By 1970, the highest rates of divorce and remarriage ever recorded occurred (Norton and Glick 1976). Since then, the picture has begun to change somewhat. "The divorce rate has undergone a leveling off period and appears to be on the decline, and remarriage is more often delayed and avoided by women of high educational, occupational, and economic levels. Liberalization of divorce laws, as well as changes in attitudes and sex roles, have contributed to the divorce boom" (Lipman-Blumen, 1976:71). By 1974, divorces totaled 970,000 in the United States, a 6.2% increase over 1973.

Partly as a result of the increased incidence of divorce, there has been a significant rise in female-headed families. Of the 55 million families in the United States in 1974, 6.8 million were headed by women. There was a 40% increase in female-headed families between 1960 and 1970, with the most growth attributable to the rapidly increasing divorce rate during that period. By 1974, approximately half of all women heads of households were divorced, an increase of close to 6% since 1968 (U.S. Department of Labor, Women's Bureau, 1975:20).

The financial strain experienced by female heads of households is only imperfectly reflected in the fact that 54% of these women are in the labor force, compared to 45% of all women, and 43% of women with husbands present. Perhaps even more telling with respect to financial strain is the fact that 35% of female family heads are the only persons in their respective family groups currently employed.

The unemployment rate of female family heads is more than double that of male family heads, 6.4% versus 2.7% respectively. Among unemployed female family heads, only 18% had an employed family member to absorb some of the financial burden. The difficulties that divorced mothers of young children face in caring for them and simultaneously working are reflected in the 70% labor force participation rate of female heads of households ages 45 to 54, most of whose children are old enough to permit the mother relative freedom to enter the labor force.

These demographic trends point clearly to the growing importance of divorce as an expectable life crisis that more and more women and their children will face. These sociological trends suggest the need for increased concern about the prevalent crisis that women face—the second dwindling into divorced wives and mothers.

THE CRISIS OF DIVORCE: RISK AND OPPORTUNITY

In the present chapter, divorce will be examined within the framework of a crisis orientation in an effort to understand the dynamics of role changes that divorce brings. Most crises are not solely unmitigated catastrophes; they often contain within them the seeds of positive events, attitudes, and behaviors.

The Chinese symbol for crisis has two elements, one representing danger and risk, the other opportunity. Divorce, realistically considered, encompasses both these aspects: vulnerability both to destruction and development. Historically, society has emphasized the dangers inherent in the divorce cycle. This was only reasonable, in view of the difficulties that women historically confronted and even today commonly encounter. The dangerous and destructive aspects of divorce have been the foreground, looming large and clear. The opportunities for growth, development, and redirection have been in the background, often difficult to see in any detail.

The predominance of the negative aspects of divorce is still evident today, and it would be unrealistic if this chapter did not reflect that condition. In large part, this chapter will focus on the problems that women face in the process of changing their roles to join the ranks of the "formerly married." We shall try to delineate the range of problems and vulnerabilities that women experience in this very special life crisis of divorce. Disentangling the delicate skeins of opportunities and new options from the tangle of difficulties and risks that divorce usually presents is an arduous task; however, in the final section of this chapter we shall turn to a discussion of the possibilities for converting the problems arising out of the divorce crisis into new role and life possibilities.

A THEORETICAL FRAMEWORK

As mentioned above, this chapter attempts to apply a theoretical framework involving aspects of crisis to the problems of divorce. Elsewhere (Lipman-Blumen, 1976) I have applied this framework to the problems of marriage, divorce, and remarriage from a *macrosociological* perspective, using census data to test hypotheses derived from the framework. Here I shall be dealing closer to the *microsociological* level, looking at the ways in which individuals can respond to the crisis of divorce. Hopefully, such an analysis eventually will lead to the development of a model for predicting role changes in divorce at the individual level.

In order to develop this analysis, I shall begin by defining the concept of "crisis." Then I shall examine at least 10 dimensions by which any crisis—including divorce—can be characterized and apply these to the case of divorce. After that, I shall set forth those aspects

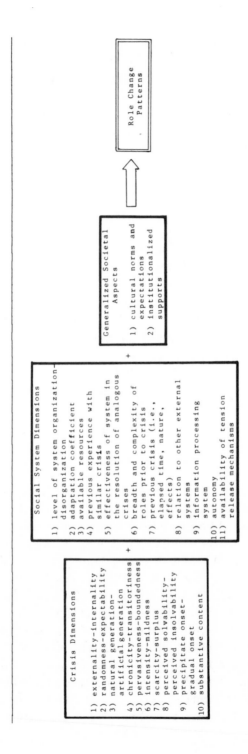

FIGURE 1: System Responses to Crisis

of a social system—here, the family—which, combined with the exact nature of the crisis, can lead to predictions about the nature of role changes to be expected at the acute phase of divorce and in the usually more protracted reconfiguration or resolution period. Finally, I shall examine briefly certain generalized societal aspects which tie a band of constraint or elasticity around the divorce process.

DEFINITION OF CRISIS

Crisis may be defined as any situation recognized by the individuals involved as a threat to the well-being, sustenance, or survival of the system, whose problem-solving mechanisms and resources are strained or inadequate to resolve effectively the problem confronting it. As I have described elsewhere (Lipman-Blumen, 1973, 1975b, 1976), role change is one of several possible system responses to crisis. The actual type of role change that occurs depends upon relationships between the nature of the crisis and the state of the system—in this case, the family—at the time of the crisis and is further conditioned by certain general societal aspects, including cultural norms and expectations.

DIMENSIONS OF CRISIS

The nature of any given crisis—in this case, divorce—can be described in terms of 10 dimensions. An analysis of any given divorce situation using these dimensions—and relating them to the state of the particular family involved—will lead to predictions regarding the types of role changes that can be expected. In this way, a model of role changes resulting from varying divorce situations can be developed.[2]

Internality/Externality. The first dimension[3] of crisis—internality/externality—refers to the major source of the divorce cause. Most family therapists would agree that *all* marriages that end in divorce have some internal dysfunction(s). Nonetheless, here we are distinguishing between divorces that result from problems specifically *intrinsic* to the relationship between the two partners (i.e., constant disagreements, alcoholism of one or both partners, sexual incompatibilities, etc.) and problems which are primarily *extrinsic* to the marriage (i.e., relationships with individuals outside the marriage, economic disaster, etc.).

Clearly, there are links between problems that occur inside and outside any marriage (i.e., sexual boredom or dissatisfaction inside can lead to sexual liaisons outside the marriage relationship). Nevertheless, in most cases of divorce, the immediate "cause" can be described as primarily internal or external. The greater control often (but not always) associated with internal problems may lead to greater control over the type and pace of role change than when the cause is seen as externally generated.

Precipitate Onset/Gradual Onset. A second related dimension is precipitate versus gradual onset. Most divorce situations have fairly deep roots; however, these roots may be well buried beneath the numerous ritualizations of behavior characteristic of marriage. Although the cues are all there, one or both individuals may fail to read or acknowledge them. Thus, a not uncommon divorce scenario involves the spouse who is "shocked after 30 years of marriage" when his or her partner wants a divorce. For purposes of classification, we would consider this a crisis of precipitate onset, since that is how it is perceived by at least one spouse.

There are times when the onset of the divorce situation may be experienced as sudden by both partners. For example, "infidelity" of one partner may cause the other spouse to "demand a divorce," despite the fact that the "unfaithful" partner did not plan to replace the marital with the extramarital relationship.

The meaning of both the suddenness factor and the previous dimension (internality/externality) for potential role change lies in the degree to which prior awareness of an impending marital crisis could promote preparation for role change—either by attempting to salvage the marriage or by beginning a new "unmarried" life.

Marital discord that grows over time, periodically forcing the partners to consider, consciously or otherwise, the possibility of divorce, allows and promotes preparation for role change—within the context of either marriage or divorce. When there is less preparation for divorce, the danger side of the crisis equation is most apparent. In cases where the "buildup" has been gradual, coping mechanisms —ranging from emotional distancing to occupational training preparatory for entering the labor market—may be developed and possibly already in use.

Chronicity/Transitoriness. A third dimension of divorce crisis is chronicity/transitoriness. For those individuals whose divorce plans are spearheaded by remarriage plans, the role of divorce is perceived as a transitory state. As a result, serious role changes that usually accompany transitions in marital status changes may not occur; instead, marital *identity* problems may predominate. Thus, Ms. X need not begin to prepare herself (and possibly her children) to live as a female-headed family, but rather as a family with a new husband-father.

In the remaining cases, where the length of time that the woman will remain in the divorce category is uncertain, the divorce crisis is marked by at least potential chronicity. If we are to extrapolate from current demographic shifts, more women—particularly women with high educational and occupational levels—are choosing to maintain their "divorced status" on a permanent or at least long-term basis. Thus, new long-term roles—as breadwinner or as mother-father—may be planned or at least expected by the former wife. In some instances, these "changes" merely represent formalization and/or continuation of an existing situation. For example, divorces sought by wives of veterans returning from overseas duty may be the legalization and institutionalization of an existing condition. Such "formalization divorces" have reversed order—the major role changes *precede* the divorce.

Solvability/Insolvability. Solvability/insolvability refers to the degree to which the divorce crisis can be resolved without total dissolution of the marriage. Some marriages confronted by a "divorce crisis" can effect enough adaptations to avoid or postpone the divorce.

In many cases, the divorce "goes through" and solvability questions begin to surround the new problems ushered in by the state of divorce. Thus, solvability becomes defined, not in terms of reconstituting the former marriage, but in terms of developing the divorce relationship between the two former spouses, as well as developing new roles and relationships emerging from the divorced woman's new life. No well-defined positive model for divorced roles for former spouses vis-à-vis one another have as yet been articulated.

Intensity/Mildness. Intensity/mildness is another dimension that is linked to the issues of preparedness and awareness of the impending divorce. A crisis will more likely be experienced as intense if no preparation has occurred. When individuals gradually have prepared for divorce, they are more likely to experience relatively less trauma.

An underlying assumption suggests that all divorces—even those sought and/or wished for over a long time—are traumatic in various ways to the individuals concerned. Thus, when I present the intensity/mildness dimension, I caution the reader to recognize that I am speaking in relative terms.

Natural Generation/Artificial Generation. Natural generation/ artificial generation in the case of divorce crises refers to the evaluation by the partners of the inevitability of the situation. Natural generation divorces would appear to be associated with intrinsic characteristics of the individuals, their relationship or unavoidable and unchangeable circumstances of their marriage.

When one or both partners feel that the divorce was not unavoidable, guilt and depression are likely concomitants affecting the degree to which the range of new divorce roles can be carried out effectively. In some instances, where both partners feel a solution other than divorce should have been selected, it is possible they will remarry one another or develop a "new" relationship between them. This is not to suggest that depression and guilt do not characterize even those divorce situations that both partners think were unavoidable.

Perception of artificially generated causes—for example, a troublesome in-law—may lead to incipient coping mechanisms to be used if ever the individual remarries. Problems characterizing a specific marriage that the partners feel inevitably led to divorce—for example, an alcoholic spouse—may be recognized as factors to be avoided in future relationships.

Randomness/Expectability. Randomness/expectability is a dimension that refers to the degree to which a given crisis can be expected to occur or is totally unexpected. Crises that all individuals expect to encounter include the life crises of birth, illness, adolescence, marriage, and death. Widowhood is becoming an expected life crisis as American women's longevity surpasses men's by approximately eight years.

If the divorce trend continues its current trajectory, more women may begin to look at divorce as an expectable occurrence, compared to earlier generations of women for whom divorce was a random, unscheduled life crisis. As more young females recognize simply the statistical possibility and expectability of divorce in their own lives, they may begin to plan their lives in a more realistic way. Occupational training and planning may take such a possibility into account, even before a marriage partner is found. Child-spacing, marriage contracts, prenuptial agreements, divorce insurance, divorce trust funds, planned job-renewal training, and additional education periods are all possible long-term strategies designed to prepare for the possibility of divorce even when the marriage is at its strongest.

Scarcity/Surplus. Scarcity/surplus is still another crisis dimension meaningful in divorce. Overall, most divorces tend to create scarcity of many important elements—companionship, love, sex, money, time, material goods, social networks—to name a few. The very surpluses that divorce creates (i.e., additional, often burdensome tasks that were part of the former partner's role, loneliness, emotional difficulties of any or all of the individuals involved) tend to be heavily weighted on the "negative" side.

In some cases, for former wives, divorce commonly leads to a surplus of responsibilities and a scarcity of resources necessary to meet them. The resulting strain can lead the former wife to seek additional financial, personal, and social resources. This may take the form of entering new or additional occupational roles, returning to the early family (i.e., reassuming the "daughter" role), or seeking a swift second marriage. More recently, some younger divorced women are seeking simultaneous solutions to several of these problems by joining communal living groups whose combined resources of people and material goods may ease the strains and costs of these new responsibilities.

Boundedness/Pervasiveness. Boundedness/pervasiveness is a ninth dimension of crisis. In divorce problems, the crisis may be bounded if it is still in the "threat of divorce" stage. The crisis is pervasive to the family involved if the divorce does, in fact, come to pass.

Boundedness/pervasiveness may have still another meaning for former wives: the degree to which her divorced status permeates all her attitudes and behaviors. If all her choices in life are based upon her divorced status—and some inevitably must be—then we would characterize the divorce crisis as pervasive. If only some of her choices are contingent upon the former wife's divorced status, then she experiences a "bounded" crisis.

Probably the most characteristic course of the "divorce syndrome" is for pervasiveness to characterize the early stages of divorce, and boundedness the later period of crisis adaptation or resolution. Women whose lives continue to be pervaded and dominated by their divorced status may prevent themselves from undertaking new roles and new directions with any clarity and strength.

Substantive Content. The final dimension of crisis is substantive and differs from all the previous dimensions, which were content-free. The substantive dimension of divorce may and usually does involve *several* substantive domains—emotional, sexual, financial, religious, social, and legal—to name some common ones.

It is the substantive dimensions which specify the content of any individual divorce. To illustrate, let us compare two women divorcées. One woman is from an upper-class Protestant background with a substantial trust fund; the other is from a working-class Catholic background with four children and a factory job. The first woman faces a social, psychological, perhaps sexual problem. Her social life may undergo some disruption, with some friends drifting away, perhaps remaining within her husband's social network. The psychological trauma may be great, but she can seek the services of a private psychiatrist or counselor. Depending upon the sexual mores of her own social group, although her sexual relationship with her husband may be disrupted, her opportunities for establishing other sexual relationships may be adequate. Her economic resources make it possible for her to rearrange her life with somewhat better control than her working-class counterpart.

The second woman faces the social disruption, the psychological loss, the sexual deprivation. In addition, her religious beliefs may contribute an added level of dissonance, creating more difficulties of grief and uncertainty. Her religious beliefs may preclude acceptance of the legitimacy of a civil divorce and the possibilities for a new marital relationship. They also may militate against the establishment of nonmarital sexual liaisons. Her lack of economic resources constrains her ability to mobilize still other resources that could ease some of the burdens of running the household and caring for the children. The presence of children may add serious responsibilities to the less advantaged woman, whose reduced resources may restrict the amount of outside help—babysitters, counselors, medical experts— that she can commandeer. Of course, this is an oversimplication; however, we simply wish to convey that the content of the divorce problem may differ from woman to woman depending upon each individual's specific circumstances.

Similarly, in an overall sense, each divorce will be experienced as a highly individualized crisis according to where each divorce fits on the *crisis dimensions* discussed above. The *state of the specific family system* that the divorce affects plays an important role in determining how the family, or the individual wife, can respond to the divorce crisis. In addition, *generalized societal aspects,* such as cultural norms and institutions and the availability of institutionalized supports, add still another crucial element, as I shall discuss below.

SOCIAL SYSTEM (FAMILY) DIMENSIONS

There are several key aspects of a family system which are crucial in its ability to react to the crisis. The relationship between the nature of the crisis (i.e., determined by the dimensions of crisis) and the state of the family (i.e., determined by the dimensions of the social system involved) will influence the type of role changes that the woman can or might undertake.

Organization/Disorganization. The first dimension of the family that is relevant to crisis resolution is its level of organization or disorganization. By organization, I mean the degree to which the family members are organized into an integrated, functioning group. If the husband has been an important, integrated member of the family, more serious problems confront the wife who is left to assume his former responsibilities. This is particularly so if there are children and if the husband has been involved in their upbringing, schooling, and everyday lives. As more men obtain custody of their children, they may begin to face even graver problems in trying to take over the wife-mother's previous child-rearing and homemaking tasks.

Adaptation Coefficient. The second structural dimension of the family is its adaptation coefficient or degree of flexibility, by which I mean its ability to adjust its organized pattern to new situations by creative, meaningful, and effective realignment of its parts. When there are no children, the degree of family reorganization necessary may be very limited. The family, as such, becomes atomized into two separate individuals. If there are children, depending upon their ages and abilities, one or more of them may be enlisted to assume part of the husband-father's role. Where children are very young, the mother may have to turn to other relatives or friends to absorb part of the former husband's role.

The nuclear family, in its sparse outlines of two married adults with their children, leaves little room for adaptation within the family structure. In societies characterized by the extended family structure, such as Japan, divorce is experienced as a phenomenon relatively absorbable by the family. The adaptation coefficient of extended families usually far exceeds that of nuclear families, whose limitations produce severe consequences for wives.

Resources. The third structural dimension of the family is available resources. Resources are broadly conceived here to include money, such other material goods as cars, shelter, and furniture, and nonmaterial goods such as credit, status, and information. Ordinarily, a divorce, like all other crises, requires reallocation of resources in order to meet the threat to sustenance or survival. The wife who has adequate material and nonmaterial resources can make the transformation to former wife with comparative ease.

Unfortunately, the majority of divorced women have relatively little in the way of resources. Even those women who are employed outside the home usually find that their single incomes are not adequate to cover expenses. Some states do not award alimony, and, even in those states where both alimony and child support are technically awarded by the courts, the practical difficulties encountered in collecting alimony or child support may make it a pyrrhic exercise. Several studies have suggested that even during the first year such awards are difficult to collect, and the collection rates go down precipitously thereafter.

Resources are further restricted by the difficulty of obtaining credit, a situation that has been eased somewhat recently by law, but mostly for women with salaried positions or demonstrable collateral. This does not help the working-class woman without a job and with small children.

The degree to which the woman can develop new resources, sometimes by recognizing or redefining formerly untapped resources, will affect her ability to cope with the divorce situation. Control over resources and the ability to accrue resources are at the very heart of the matter for many women who could deal with the situation if their very existence were not threatened by lack of resources.

Nonmonetary resources also are important in the divorce crisis. Psychological and physical health and strength, friends, talent, family status, religious faith, all may be conceptualized as part of the panoply of resources that may come into play for the divorced woman.

Experience with Similar Crises. Previous experience with similar crises is the fourth dimension of family structure that is relevant to crisis resolution for the divorced woman. Close-hand knowledge of friends' or relatives' or even one's own previous divorce may help the woman to develop coping strategies that ease her predictable role transformation.

Experience with Analogous Crises. A related dimension is the effectiveness of the family in the resolution of analogous crises (i.e., sometimes a death or illness of a family member may contribute to the development of coping mechanisms). Previous ineffectiveness, however, may not necessarily lead to a more positive adaptation in the latest crisis. Earlier ineptitude in the face of crisis can seriously damage the family's ability to cope with the divorce problem.

Breadth and Complexity of Roles Prior to the Crisis. The sixth dimension, breadth and complexity of roles prior to the crisis, is an important aspect of the family structure relative to role changes demanded by divorce. As suggested above, if there is simply the married couple, who live alone without children or other relatives, the demands for role change are simpler, more direct, and more stark. The wife may dwindle into a nonwife, without benefit of any handicaps or help from additional family members. Legal constraints may accelerate the "second dwindling," so that the woman may find that she is worse off than before she was married. To illustrate, a single woman often must give up credit in her own name when she marries; however, when she subsequently divorces, she may be refused credit in her individual name. She cannot even return to the few legal privileges accorded her in terms of credit before her marriage. Serious efforts on the part of the women's movement have begun to make discrimination on the basis of marital status illegal.

Where very young children are part of the family and where no other adult members, such as a grandparent or aunt, are part of the family unit, the divorced mother has additional responsibilities if she gains custody of the children. When children are older and can assume some of the husband-father tasks—breadwinning, caretaking, etc.—the divorce-induced changes in the mother's role may be less severe. If other adult members live with the family, such as a grandparent, aunt, uncle, or housekeeper, the role transformations demanded of the wife-mother may be relatively inconsequential. In most American families, however, the wife is left alone with her children to fend as best she can, to become total breadwinner, total caretaker of children and home, and total emotional support. In view of the high geographical mobility rate of Americans, this problem often is exacerbated by the fact of living in a relatively "new" community, far from close friends and relatives.

Effects of the Last Crisis. The eighth dimension is the occurrence of the last previous crisis. The nature of the last crisis, the elapsed time since its resolution (if, in fact, it has been resolved), and the residual effects of that previous crisis have an impact on the way in which the current crisis may be handled. If the last crisis created a serious drain on family resources—psychological, financial, physio-logical, etc.—the family may be in a relatively weakened condition, with impaired coping mechanisms. In the event that the last crisis was easily resolved and important strategies for coping with crisis were developed, such as the adoption of new roles by one or more family members, the previous crisis may have provided preparatory conditions for moving swiftly into action. Sometimes the previous family crisis involved the reduction in the number of family members by marriage, geographical move, death, hospitalization, or incar-ceration. While intrinsically such a previous crisis might have drained the family resources, the reduction in family size also may have reduced the number of responsibilities the wife-mother now faces in her new position of divorcée.

Family Relations with External Systems. The next important structural dimension is the relations of the family to other external systems. Here we include a wide range of other social systems, particularly the extended family, friendship networks, occupational organizations, religious institutions, political groups, social welfare or other community support groups, and the entire range of potential support systems. The degree to which the wife faced by divorce has access to other support groups, external to the family, will determine, in large part, the degree to which she will be able to develop new avenues to resources. The basic assumption here is that the greater the network of relationships to other external systems, the greater will be the ease with which the divorced woman can effect the role transformation demanded of her in her new situation.

Information-processing System. The ninth dimension of family structure that bears on the ability of the system to respond to divorce is its information-processing system. How well information is gathered, understood, and applied to the problem at hand is a serious factor in the response patterns that can be developed.

The ability to gather, store, retrieve, evaluate, and apply information is an important means of adaptation. Women who have been part of families in which the acquisition of important information for family continuity was a standard coping pattern are able to rely on a developed methodology that now can be used to develop legal, financial, and occupational information to meet new goals demanded by the divorce situation. Women from families in which such information-processing systems did not exist are faced with the added difficulty of developing such mechanisms in order to assess how best to deal with the new complication of divorced living.

Where an organized information-processing system exists, it may be used to develop necessary resources and additional control over the problem. New resources may be recognized as the result of information gathering. Social institutions may emerge as potential absorbers of elements of the departed spouse's role. For example, a social welfare agency, previously unknown, may help to assume the economic function of the husband-father role as well as a portion of the child-caring role of the wife-mother.

One of the most important functions of the information-processing system of the family facing divorce is the assessment of how well the crisis goals are being met. If the evaluation is negative, the information system should be able to provide alternative suggestions for goal achievement.

Autonomy. The degree of autonomy of the family is the tenth dimension that is meaningful to the outcome of the divorce crisis for the individuals involved. The family which has developed an autonomous style—a capacity for independent decision-making and the exercise of control—may be able to sustain it in the face of crisis, if other factors, such as resources, flexibility, and the information-processing system, are accessible. When autonomy has *not* previously characterized the family structure, it may be even more difficult to begin to develop patterns of independent decision-making and control in the acute phase of divorce.

The question of autonomy is complicated, particularly in light of the fact that nuclear families, with their greater isolation, may have developed stronger autonomy patterns but fewer relationships with external systems. Its very autonomy may have separated the family unit from other sources of strength and help, such as extended family structures, friendship networks, and religious institutions. How the individual woman faced with divorce handles the autonomy aspect of the situation will have a very important bearing on the types of role changes that she selects in divorce.

Tension Release Mechanisms. The last dimension of the family system that we shall discuss is the availability of tension release mechanisms. Role changes in themselves are tension release mechanisms; however, here I mean to refer to other types of tension release possibilities that exist in addition to role change. The greater the number and diversity of such mechanisms, the less need for tension release through role change. Such tension release mechanisms may act as a safety valve to prevent the actualization of divorce. Tension release possibilities exist in terms of alternative relationships, alternative living arrangements (such as clubs or weekend homes), and alternative interests and avocations, including athletic activities.

The relaxation of usual negative sanctions is another important tension release mechanism. While the availability of tension release mechanisms can act to forestall the crisis, in the event that the divorce still takes place, such mechanisms can be used to ease the strain of the divorce process. New tension release mechanisms may be developed during the acute phase of the divorce period, only to be replaced by other comparable but more suitable ones during the later resolution period of the divorce process.

GENERALIZED SOCIETAL ASPECTS

There are at least two generalized societal aspects that overarch and condition the relationship between the type of crisis and the state of the family system at the time of crisis: institutionalized supports and general cultural norms and expectations.

INSTITUTIONALIZED SUPPORTS

Institutionalized supports are important during role change. Such supports can act to prevent the perpetuation of crisis even during orderly role change. The relationship between crisis and role change is very complex. So far, I have focused upon crisis—in this case, divorce—as a precipitating condition of role change. As I have noted elsewhere (Lipman-Blumen, 1973:124), "it is an undeniable paradox that in certain instances planned or non-crisis (role change) can precipitate crisis. Here it is important to note the significance of institutionalized structural supports during periods of crisis and non-crisis (role-transformations)."

One type of institutionalized supports is *rituals*. Rituals associated with life crises provide an excellent example of structural supports that protect the individual and the group at life crisis points when the dangers associated with role change are greatest. Rituals commonly mark the beginning and end of certain crisis periods and therefore keep the crisis from continuing indefinitely. Rituals often specify the mechanisms of support by which the larger society may come to the aid of the individual(s) undergoing role change. For example, in bereavement periods, neighbors and friends customarily prepare food for the widow and her children. In addition, they temporarily, and for fairly specified periods of time, take over other daily functions, such as shopping and childcare.

Rituals symbolize that the society is involved in the individual's crisis, and thus convey to the individual that he or she is not alone in this trying period. Rituals signify the society's stake both in the crisis and in the return to society and normal social life of the persons involved.

Most life crises are marked by rituals—the rituals of birth, puberty, marriage, and death. At least two life crises in American society are lacking in rituals: adolescence and divorce. There are at least two possible reasons for the occurrence of life crises that are unmarked or only insignificantly marked by rituals. One, the life crisis is a relatively new historical phenomenon—such as adolescence in modern society. Two, the life crisis is one which the society does not officially sanction or one which actually it negatively sanctions—such as divorce and excommunication, respectively.

Divorce, in its increasingly prevalent state, is a relatively recent historical phenomenon. In addition, it is a life crisis which society has no desire to promote. Thus, the comforts of social rituals are largely absent. What rituals have existed historically are primarily of a religious and legal nature and tend to emphasize the isolation of the individual from the group. They stand in sharp contrast to the rituals associated with marriage and widowhood, which underscore the individual's solidarity with the group. The few existing religious rituals and the legal rituals associated with divorce have tended to emphasize and symbolize the wife's "second dwindling" into a divorcee.

The courtroom proceedings that mark a divorce case may be

interpreted as the type of ritual that emphasizes the individual's isolation and diminution by societal rules. It is the ritual whereby the individual is stripped of her "wifely prerogatives" and legally marked as a nonwife.

The lack of institutionalized supports for divorce, particularly in the form of social rituals, has made divorce even more difficult to bear for most people. The outlet for emotion and tension available through rituals (e.g., the funeral) is denied the divorced person on any institutionalized societal basis. It is not surprising, therefore, that in modern American society psychotherapy has come to fill that vacuum for many individuals undergoing divorce. The scenario of both former spouses and often their children meeting the weekly therapy appointment is very common for families caught in the throes of divorce.

Psychotherapy serves as an institutionalized support, whose highly ritualized aspects—the punctuality and specificity of the appointed time, the exactness of the 40-minute therapeutic hour—in some ways begin to meet the need for comforting ritual. Psychotherapy, in the context of divorce, can be conceptualized as a grieving ceremony for a dead relationship. It is the ritual (i.e., funeral) marking the burial of a bad marriage.

On another level, the relationship with the therapist often temporarily replaces social networks and other support systems commonly broken as the result of divorce. Psychotherapy acts as a *rite de passage*, indicating both the appropriate period of mourning and the proper time for the former wife to undertake her new nonwife roles in society.

Another important category of institutionalized supports is *social policy*, which until recently was of little help to divorced women. Only since feminists have become active in the realm of social policy has the question of supports for the divorced woman and her children gone beyond the primitive stage of a kaleidoscope of state laws. Paradoxically, certain types of social policy have contributed to the marital dissolution rate by requiring the absence of the father in order for the children of the poor to obtain certain economic aid.

The adversary system of law characteristic of the American judicial system perpetuated the "guilt principle" whereby one of the parties had to be considered legally responsible for the marital breakdown. Such a system could only contribute to the sense of guilt, shame, and isolation that historically has characterized

American divorce. With the advent of the California "no-fault" divorce legislation in 1970, things have begun to change somewhat. Numerous states have initiated reform of divorce laws to eliminate the concept of the "guilty party." But in doing so they have frequently eliminated the chance for a dependent wife to receive an equitable settlement. Many problems still remain.

The most recent revision of the Social Security Act (Public Law 93-647) has empowered the federal government to enforce and collect court-awarded alimony and support owed by government workers. Recipients of social security payments and veterans' benefits also are subject to this legislation (U.S. Department of Labor, Women's Bureau, 1975).

More promising in some respects is the recently introduced Displaced Homemakers' Bill, through which spouses who have focused their major time and energies on homemaking may have an opportunity to receive special occupational training and other counseling preparatory to entering the labor market. These are just the very first steps that must be taken to provide institutionalized supports for the divorced person. A broad range of institutionalized supports, including recognition of the human needs for approval and inclusion in the general community, are necessary to ease the pain and difficulties that confront the divorced person.

GENERAL CULTURAL NORMS AND EXPECTATIONS

General cultural norms and expectations set the parameters within which adaptations to changing life situations can be fashioned. Expectations and norms for behavior and attitudes of the divorcée have cast a pall over her real life options. The underlying concept of sex role differentiation has created the expectation that a single parent cannot effectively rear children. Thus, predictions of juvenile delinquency, as well as social and emotional deviancy, associated with "broken homes" often have created self-fulfilling prophecies. More recent analyses suggest that single parent homes per se are not necessarily associated with juvenile delinquency (Ross and Sawhill, 1975); rather, it is the poverty level often associated with such family structures that is linked to juvenile delinquency.

The very language—"broken homes"—used to describe the family structure created by divorce is pejorative and connotes societal disapproval. Much of the language associated with divorce reflects similar social disapprobation.

Subcultural norms and expectations, associated with specific religious, ethnic, or racial groups, may introduce an additional level of strain or the possibilities of strain reduction. For example, Roman Catholic disapproval of divorce imposes a special constraint upon Catholic families even when the larger social context in which they live may be less restrictive.

On the other hand, subcultures characterized by extended family structures may have normative systems that absorb the difficulties of divorce and reduce the strain and isolation otherwise experienced by the divorced woman and her children. Earlier, we cited Japanese culture as just such an example. In addition, when subcultural and generalized cultural norms and values conflict, the strain is exacerbated.

Cultural norms about the types of adaptations that are acceptable —heterosexual remarriage, return to the parental home, communal living with nonrelatives, nonmarital heterosexual cohabitation, lesbian marriages—vary widely from region to region, and even from community to community. They are further fashioned by social class and occupational constraints.

Generalized social expectations that the formerly married woman will be lonely and isolated may act as a self-fulfilling prophecy. The ideological underpinnings of this concept suggest that single women must or should be isolated and, therefore, lonely. As a result, these women may begin to feel guilty and deviant if they are *not* isolated and lonely. Their relatives, friends, and colleagues project such expectations upon them, begin to exclude them from previously shared activities, and treat them as deviant, strange, or "shameless" if these formerly married women break through this stereotype and appear active, happy, and integrated into the larger social structure. In this way, formerly married women are practically forced into structural isolation from friendship networks, and the self-fulfilling prophecy about the loneliness and isolation of divorce occurs.

As divorce becomes more prevalent in our society, affecting more and more families, cultural expectations and norms, traditionally negative and constraining, may begin to change. In certain regions of the country, particularly the more industrialized, urbanized areas, such changing cultural norms and expectations already are apparent. As these changes occur, the types of adaptations to the divorce crisis that the individual woman can make broaden in range and flexibility.

Presumably there are other dimensions—of crisis, of the state of the family, and of general cultural expectations—that may influence the type of role change that occurs in divorce. The aspects that we have outlined here, nonetheless, act in confluence to determine in large measure the range and type of role transformations that the divorced woman has available to her. When the crisis is relatively controllable, when the family system is reasonably strong in a broad range of the outlined dimensions, and when the cultural norms and expectations are supportive rather than isolating and destructive, it is likely that the divorced woman will adapt more readily to the divorce phenomena that constitute a major life crisis for most women today.

DIVORCE AS AN OPPORTUNITY

Despite the many risks, deprivations, and difficulties associated with divorce, the seeds of opportunity for growth and new life exist within this crisis. As divorce affects more individuals, the impact on the larger society will open new avenues for development and change in the lives of the formerly married.

Demographic trends—including lower first-marriage and remarriage rates, increased age at first marriage, decreased fertility rates, higher levels of education—have been noted. They have serious implications for future family, occupation, and neighborhood structures. Concern for conservation of natural resources, coupled with reevaluation of land use, very well may lead to more heterogeneous neighborhoods.

Neighborhoods segregated by age and by marital and parental status, as well as by race, are everywhere in evidence at the present time; they may eventually become more heterogeneous when costs of single-unit dwellings and gasoline begin to change our living patterns. Such possibilities are a hopeful sign for formerly married women and their children.

In neighborhoods where young and old, married and unmarried, parents and nonparents live together, there is more possibility for interaction and cooperation among households. Neighbors can assume quasi-familial roles. For example, the aging widower living alone is not an unlikely candidate for a quasi-grandparental role vis-à-vis young children living nearby. Retired senior citizens can take an active part in the lives of divorced women and their children, and vice versa. As the distinctions between the never married, the married pair, the unmarried couple living together, the divorced individual with or without children, and the mixed groups living in communal arrangements begin to diminish, modes of interaction can begin to emerge that will lead to greater diversity and less isolation of individuals living alone or with other people.

New configurations of the adult-parent role are emerging. The number of female heads of households, we have noted, has increased enormously in the last decade. This represents merely one pattern for reconstituting the household unit. Women living with other women, with and without children, offer opportunity for cooperative arrangements. Such arrangements could free the divorced woman to enter a more demanding occupational role, to engage in recreation, to interact within her own living space with other adults. Sharing costs in such an arrangement is an added attraction.

Similar living patterns can be developed with parent and child groups, without regard to the sex of the parent. As more males seek the custody of their children, the door will open wider for heterosexual community living without the individual "family unit" sacrificing its "familial integrity."

The "singles" culture continues to grow and increasingly encompasses a wider age span. Social support mechanisms, such as Parents without Partners, begin to crop up to help routinize the common problems of divorce. As the stigmata associated with divorce gradually fade, many of the usual problems associated with divorce will shrink to manageable proportions. With eroding social disapproval, the status of "formerly married" may become preferable to that of "remarried." There will be less social pressure, direct and indirect, to remarry.

We have looked fairly intently at the direct pressures that the divorced individual faces. The indirect pressures are pervasive and require serious attention for reforms. The "couple orientation" of our society still makes social interaction more problematical for the "unattached" female, although this, too, is giving way. In private gatherings, unescorted women more and more are welcome guests. As the women's movement spreads awareness, the dread of the "single woman" syndrome is beginning to dissipate.

The advent of "the pill" and other contraceptive measures, including abortion, has gone far to relax the informal sexual pressures for the formerly married woman. Thus, one more indirect pressure toward remarriage is gradually being eliminated.

As the social pressure to remarry diminishes, divorced women with children will have increased opportunity for social interaction with men. Previously, "the divorcée with three kids" was an individual with whom romantic entanglements were best avoided. As men begin to recognize that not all divorced women are eager to remarry, they can begin to relax and just enjoy relationships, allowing these relationships to develop more naturally.

Social policy is gradually paving the way for greater opportunities for women. Legislation that bars discrimination on the basis of sex and marital status is creating opportunities for education, work, credit, and housing. Jessie Bernard has indicated the legal losses that women suffer when they enter marriage. The legal losses that they traditionally suffered when leaving marriage were even greater. Some of those inequities are beginning to be redressed—but very slowly.

Social policy changes with glacial speed. But awareness and demands can shape policy. Changing age limits on scholarships and fellowships, as well as in admission requirements in educational programs, creates a new range of possibilities for divorced women, particularly women who have been married for long periods of time. Legislation for "displaced homemakers" and court decisions have begun to recognize the need to reciprocate to women the contributions that they have made to their families and to their husbands' careers by sacrificing their own educational and occupational opportunities. Counseling programs to help women select among new options are necessary adjuncts. The Equal Rights Amendment, when it is finally passed, will help to ease the way for women in these areas.

Day-care centers would be a definite asset in aiding divorced women to reconfigure their lives. Well-run day-care and after-school centers, patterned on the Swedish model, can relieve the divorced mother of guilt and concern about leaving her children during working or recreational hours.

Divorce insurance to cover the costs of divorce and to replace or supplement alimony and/or child-support payments should be available to all couples applying for marriage licenses. Premiums could be based upon their ages at marriage, the educational and occupational histories of both partners, as well as other relevant factors. The availability of divorce insurance should not provide greater impetus to divorce, anymore than life insurance increases the possibilities for early death. Since we have managed to deal with the notion of risk in the case of life insurance where death is ultimately inevitable, the risks of divorce, which are less universal, should not present insurmountable problems. Divorce insurance should be available to both women and men and would go far toward relieving some of the economic and related burdens of divorced life.

Gradually, social policy is being designed to get at the more subtle difficulties that divorced women face. Discrimination against women in housing, particularly divorced women, and even more particularly divorced women with children, is under attack. Legislation that demands that the wife's alimony and child-support payments be counted as legitimate income in credit situations is one small step in the right direction. But the *mechanisms* for *implementing* this and other legislation remain to be developed. Labor unions must be galvanized to bring their negotiation powers to bear on implementing social policy.

The growing political power of women makes political candidates and legislators more sensitive and responsive to the articulated needs of women. As women develop strong political awareness and organizational strength, their demands will be heard more clearly.

The need to deal with the problems that characterize divorce is great. The task we face in helping women who confront the crisis of divorce is enormous. The opportunities to create new lives, new roles, new visions for these women and their children are just beginning to flourish. As Virginia Woolf understood, we cannot afford to lose "the moment."

NOTES

1. This is not to gainsay the multitudinous work on other aspects of divorce: Bernard, 1972; Burgess and Cottrell, 1939; Davis, 1950; Ferriss, 1970a, 1970b; Glick, 1949; 1957, 1973, 1974; Glick and Norton, 1973; Goode, 1951, 1963; Jualerry, 1971; Kephart, 1955; Kunzel, 1974; Monahan, 1962; Newman, 1949; Nye et al., 1973; Pinard, 1966; Roussel, 1970; Thomas, 1927.

2. In this chapter, the discussion will be confined primarily to changes in the wife-mother role, although I recognize that the father may undergo equally serious role shifts.

3. Each dimension may be conceptualized as a continuum presented here in terms of its polar opposites. A particular crisis can be placed at any point along the continuum.

REFERENCES

BERNARD, J. (1972). The future of marriage. New York: Bantam.
BURGESS, E.W., and COTTRELL, L.S., Jr. (1939). Predicting success or failure in marriage. New York: Prentice-Hall.
DAVIS, K. (1950). "Statistical perspective on marriage and divorce." Annals of the American Academy of Political and Social Science, 272(November):9-12.
FERRISS, A.L. (1970a). "An indicator of marriage dissolution by marriage cohort." Social Forces, 48(3):356-365.
——— (1970b). Indicators of change in the American family. New York: Russell Sage Foundation.
GLICK, P.C. (1949). "First marriages and remarriages." American Sociological Review, 14(6):726-734.
——— (1957). American families. New York: John Wiley.
——— (1973). "Dissolution of marriage by divorce and its demographic consequences." Paper presented at the International Union for the Scientific Study of Population, International Population Conference, Liege.
——— (1974). "A demographer looks at American families." Burgess Award Address presented at annual meeting of the National Council on Family Relations, St. Louis, October 25.
GLICK, P.C., and MILLS, K.M. (1974). "Black families: Marriage patterns and living arrangements." Paper prepared for the W.E.B. DuBois Conference on American Blacks, Atlanta, Ga., October 3-5.
GLICK, P.C., and NORTON, A.J. (1973). "Perspectives on the recent upturn in divorce and remarriage." Demography, 10(3):301-314.
GOODE, W.J. (1951). "Economic factors and marital stability." American Sociological Review, 16(December):802-812.
——— (1963). World revolution and family patterns. Glencoe, Ill.: Free Press.
GLASS, G.V., TIAO, G.C., and MAGUIRE, T.O. (1971). "The 1900 revision of German divorce laws: Analysis of data, as a time-series quasi-experiment." Law and Society Review, 5(4):539-562.
KOOY, G.A., and CRAMWINCKEL-WEEDA, I. (1975). "Forced marriages in the Netherlands: A macro-sociological approach to marriages contracted as a consequence of unintended pregnancies." Journal of Marriage and the Family, 37(4):954-968.
JUALERRY, E. (1971). "Les dissolutions d'union en France, etudiés a partir des minutes de judgement." Population, 21(June):143-172.
KEPHART, W.M. (1955). "Occupational level and marital disruption." American Sociological Review, 20(4):456-465.
KUNZEL, R. (1974). "The connection between the family cycle and divorce rates: An analysis based on European data." Journal of Marriage and the Family, 36(2):379-388.
LIPMAN-BLUMEN, J. (1973). "Role de-differentiation as a system response to crisis: Occupational and political roles of women." Sociological Inquiry, 43(2):105-129.
——— (1975a). "A crisis framework applied to macrosociological family changes: Marriage, divorce, and occupational trends associated with World War II." Journal of Marriage and the Family, 37(4):889-902.
——— (1975b). "A crisis perspective on emerging health roles: A paradigm for new occupational roles." Paper presented at the symposium on Critical Issues in Emerging Health Roles at the annual meeting of the American Association for the Advancement of Science, New York, January.

——— (1976). "The implications for family structure of changing sex roles." Social Casework, 57(2):67-79.

MONAHAN, T.P. (1962). "When married couples part: Statistical trends and relationships in divorce." American Sociological Review, 27(5):625-633.

NEWMAN, S. (1949). "Needs and future prospects for integrating marriage and divorce data with other vital statistics." American Journal of Public Health, 39(September): 1141-1144.

NORTON, A.J., and GLICK, P.C. (1976). "Marital instability: Past, present, and future." Journal of Social Issues, 32(1):5-20.

NYE, F.I., WHITE, L., and FRIDERES, J.S. (1973). "A preliminary theory of marital stability: Two models." International Journal of Sociology of the Family, 3(1):102-122.

PINARD, M. (1966). "Marriage and divorce decisions and the larger social system: A case study in social change." Social Forces, 44(3):341-355.

ROSS, H.L., and SAWHILL, I.V. (1975). Time of transition: The growth of families headed by women. Washington, D.C.: Urban Institute.

ROUSSEL, L. (1970). "Les divorces et les separations de corps en France (1936-1967)." Population, 25(2):275-297.

THOMAS, D.S. (1927). Social aspects of the business cycle (Demographic monographs, Vol. 1). New York: Gordon and Breach.

U.S. Department of Labor, Women's Bureau (1975). 1975 Handbook on Women Workers (Bulletin 297). Washington, D.C.: U.S. Government Printing Office.

11

WOMEN INTO MOTHERS
Experimental Family Life-Styles

MADELEINE KORNFEIN
THOMAS S. WEISNER
JOAN C. MARTIN

Women in this country are actively experimenting with alternative forms of family composition, affiliation, and setting. Some families are new versions of familiar models, while others have been newly invented (cf. Keniston, 1965). These new family arrangements vary in their utility and success, but they do suggest possible alternative paths for increasing numbers of women. Family experiments also suggest policy areas where legal and institutional changes may be timely.

This chapter explores the diverse ways that women are using these alternative forms to manage the many concerns facing them as they become mothers. First, the resources for basic survival must be adequate and secure—food, shelter, medical care, and the like. Second, new and different social networks and sources of information usually are needed, especially by the woman no longer located in a comfortable matrix of neighbors and relatives. Third, housebound tasks multiply just at the moment when time must suddenly be devoted to a new and insistent social relationship with

AUTHORS' NOTE: This chapter is based on UCLA's Family Lifestyles Project, which is supported in part by the U.S. Public Health Service Grant No. 1 RO1-02 MH 24947 and the Carnegie Corporation Grant B-3694. Bernice T. Eiduson Ph.D., is Principal Investigator. Senior Investigators include Jannette Alexander, M.S.W., Jerome Cohen, Ph.D., M.R. Mickey, Ph.D., Thomas S. Weisner, Ph.D., and Irla Lee Zimmerman Ph.D. (See Alexander, forthcoming; Eiduson, 1974; and Cohen and Eiduson, 1976, for additional information.)

her infant. Also, the woman now has an entirely new role—the responsibility for the nurturance and socialization of a child, which is above and beyond the mere expansion of tasks and concerns—and she has a concomitant need to find a setting in which to fulfill this role. A woman becoming a mother is also usually compelled to reexamine her relations to men or to a particular man; she may want to add or subtract a man in her life or redefine an existing relationship. Finally, the woman as mother must somehow learn to balance these new and greater concerns against the sometimes competing, sometimes complementary personal need to express herself as a productive being.

For many women, these needs can be met in a conventional family setting, but for others the availability or desirability of this path is limited. Particular life-style choices usually solve some problems and exacerbate others. Furthermore, the appeal and success of different family forms may be life-cycle specific. That is, a given family style may turn out to be a practical solution for a woman at a particular point in her life or in the child's development, while a different one may be appropriate later on. This chapter considers the family and the mother at a particular turning point—the birth of a new child—and follows the woman from that stage of the life cycle.

We have assumed the point of view of a woman embarking on the road through parenthood, dealing with the problems, opportunities, and choices that she will encounter. Despite the raised consciousness and role restructuring brought about by the women's movement, mothers are still more likely to be living with children than are fathers. However, any parent or set of parents will be able to identify with most of the concerns and alternatives described. They are the common province of parenthood. Furthermore, although we are looking at life-styles from the perspective of parents, there are women and men who do not choose to be parents, but who share the needs for survival, support, and self-expression that some alternative life-styles are designed to satisfy. For them, this chapter can provide information about the many possibilities for alternate designs of individual and group living.

A LONGITUDINAL STUDY OF FAMILY ALTERNATIVES

The description of families and the empirical data referred to in this chapter come from our work with the Family Lifestyles Project at the University of California, Los Angeles. This project was conceived and initiated with a pilot study in 1972 involving a preliminary sample of 50 families. This was a time when many countercultural men and women were becoming parents. These new families were challenging prevailing assumptions and institutions, and some of these parents began to experiment with alternative ways of rearing children. Experiments in collective living became more public as well as more numerous. Pride and public avowal by unmarried couples and single mothers replaced the shame and secrecy of previous decades. They decried negative labels such as "fatherless" or "broken" homes. The birth of children into these families compelled new interest in child development and child welfare. How would their ideals and life-styles be affected by the rigors and responsibilities of child-rearing? Would the ways in which they designed and chose their environments, lived their daily lives, earned a living, and taught their children differ from the ways of their parents? Or would they converge toward more conventional patterns after all? How would the children fare, given both the hopeful and fearful predictions of the experimenters and their critics? These broad questions, and the many theoretical and practical issues they raise, are the central focus of the Family Lifestyles Project.

To best encompass the breadth of our concerns, the project is interdisciplinary and longitudinal, bringing to bear the perspectives of psychology, sociology, and anthropology in a year-after-year focus on 150 children growing up in alternative families and a comparison group of 50 children in more conventional families. These 50 comparison families are legally married, two-parent nuclear units. Since alternative family constellations vary along many dimensions —size, seriousness of commitment, ideology, to name a few—there is always some arbitrariness in differentiating them into groups and labeling them. However, we have selected three structural foci around which many families living alternative styles do appear to cluster: (1) single motherhood, (2) "social contract" relationships (two-parent units without legal ties), and (3) collective living arrangements of various sorts.

The criteria for inclusion in one of the four sampling groups are purely and purposely structural. We did not want to make judgments about, for example, a family's "traditionality" or "uniqueness" as a condition for inclusion, partly because no reliable indicator has been identified for on-the-spot labeling and also because we wanted to cast a broad net in our sampling of the universe of alternative family styles. As a result, there is considerable diversity and variability within as well as among the four groups.

In the research design, children, not mothers, are actually the central focus. We follow babies born into these various kinds of families wherever they lead us, developmentally and geographically. Nonetheless, while the overall focus is on the child and while family style and home environment are seen as the child's milieu, the woman's concerns and outcomes as she experiences her own birth into motherhood are also well documented.

We began the study by selecting women in the third trimester of pregnancy who were living in one of the four specified family structures and who satisfied certain demographic criteria (Caucasian, aged 18-35, with a middle- or working-class upbringing) that were needed to control for other factors. We located these women through a combination of professional and network referrals and responses to posted advertisements. For each group, 50% were sought in the greater Los Angeles area, 20% in and around San Diego, and 30% in the northern half of California (Monterey to Eureka).

Fifty women from each specified family form began their participation with an interview about their attitudes, philosophies, personal histories, and expectations as mothers. Where possible, the fathers were interviewed as well (145 cases). Over the years of their participation, repeated interviews will trace the evolution of their development as women and as parents. Visits to their homes by trained observers will document their environments and child-rearing practices. Testing by child psychologists and pediatricians will assess the physical, cognitive, emotional, and social growth of the child.

Presently, all 200 babies have been born; the oldest is now 2½ years old and the youngest is just 6 months. Complete data are therefore available through 6 months of age. What is reported in this paper is drawn primarily from the early contacts with the mother —one interview in the third trimester of pregnancy, a second immediately after the birth, and the sixth-month interview and home observation.[1]

The women averaged 25 years old at the time of the birth, ranging from 18 to 32; fathers were a little older, averaging 28 with a range of 19 to 42. For two-thirds of the women, the child in our study is their first. Seventeen percent were living in rural or semirural areas at the time of their pregnancy, and the other 83% in various towns and cities. Twenty-nine percent have at least a college degree (B.A.), and 91% graduated from high school.

As well as differentiating the four structural life-style categories, one can also differentiate internally in each of the three alternate family life-styles, according to the dynamics and motivation of women becoming mothers in such families. We have identified three kinds of single mothers, which we have called Nestbuilders, Post Hoc Adaptors, and Unwed Mothers. Each type is defined according to when and for what reasons the decision to bear the children was made and how the mothers carry out their new role. We have identified two types of women in social contract families. Women in Committed Social Contract families have an ideology about non-marriage—they either are making a political statement against institutional interference in family life or believe that legal ties weaken more important emotional bonds. Women in Circumstantial Social Contract families would like to marry but have not done so because of practicalities, doubts about a particular man, or some other nonideological consideration. Collective living arrangements, because of their great diversity, can be compared in many ways, but we will differentiate in this chapter between women in Creedal Living Groups, in which the group's goals and philosophies are central to family life, and women in Domestic Living Groups, which have been formed either out of practical or social needs or out of a commitment to group living rather than to a specific "higher" ideology.

The following discussion describes the mother's role in each family life-style and how each life-style meets the common problems of (1) the provision of basic resources, (2) the organization of domestic tasks, (3) the responsibility for child nurturance and caretaking, (4) access to social supports for the mother herself, and (5) the mother's relationship with the father and/or other men. These problems are pivotal ones for new mothers. They profoundly affect and are affected by the choice of family life-styles.

SINGLE MOTHERS

Since the availability of birth control and legal abortion in California makes childbearing almost completely optional, single motherhood is increasingly a voluntary condition, different from the involuntary "unwed mother" of past generations. Empirically, however, we find that women differ in the nature, timing, and perception of their choices. One-third of the single mothers in the current study planned their pregnancy; the others chose to become mothers by not availing themselves of abortion or adoption. Likewise, women vary in their attitudes toward remaining single. Half hope to marry eventually; the others feel that marriage is irrelevant or undesirable.

The three types whom we call the Nestbuilders, the Post Hoc Adaptors, and the Unwed Mothers are distinguished by the degree of planning and choice in their pregnancy and on related attitudes, resources, and resourcefulness that the woman brings with her in the transition into motherhood. These dimensions are particularly relevant since the single mother faces even more acutely the general concerns of all mothers. She has sole and unshared responsibility for her child. She does not have the standard, taken-for-granted solutions or arrangements provided more or less automatically in the legally married family. She often must come up with creative and experimental solutions of her own devising and, in fact, may try out several such family arrangements.

THE NESTBUILDERS

One group of single mothers sees single motherhood as a defined and desirable role, even as a solution. These women are often older (28 to 32 years) and feel that they are ready for a child, but they have no mate. Many are disenchanted with men and marriage. Others may still hope for marriage but are willing to reverse the usual sequence of marriage and motherhood (cf. Klein, 1973). Meanwhile, they seek out men whom they personally perceive as good biological fathers, sometimes hoping for, but rarely expecting or receiving, involvement beyond their brief sexual relationship. Six months after the baby's birth, most Nestbuilders have minimal or no contact with the baby's biological father. In many cases, they see him less often than prior to the pregnancy. These men were usually friends or colleagues, sometimes married to someone else. A few have some contact, showing pictures of the baby or describing developmental details.

These women build a foundation for single motherhood. They

consciously prepare themselves financially by obtaining good jobs and providing for insurance needs. They make a wide variety of contacts in search of information and social support. They reject the idea of dependence on welfare, the father, or even their own kin. From the beginning, these women expect, accept, and, in some cases, want total responsibility for their child.

While our statistics show that by the end of their pregnancy, two-thirds of our single mothers receive Aid to Families with Dependent Children (AFDC) and continue to receive this aid six months later, this is not characteristic for the one-third who are Nestbuilders. Typically, they have college degrees and stable jobs. Most of them worked right up until delivery date; likewise, they were working again six months later. This spirit was reflected in the ways they anticipated and managed the postpartum period—a time they preferred to spend at home with their newborn. Several women consciously prepared for this period by soliciting temporary work assignments in the home that utilized their training and skills. For example, a commercial artist arranged to paint dolls and make designs for T-shirts at home. Another woman, employed on a research project, wrote a grant application from her home.

Our society's severance of domestic from financially productive work proves somewhat troublesome for the Nestbuilders who live alone. A few have hired household workers. Most, however, do all domestic chores by themselves. Day-care homes usually provide child care once the Nestbuilders return to jobs away from home. The mothers frequently have ambivalent feelings about these arrangements. Day-care usually means that a baby must be bottle fed, although several women, reluctant to give up completely, continue to breast-feed for the early morning and late evening feedings. They complain about the lack of day-care choices and feel frustrated if the caretaker's child-rearing philosophy and practices are not in complete harmony with their own. Even those who enjoy their work miss their infant during their long working day.

As a result of these pressures, some Nestbuilders are seeking permanent ways to earn a living from home. One mother is trying to write a screenplay; another is looking for a position as a resident manager of a large apartment building. They seek work which has some flexibility of time and can be performed at home and can thus reintegrate the domestic and economically productive work settings.

Many of these mothers intentionally seek out a system of social support. Those separated geographically and in some cases emotionally from their own parents extend their own social ties by expanding relationships with friends, neighbors, the community, and professional associates. One mother's older neighbors are called and consider themselves "aunts" and "uncles." Some of these fictive kin were even present for the baby's home delivery. Some have a friend (male or female) close enough to attend natural childbirth classes and assume the "father's" position as a labor coach. Most Nestbuilders are active seekers of information, reading numerous childbirth and development books, consulting experts, and attending childbirth preparation classes.

THE POST HOC ADAPTORS

For Post Hoc Adaptors, pregnancy is a problem, not a solution. In contrast to the Nestbuilders, Post Hoc Adaptors did not seek to be single mothers. Usually the pregnancy was unplanned; in some cases, the pregnancy was planned, but the mothers did not intend to be single. In most cases, the baby's father encouraged an abortion or adoption, but instead these women elected to bear their child and raise it alone.

These women tend to be younger than the Nestbuilders. As a partial function of the age difference, they also have less formal education. Although some have a stable working record, many have not yet established themselves in a particular occupation. Frequently, the pregnancy at least temporarily interrupts their school or career plans.

Post Hoc Adaptors typically rely on AFDC for their financial support. While some view AFDC as a source of income indefinitely, most consider it a necessary but temporary solution to their financial needs. While grateful for it, many would prefer to get off the "welfare cycle" and earn a living. Some quietly supplement their income by selling handcrafted items. Many feel that the low salaries that they could earn would be eaten up by child-care expenses. They also see this as a poor exchange for being separated for long days from their infant. By six months, some have gone back to school part-time with a clear vocational purpose in mind.

Child care for those who return to school or who simply need some time of their own away from the baby is provided in a variety of ad hoc ways, contingent upon the mother's setting. Some mothers, perhaps previously estranged from their own parents, enter a state of peaceful coexistence with them. They purposely move nearer, although rarely into the grandparents' home. Post Hoc Adaptors separated from their family often seek out other women in similar circumstances. They find acquaintances and support in natural childbirth classes, La Leche League groups, and the like. These are avenues of support and information available to and used by mothers in all life-styles, but particularly appreciated by single mothers. They often maintain these contacts and later form cooperative "play groups" for their infants, which are used for baby-sitting, as an opportunity for the mothers to exchange ideas and information about child-rearing, and as a source of playmates for their children.

Another possibility for the Post Hoc Adaptor is some sort of collective living arrangement. Some live with a roommate, generally female, but this arrangement is usually for financial reasons only and not particularly long-lived. Roommates characteristically help with general household tasks and occasionally baby-sit after the baby is asleep. Overall, roommates are a temporary expedient and are minimal in their potential to satisfy the mother's long-term needs.

Seven single mothers in the project were in one or another kind of living group. It is important to note that collective living is an attractive choice for the Post Hoc Adaptors. For a woman with limited resources of her own, collective energy, resources, and help are particularly useful. This living situation seems to alleviate many of the problems that women often look to a husband to solve. Nonetheless, many Post Hoc Adaptors, though accepting and making the best of their single status, would prefer to be married or at least in a serious relationship with a man.

UNWED MOTHERS

A third group of single mothers never quite accepts single motherhood as a positive role nor views it as an alternative life-style choice. They seem passively resigned to their situation, often regarding themselves as victims of men or fate. Since they resemble the familiar model of single motherhood of their parents' generation, we call them the Unwed Mothers. They even at times refer to themselves by this term. Most of the Unwed Mothers are anxious to be married and try countless times to get together with the usually unwilling or uncommitted father, himself either young and unprepared to take on the responsibility of a family, or older and otherwise committed.

These women tend to be the youngest of the single mothers. Many are just 18 and have not had the time to educate themselves and/or expand their job skills or experience. They are barely out of their own nest, still in the habit of turning to their parents for support. Most families, though deeply disappointed, do come to the rescue. Typically, the Unwed Mothers live in or return to their parents' household. Those who receive AFDC contribute their check to the household economy; other needs are taken care of by the mother's parents. Her parents and siblings may be available to baby-sit, although these women often sadly complain that they have no place to go. The mothers do get help raising their child—not only baby-sitting but lots of advice (sometimes too much) on how to bring up the baby. Often, the maternal grandmother relates to the new baby as the youngest member of her own family, with the dependent young mother acceding to this tacit redefinition of status. The mother usually does a significant share of the total housework, as well as supervise younger siblings, nieces, or nephews in exchange for room and board.

CONCLUSION: SINGLE WOMEN INTO MOTHERS

The conscious choice of single motherhood is a key variable determining the roles that these women define for themselves. External circumstances are, of course, of great importance in shaping the women's roles, particularly age, life cycle, and income-occupational differences among the women. Yet the autonomy and self-reliance of the Nestbuilders stands out regardless of economic advantages or life experience factors, in contrast to the dependency and lack of reformulation of familial relations characteristic of the Unwed Mothers. The Family Lifestyles Project is examining the long-term influences of these variables on both mothers and their young children.

WOMEN IN SOCIAL CONTRACT RELATIONSHIPS

A social contract couple is a family unit in which the man and woman are not legally married. The term "social contract" connotes a sense of serious commitment, which differentiates this life-style from "living together" and from the "shacking up" of their parents' generation. Even though they themselves experience a strong sense of commitment to each other, these couples continually fend off the pressures of social convention and of their own families to formalize the commitment and "really get married." For many of the women and men in these relationships, legalization and lifetime vows are undesirable. There is the persistent belief that separation, for better or for worse, is easier without the complication of legalities.

By the women's third trimester of pregnancy, one-third have been with their present partner, or compeer, three years or longer; half, from one to three years. More than half of these couples planned the pregnancy of the child studied in our project; in a few cases, this is the second child in the family unit.

Though resembling the legally married nuclear family in outward form, these alternative families do seem to be different in a number of ways. To begin with, one-third of the social contract partners, both women and men, have been previously married—twice the rate as among their married peers. Forty percent of legally married fathers have had some graduate education, compared to 14% of social contract fathers. The legally married family's income is also commensurately higher. Social contract families earn $3,000 to $20,000 per year, with a mean between $7,000 and $8,000; legally married families earn $6,000 to $30,000, with a mean between $12,000 and $14,000.

In background as well, social contract women and their compeers differ from the legally married. As children, they made many more residential moves. They were also less likely to feel close to their own parents and significantly more likely to feel close to their brothers and sisters. This is particularly significant in terms of their avenues of social support as they become parents. As one finds often with these alternative-seeking parents, women in social contract relationships are more likely to be estranged from their own families of origin. Half of these mothers see their own parents only twice a year or less (25% see them not at all), as compared to legally married mothers, half of whom see their own parents at least several times a *month*.

We have also found empirical differences in their family style. During a comprehensive sixth-month home observation of the families, 58% of the fathers or other males were present and caretaking, compared to 14% in the legally married family settings.

This finding reflects the fact that social contract families more often have a flexible, egalitarian division of responsibility. This tendency may be partly a function of the absence of a legal vow. Without a formal long-term commitment, there is a concern for not allowing either person to become overly dependent in any area of responsibility, and there is a desire for an accounting in the here and now.

The more egalitarian nature of social contract relationships may also be a function of the type of people who seek out such relationships. Most of the women, more than those in other life-styles, reported that they were in sympathy with the women's movement. Eighty percent of these women said that as parents they will not emphasize sex role differences and that they will try to treat sons and daughters similarly (compared to 59% of women in legal marriages). Their compeers are similar: 60% of these fathers, compared to 36% of their legally married peers, said that their lives had been changed by the women's movement. Women in social contract relationships also differ from the married participants in the higher priority they place on both creative and humanitarian pursuits. Again, the values of their compeers were in harmony with their own; men in social contract families most frequently ranked humanitarianism as their first or second most important value—three times as often as men in legal marriages, who instead valued career and financial success.

Just as with single mothers, women in social contract relationships differ in their reasons for entering into their particular family style. Some women actively choose the social contract status for reasons of personal or political philosophy, even though it often requires an exertion against the expectations of their parents and against the system and all its institutions. In this way, they share a certain spirit with Nestbuilders. We call this family style the Committed Social Contract. There are also women who are confined to this status only out of legal, economic, or other pragmatic considerations and would ideally like to marry. These women form what we call Circumstantial Social Contracts. These quite different motivations tend to outline the form of the relationship and the characteristic style in which the woman approaches and solves the general problems of her transit into motherhood.

THE COMMITTED SOCIAL CONTRACT COUPLES

For some women in social contract relationships, refusing to marry is a political statement, a positive act against governmental interference in personal affairs. They reject a system of laws that dictates who, when, and by whom a family commitment can be made and the complicated process by which it can be undone. Others choose a nonlegal status mainly out of concern for the quality of the relationship itself. They feel that legal marriage, usually regarded as a requisite for an enduring bond, has instead a deleterious effect on the quality of the relationship; because of long-term commitment and absolute vows, legal marriage allows people to take each other and the relationship for granted. Women in this family style often emphasize that relationships are fluid and in process, and they prefer to stay in a relationship only as long as it is rewarding in the present. Thus, their relationships are by definition open to change and are purposely not bounded by roles and vows. Typically, these are not transient relationships, but serious attempts to experiment with a form of family organization. The assumption in legal marriage that one must have a reason for separating is turned around; Committed Social Contract couples insist that there must be a reason to be together. People should be together because they want to, not because they have promised to. Self-expression, spontaneity, and interpersonal honesty are highly valued, and they feel that these values will be corrupted in the stifling presumptions of legal matrimony.

Typically, Committed Social Contract couples also question and redefine the roles associated with marriage and feel especially committed to an egalitarian division of labor in the family. In contrast to legally married couples, in which the women reported and were observed doing most domestic tasks alone, these social contract families were significantly less likely to stereotype domestic and financial tasks by sex. Tasks tended to be unplanned and shared in a flexible, variable manner.

Preliminary data indicate that this difference in flexibility of domestic tasks carries over to some extent into child caretaking roles; i.e., there was more variability in who performed caretaking functions in these families than there was among their legally married peers, among whom the mother was typically the sole caretaker. Some of this is a consequence of the fact that fewer social contract fathers were working at jobs outside their homes and therefore were more available to do child care. However, in some of these cases, the father purposely chose to stay home, consciously forgoing additional income, in order to help raise the child.

Financially, most of these women have a clear sense of their own economic contribution to the household. Six months after the baby's birth, 25% of the women were earning at least a part-time income. Those who have moved into rural areas often turn their gardens into a primary source of sustenance and sometimes raise chickens and goats as well. Like many of the single mothers, those who receive AFDC often view public assistance as a temporary solution in an economy in which jobs are scarce and require long hours of separation from their infants. Meanwhile, these women consider their AFDC checks as their personal income contribution to the household.

Some couples make a conscious effort at egalitarian reform. One family has a negotiated understanding about income and equal work sharing such that neither feels a total dependence on the other in any area of responsibility. They each are responsible for the baby's care and concurrent household tasks three days a week. This arrangement is seen not only as a matter of equity but also as a calculated effort to correct a personality imbalance that traditional roles are seen to create. These parents believe that child-care responsibilities for the man will foster the growth of his nurturing qualities and that income and decision-making responsibilities for the woman will promote assertiveness and a sense of self-reliance for her. It is interesting to note that a year after the baby's birth, when financial pressures necessitated that both parents give up the "luxury" of working less than full time, they are still trying to maintain some semblance of this arrangement. They still each have days that they are in charge, but now dressing and feeding the child are followed by packing her day's paraphernalia and taking her to the sitter's, then picking her up in the evening.

Another well-established social contract couple has formed a productive and close-knit family life with their two children during the 10 years of their relationship. In the wooded hills where they live they have designed and built a unique and beautiful home primarily of natural local materials, brick by homemade brick, and piece by salvaged piece—an ancient stove, a bowling alley lane, railroad ties. On the slopes around the house they have planted and hybridized a fruit orchard and an extensive vegetable garden and maintain a goat and poultry; from these they derive most of their food. They have minimal contact with the "conventional" world, utilizing its cash economy and institutions as little as possible. The semirural area where they live is peopled by a network of like-minded friends, who not only are an effective source of social support for the mother and her values but also have established a successful alternative school. The school is taught by all the parents and attempts to completely integrate curriculum with daily life, parents' work with the children's learning, and the natural world with the school environment. The couple's rejection of legal marriage, employment, and public school is rooted firmly in their commitment to a life that is simpler, more peaceful, and harmonious and open to whatever changes the future may bring. Their personal bond to each other and to the careful upbringing of their children supercedes and replaces the usual legal contract.

Many of these couples have applied this same spirit of critical evaluation, serious study, and experimentation to other aspects of their lives. One-third of these mothers carefully planned and carried out home deliveries. This method was chosen because they wished to ensure the father's full participation, and because they believed it superior for the mother and the infant. Nutritionally, too, these mothers often critically evaluate conventional diets and habits. They make an effort to avoid foods with additives or preservatives, and a significant number are vegetarians because they feel it to be more healthful. They frequently reject commercial canned baby food, preferring instead to make their own according to nutritional principles that they have studied. Some have also experimented with unconventional housing forms for their families. A few live in purposely primitive settings without running water and electricity. Some have built their own homes. These are generally not haphazard assemblages, but rather represent many hours and even years of study and planning to efficiently and economically utilize available resources.

Because of the emotional or geographical separation from their families of origin, many currently cluster in "counterculture" areas of a city, where their life-style is unremarkable and where they can get information from people whose values are similar to their own. For example, it was in local self-help clinics and birth centers in these areas where these women found out about home deliveries and gained access to midwives and doctors for such a delivery and also where they linked into the available social support of mothers and others with similar ideas. In this setting, social contract women are typically quite open about their nonlegal status, often retaining their own name and making it part of the child's surname.

THE CIRCUMSTANTIAL SOCIAL CONTRACT COUPLES

There are also in the social contract sample women for whom nonmarriage is less a matter of principled choice than of practical circumstance. The woman may genuinely want to marry her compeer, but be restrained by some exigency—such as waiting for a divorce to be final or preserving some tax or income advantage. Other women are being cautious; their relationship is in a trial period, as a precursor for legal marriage. Sometimes marriage itself is valued, but not with this partner. In one family, the mother finds it expedient to stay with the baby's father because he cares for the child while she attends classes; eventually she hopes to marry someone else. In other cases, it is the woman who wants to marry, but the man who is unsure or unwilling. The women in this category ultimately expect to marry either the baby's father or some other man; therefore, in spirit and style, these families often closely resemble the legally married. They view the concerns of becoming parents in a similar manner, yet without the sense of security and the protections of property provided by a legal contract.

Sixty percent of all social contract women receive AFDC, and a number are postponing marriage partly to avoid losing this support. Either their income level is so low as to necessitate this strategy, or they feel strongly the need to have some degree of financial independence from their compeer. Since many of these fathers are still unemployed when the baby is 6 months old, many of these women were thinking in terms of providing their own financial support in the interim, until the man becomes a stable provider. For these women, earning an income is an expedient. They differ in this sense from the Committed Social Contracts and also from the Nestbuilders, both of whom value and plan to continue in their sole or shared breadwinning capacity.

In terms of child-rearing and the performance of domestic tasks, these families more closely resemble the legally married, with a division of household labor along sex-stereotyped lines. Some exceptions to this occur in cases in which a woman is staying with this particular man precisely because of his helpfulness. Likewise, when the father is unemployed, he becomes more available to help, at least on a pinch-hit basis.

Women in circumstantially unmarried couples often present themselves as married and may wear wedding bands and use the father's last name. These couples also often live in conventional neighborhoods where there would be less likelihood of acceptance of their nonlegal marital status. Where the mother's own parents know the couple is not legally married, disapproval is common. All these factors combine to provide less social support for many of these women, caught as they are in a grey area, neither legally married nor truly committed to the social contract ideal of family life.

WOMEN IN COLLECTIVE HOUSEHOLDS

Collective living can take a variety of forms, differing on such dimensions as size, membership, design, beliefs and practices, and degree and kind of communality, to name only a few. The collective living groups sampled vary in size from three adults to hundreds. Out of a total of 50 living group mothers, 33 were legally married, 10 had social contract arrangements, and 7 were single mothers at the time they joined the project. The groups vary in what they share, ranging from the simple practicalities of daily life, to joint ownership of properties, to total life philosophies. A group may regard itself as one large "family" of brothers and sisters, perhaps under the stewardship of a charismatic or spiritual leader. Nuclear ties are at times intentionally diminished, with children separated from their parents or parents from each other. As a corollary, children may be regarded as everyone's children, with the responsibility taken from the parents and lodged with the group as a whole. In other groups the nuclear family unit is preserved intact; families enter, live in, and leave the group as a discrete unit.

There is no typical design for a communal dwelling. This is partly because collectives vary so greatly in size and structure, but more importantly because housing was never designed with collective living in mind. These groups have had to take the existing structures and adapt them to their needs. Occasionally they build from the ground up, but generally an adaptation is ingeniously devised. The use of space is reinterpreted such that abandoned mansions, no longer economically feasible for most nuclear families, are revived and put to new use. Apartment complexes, duplexes, or triplexes, especially those with some central court or other centripetal space, are taken over completely. Rows of houses become a communal "neighborhood." Tents, buses, and shacks are drawn into a wagon circle in the open countryside or the woods. An abandoned motel is unboarded and reawakened. A farm is reorganized for people more than for animals and farm functions, so that the outbuildings become bedrooms even while retaining their colorful original names: "the Brooder Shed," "the Pumphouse," "the Springhouse."

Household tasks and income production are assigned and organized in many different ways. In some groups, sacred texts, leaders, or governing boards make these decisions. Other groups are explicitly democratic and experimental; decisions are made and enforced by house meetings, with posted rules and schedules; typically there are periodic reassessments. In these latter groups, diversity and change are accepted, even taken for granted.

For the purposes of obtaining a great range of types of collective households for the Family Lifestyles Project, the selection criteria were minimal: the household had to contain some number of people above and beyond the mother and her husband or compeer, and some degree of economic and/or value bond had to be in evidence.

COLLECTIVE LIVING AS AN INTEGRATED SOLUTION

At every income level, there are potential economic benefits to communal living. Buying power in housing, food, and utilities can be maximized. In the inflationary housing market, young families who cannot independently afford their dream of a home and a yard can realize it if they share resources with one or more other families. If two families share one large household, there can be one washer and dryer, one vacuum, one stove instead of two. For many women this is desirable not only as a simple savings, but also as an ecologically sound use of resources. Welfare payments in this setting can stretch to a more livable income. Child-care costs can be reduced to zero. A mother who wishes to work outside the home is often freer to do so, and a mother who does not is often relieved of the necessity to do so. For the relatively affluent, conveniences and luxuries such as a swimming pool, grand piano, or library are more financially feasible.

In all groups, there are private tasks and common tasks. Each person or couple has responsibility for their own space, be it sleeping mat, room, or apartment. We observe that the average number of tasks that the mother does alone is less than half the number in other life-styles. In addition, teamwork alleviates the monotony and isolation associated with housework. "Just housework" becomes elevated to the status of "Work," publicly defined and publicly recognized as an essential contribution (cf. Oakley, 1974).

The presence of other parents and children in 71% of the living groups provides access to playmates for the child and the possibility of shared caretaking for the mother. Whether to go to work, take a class, or just have a long bath, the mother can call on someone who knows and cares about her child. At the sixth-month home observations we found these children having more caretakers and more changes of caretakers than in other living arrangements. As a simple index, twice the number of people were generally within view of the child during these observations as in other family settings.

The pattern of assistance in which the mother retains full primary caretaking responsibility is the most common arrangement. But some groups have appointed or hired chief caretakers. In other groups, members take turns (either all group members, all parents, or all who are willing) in some sort of schedule of shifts, with a written log of each child's behavior handed from caretaker to caretaker. Some groups have only a general agreement that whatever adult happens to be present assumes the responsibility for supervision.

The needs for and types of relationships with men are influenced by communal residence. For example, none of the single mothers in our project who live in collective households report that marriage is important to them, whereas half the single mothers outside such groups do value and want marriage. Living groups offer security to women which can reduce some women's desire to marry; these women may feel greater freedom to choose single motherhood or a social contract status. In addition, relationships between couples are altered due to the immediate group support that each member can draw on. For instance, both parents can gain more free time once responsibility for income production, household maintenance, and child care are shared. Some couples find it easier to practice sex-role egalitarianism when there is group solidarity and pressure to change old habits. Explicit ideals, group decision making, and public posting of rules and tasks can encourage change. In some groups, fidelity and kindness between spouses is valued and publicly enforced with group pressure. Bolstering, exhorting, and nagging can be diffused from the couple to the relatively impersonal group framework of rules and sanctions.

In our sample, women in collective households tend generally to be more alienated from their families of origin and seem to have substituted the group matrix as a kind of self-selected extended family. The alienation is graphically evident in the third trimester interview. Only half as many mothers in living groups as in legal nuclear residential arrangements report good relations with their own mothers and fathers. Only a third of the parents of living group women feel good about their daughters' life-style, and a full third feel negatively. At the time the baby is 6 months old, far more living group mothers have "infrequent" (less than once a month) contact with their own parents than the legally married participants in nuclear households. The substitutive social support function of the group is also clearly demonstrated by the fact that one-third of these mothers had home deliveries of their babies within the living group setting.

Collective living can create problems as well as solve them. For instance, not all groups allow or value children, and some offer only minimal help or support to the mother, in spite of the great potential for mutual assistance. Groups may alleviate isolation, but the members sacrifice privacy. Some aspects of group life can stress the parents' personal relationship—e.g., reduced privacy, other relationships competing for the mate's time, or pressures to change familiar patterns. Some marriages and social contracts may be easier inside a group, but some will split apart. Also, one may not like or get along with certain other members but be compelled to work side by side with them. Another important drawback for some women is the demonstrated instability of many living groups; they tend to dissolve after a very few years in most cases. (Creedal groups are an exception; see the discussion below.) At the very least, personnel changes are common, with the child and the mother required to make and break attachments frequently. Finally, the inevitable diminution of autonomy is not for every woman. Women are answerable to others and, in creedal groups, to religious or ideological goals as well—such as community service to drug addicts, an unwanted move to a foreign country, or simply distasteful work assignments. Large, hierarchical groups are more stable but often require greater sacrifice of self and a confession of faith that would be unacceptable or inappropriate for many women. Choosing a compatible living group setting is clearly comparable in many respects to selecting a mate.

All these considerations about collective living—the problems, the opportunities, the variety—have a general effect on the woman's day-to-day life-style and mothering role. For all the differences and similarities among various groups, however, we can differentiate them into two fundamental types: those with a commitment to the life-style itself or the advantages and promise it offers, and those with a commitment to a creed or ideology that surmounts the life-style but which the life-style may serve to further. The former we call Domestic Living Groups and the latter Creedal Living Groups.

DOMESTIC LIVING GROUPS

Historically, communal experiments were likely to be large and internally oriented and thus relatively isolated from the larger society, often retreating to the countryside or even to new territory as pioneers (cf. Hostetler and Huntington, 1971; Muncy, 1974). These kinds of groups still exist, but a new model has also been born to meet very different needs (cf. Jaffe, n.d.).

Many of these domestic arrangements burgeoning at the present time seem to be affiliation-oriented, a conscious effort to create a hybrid of neighbors and self-selected extended family. Personal compatibility, a search for mutual assistance, and sometimes disillusion and alienation from technological values bring these people together. No shared central ideology, no particular leader, no significant joint-ownership of resources ties them to one another beyond immediate exigencies and conveniences. Most are small (3-6 adults). Some are urban and oriented toward, rather than away from, the larger society. In fact, group living is sometimes sought to facilitate career opportunities, because of the capacity to simplify household maintenance, child care, and accessibility of social contacts. Others are attempts to live close to the land and out of mainstream urban America. Another frequent characteristic is a zeitgeist of experimentation, of a search for a more humane, creative, and satisfying form of family life. Women, whether single, married, or socially contracted, are in these groups by design, seeking a better environment for themselves and their children.

For example, two Los Angeles families, one legally married, the other a social contract relationship, established a Domestic Living Group during the year prior to their entry into the project. These families had previously lived in adjacent apartment buildings. As neighbors, they had become quite friendly, frequently sharing meals and social experiences. They decided to share a home not only in order to afford a larger dwelling and space for a garden and chickens but also in order to experience the warmth of a larger "family." These four parents are all committed to personal values of cooperation and egalitarianism in the ways in which they rear their children. They felt it particularly important that their infants be cared for in their own home and by other "family" members who knew them well. Both of the women were pregnant when they moved in together. After the births the families helped each other on an informal, casual basis with the care of the infants. Housework and meal preparation were divided and rotated among the four adults. The arrangement worked well, but at the end of a year the social contract couple decided to move to northern California. This couple is now looking for a communal group in a rural setting; the married couple has returned to living as a nuclear unit, which they find they prefer.

CREEDAL LIVING GROUPS

Creedal Living Groups are distinguished from others by a system of values and beliefs that all members share as a condition for membership in the group. Sixty percent of our sample of living groups are of this type. Most of the groups are based on a religious belief system—Western, Eastern, or Western adaptations of Eastern religions. The rest of the groups are based on various other ideologies.

In the creedal groups, each person shares a defined source of their particular Truth, whether a sacred text, an anointed leader, or both. Some leaders live among their followers, some are in foreign countries, and some are alive only in spirit. Common features include rules and rituals for daily life and a clear line of authority to elders, masters, or teachers for daily guidance on behavior, diet, clothing, sex, etc.

For women living in these groups, the economic, social, sexual, and parenting problems are often regarded as the concern of the entire group, not only of the individual. Groups may pool outside income; they may operate their own manufacturing or service business. They may collectively and publicly solicit donations or receive contributions or grants. Group self-sufficiency is frequently a strongly held value, often accompanied by a pride that precludes the taking of any state aid. They may maintain an extensive enough agricultural operation to feed themselves and even sell surplus.

From the point of view of the woman with a baby, responsibility for solvency is taken off her shoulders at this critical time. Money comes in and goes out, rent is paid, provisions are purchased, while her contribution can vary with her abilities at the moment. However, while she is often free not to work, she is often *not* free *to* work if she wishes. Some groups dictate duties and the division of labor according to codified rules. For example, perhaps only minor work is allowed outside the home, or only women are allowed to do child care. To many women, this lack of choice is a disappointment, but for others it is a liberation from worry and responsibility. A woman who wants and/or can accept such a centrally organized and structured setting is provided with a stable, secure, and protective home.

Creedal group members often speak of "dying to yourself," "breaking the will," "transcending the flesh," and other exhortations to consider the other and the whole above oneself. There is in addition the pervasive notion of a "chosen people," an elite spiritual corps with a special mission. This ambiance of higher purpose is in and of itself a bulwark of psychological support. Individual members are therefore very special to one another. The individual is not just anyone. Even groups that house nonmembers in "crash pads" or halfway houses or provide other ministry services make a distinction between outsiders and insiders.

In creedal groups, division of labor tends to be traditional, with women having responsibility for household maintenance and child rearing. Furthermore, the usual practice is for the mother herself to have primary responsibility for her own young children, even though other women may take important roles. In easy reach are other "sisters" to help out or free the mother for her other tasks. Some groups, however, do not follow this pattern but experiment with nontraditional caretaking arrangements. They may employ men as caretakers, have nonmother primary caretakers (as the *metapelet* on the kibbutz—Spiro, 1965) or require child-care shifts from all members.

In addition to providing personnel for child care, a group must also specify or arrive at what child-rearing philosophy and practice is consonant with or fosters the group goals. In groups following an old-established religion with written texts, great detail about such matters is often dictated. In others, in which there is no text or in which families per se were never included in the membership (for instance, in which members traditionally were all celibate priests) ideas about the proper way to raise a child are still evolving.

From the point of view of the mother, having her child in someone else's trusted care obviously relieves her of the moment-to-moment worry of a child and frees her to pursue other activities. But from another point of view she is also partly relieved of a right or privilege to rear her child as she sees fit. A great deal of trust in the concern and shared values of other caretakers is therefore needed. Even if she does all her own child rearing, she is expected to follow the established practices of the group in most cases, with social or disciplinary pressure sometimes brought to bear in the event of maternal resistance. She has somehow to reconcile her own inclinations with the rules or consensus of the group or endure public disapproval. One mother in our sample eventually left a living group because of this conflict, even though she did not leave the faith. In her case, she could not inflict the physical punishment on her child which was the creedal norm.

Even the decision to have a child in the first place may be determined by the group's need for new bearers of the faith or, on the other hand, by its need for the woman as laborer rather than parent. Sovereignty over adult personal relationships in most creedal groups also rests with the group: choice of partner, limits on premarital and extramarital relations, frequency of sexual relations, birth control, and similar matters are determined according to explicit rules of the community. At the extreme, sex even between married people is restricted to a highly ceremonial mating for procreative purposes only.

Although most of the creedal groups in the study are religious, some are frankly secular. One such group has an ideology based on maximizing sensory and material satisfaction and has a founding leader who inspires and instructs them in this pursuit of pleasure. There are branches in various cities, some of which have existed over five years. Another multiresidential creedal group, even longer-lived and also inspired by a charismatic leader, was established as a self-appointed guardian of what they idealize in America's past.

Several other creedal groups are dedicated to revising the typical sexual bonding in the family unit to include more people; this small but unique subset of living groups is called Expanded Marriages. In our sample, we have three triadic "marriages" and one group marriage consisting of eight adults. The ties are sexual, emotional, and financial, completely paralleling conventional legal marriage. Moves in and out of the expanded marriages are far more weighty than a mere change in life-style. These decisions and changes are equivalent in magnitude to any marriage or divorce. Emotional upheavals, concern for the effect on the children, and seeking marital counseling would all be likely to accompany any dissolution. All adults are viewed as each child's mothers and fathers. This concept is often difficult to mesh with the institutions of the larger society. For example, in one triad, both "fathers" wished to be present at the birth of the child, but only one was allowed into the delivery room. The expanded families tend to be viewed with suspicion by the larger community and by their own families of origin. Unlike a larger communal group, the triads cannot rely on solely within-group social support when they feel estranged from the larger community, because they simply are not big enough. Support is sometimes obtained by participation in an organization that promotes, educates, and supports people interested in alternative sexual-emotional relationships (e.g., open marriage, expanded families).

CONCLUSION—LIVING GROUP MOTHERS

There are other collective living alternatives beyond the ones that we have described, and more may be discovered as women continue to experiment with new solutions to their common concerns as mothers. What we have attempted to portray, in addition to the diversity, is the seriousness of purpose and the sense of searching that often pervades these groups. The popular stereotypes of cults of "irresponsible hippies" dominate the media and drown out the message that resourceful people are trying to create a new form of family affiliation.

WOMEN IN LEGAL MARRIAGES

Most of the legally married parents in our study were located through obstetricians randomly selected from the American Medical

Association directory in an effort to obtain something resembling "typical" or "normative" American families in the same geographical areas as the alternative families, for purposes of comparison. A smaller portion of this group was obtained through network sampling in the same way as the people in the three alternative life-styles.

For a substantial number of legally married parents, marriage is not a chosen "life-style" so much as simply the right thing to do. They may question who or when but not whether to marry. When we asked these mothers why they chose their life-style, we were often greeted with a puzzled expression. They perceive marriage not as a life-style among life-styles, but as a normal event in the life cycle.

There were, however, 14% of the married women interviewed who stated that legal marriage either never was or no longer is important to them. Some of them were married before the women's movement and other social forces encouraged women to consider arrangements other than those previously taken for granted. Some who do not value marriage are propelled into it for purely practical considerations, such as tax advantages, pacifying their own parents, or legitimizing the baby. Many of them are critically evaluating the idea and practice of marriage. In a few cases no wedding rings are worn, no last names are changed, and the couple present themselves socially as unmarried. Within these families we also frequently find less conventional role divisions.

For most of the legally married women, however, the two-parent nuclear family, legally attested and tied into an established framework of kin and neighbor relationships, is still their ideal family model. The wife is expected to maintain the domestic sphere while the man is designated as the material provider. The marriage ceremony signals a welcoming into the fold extended to the new couple on the part of the existing family network, even in cases in which the couple has been previously living together. Kin and "good neighbors" back up the woman with emotional support, information, and, at critical times, practical assistance. The legally married nuclear family has access to this ready-made blueprint for building a family: familiar models, designated roles, and socially approved patterns of behavior.

Overall, the married parents in our project are finding that the model is still viable, at least by comparison with the other family alternatives being studied; for most people it is still the more stable and reliable way to cope with the fundamental concerns of childbearing and child-rearing. More than half of the legally married sample have been with their mate five years or more, and 90% three years or more. This is longer than the typical relationship between social contract compeers and, of course, much longer than that between single mothers and their men. They are also far less likely to have been divorced; for 90% this is a first marriage. Eighty percent live in houses, as opposed to apartments or more transient arrangements. The father is almost always employed, and family income is at the national urban average, higher than in any other family life-style.

Almost half of these fathers rank "career" as their highest or second highest value. The mothers are more likely to place their highest priority on "family" and "security," and 86% assert that legal marriage is important to them. This emphasis on stability is consistent with the reality of their daily life from the point of view of such objective measures as length of relationship, residence patterns, and financial security. Furthermore, almost all these women are receiving some of the social support from families that the institution of marriage supposedly promises. Only three women out of the whole group reported anything but good relations with their own parents. Both grandparents on both sides feel positively about the parents, the life-style, and the new baby. In about half the cases, the women were seeing their own mother at least twice a month during their pregnancy. The figures are substantially the same at the time of the six-month interview.

The married participants, being demonstrably more security-minded and also involved in one uninterrupted relationship, usually have been on a stable regime of birth control for the several years of their marriage. Three-fourths of these women planned their pregnancies (many more than in the other family style groups as a whole), and very few have had previous abortions. (By contrast, half the project women in other kinds of relationships have had previous abortions.)

ALTERNATIVES WITHIN LEGAL MARRIAGE

We are not going to enumerate the conventional nuclear family roles and solutions to the problems facing new parents; this has been done many times before. Instead, we will mention certain changes that we are seeing in marital relations and role assignments. Egalitarian shifts, with women more often working outside the home and men more often sharing domestic and child-care responsibilities, are occurring in many families. Rather than simply adding employment to a woman's other responsibilities, there is beginning to be a real reinterpretation of roles and reallocation of household responsibilities. These trends are clearly visible in our sample of legally married families.

In 10 of the 50 legally married families, awareness and practice both have markedly shifted away from the previous sex stereotypes. In one case the woman supports the family financially by teaching in a junior college. She and her husband divide the other responsibilities and share the child-rearing, but he may properly be regarded as a house-husband. In another family the man's career allows him to be in his home workshop a great deal of the time. Another room is set aside for the woman's painting. With both of them doing a lot of their important work at home, they have developed an informal but very workable system of child-care in which one or the other assumes complete responsibility depending on which is available at any given moment. The other parent is therefore free to be involved with work or friends. In this family, what little housework is done is still in the woman's province.

In a more conventional example, both parents have careers away from home to which they are seriously committed, and so they have devised a different system of shared responsibility for their infant. The father has taken on the "morning shift" with the baby, changing the diaper and making breakfast and taking her to the sitter's before leaving for his job as an accountant. The mother does the evening caretaking. Each parent values this time with the child as part of a full parental role. In this family, each parent uses his or her own surname and the baby carries both.

Thus "conventional" legal marriage is undergoing changes too, as many of the values and practices of experimental families are becoming a part of American family life. This reinforces our belief that experimental families, though small in number compared to legally married nuclear families, have had and are having an influence far beyond their numbers.

as expedient, temporary solutions both qualifies our notion of choice and underscores the fact that a variety of options are indeed available.

There are other women who have clearly chosen their unconventional life-style with an experimental or pioneering spirit—the Nestbuilders, Committed Social Contracts, and many of the women in collective living groups. These are the women who are not only pursuing but also creating and further cultivating alternative life-styles. The impact of their attitudes and efforts has allowed other women to begin to look at their life-style as one among many. In this sense, marriage too is transformed into an option, a possible life-style among others, rather than a prerequisite for family life.

We do not clearly understand the relationship between life-style choice and personality. We have referred, for example, to the autonomy of the Nestbuilder, the dependence of the Unwed Mother, the independence of women in Committed Social Contract relationships, and the compliance required in some Creedal Living Groups. However, we do not know whether or how these life-styles attract or forge these types of women. Personality per se has not been a research focus of this study.

We have looked at some common needs and structural factors facing all mothers as they raise young children. These common problems not only influence the choices that women make but also are affected by those choices. We have tried to emphasize the complex interaction between life-style choices and mothers' roles. One important finding is that each life-style solves these problems differently. Women may change their life-styles or make other changes as these needs and common problems become more explicit and important for both mother and child.

Participants in our study often ask us if what they are doing is the best or the most appropriate for themselves and their children. It is premature for us to make any judgments of this nature, for we are in the preliminary stage of data analysis of a longitudinal study. The information presented in this chapter stems mainly from our earliest contacts with participants whom we hope to follow for a number of years. Furthermore, we are unsure how to ultimately evaluate these experimental family life-styles. What criteria shall we use? For example, are we to emphasize stability or change? Certainly the criterion of stability is not one congenial to many mothers who specifically value experimentation. Should we use the criterion of internal consistency? Here again it is not clear that consistency is an appropriate choice, since many of our participants value diversity. Our judgments as to the success or failure of specific life-styles may always remain relative ones. One criterion that we might use is the success with which mothers are able to approximate their own stated goals. For example, mothers who value individual autonomy and independence are unlikely to find Creedal Living Groups a viable alternative, whereas women seeking extensive social support may find that Creedal Living Groups are an attractive and successful option. Women who value autonomy and independence may view Nestbuilder-type single motherhood as an ideal family life-style because of the freedom to make decisions and to structure their lives with only limited consideration for or compromise with the needs of others. Yet even the issue of freedom is relative. Whereas the single mother has the freedom to make her own decisions, she is never free to act spontaneously with regard to her activities but must find child care. She must plan ahead each and every time. Freedom for the living group mother is usually the converse, with great freedom moment to moment in some groups, but the ever present necessity to consider others in most decisions that she faces. Here the relative judgments involved are even more complicated than if we use absolute criteria. At this point in our research, we can only document the wide range of life-style options that we have found and continue to maintain contact with our participants in the coming years. Perhaps the parents and children themselves will point us toward more satisfactory criteria and toward some understanding of the relative outcomes and successes of these diverse family life-styles.

NOTE

1. Data presented throughout this paper come from the detailed interviews, question-naires, and observations with the participants. There are actually over 50 babies in each life-style to allow for eventual attrition. Furthermore, the precise sample size varies for different variables, data sources, and time periods. Percentage comparisons between the life-style groups were selected to illustrate general group differences. More detailed and systematic presentations of these and other data are available from the authors and will be appearing in subsequent publications.

REFERENCES

ALEXANDER, J. (forthcoming). "Alternative life styles: Relationship between new realities and practice."

BERNARD, J. (1974). The future of motherhood. New York: Penguin.

COHEN, J., and EIDUSON, B. (1976). "Changing patterns of child rearing in alternative life styles." In A. Davids (ed.), Personality development. New York: John Wiley.

EIDUSON, B. (1974). "Looking at children in emergent family styles." Children Today, July-August.

EIDUSON, B., COHEN, J., and ALEXANDER, J. (1973). "Alternatives in child rearing in the 1970's." American Journal of Orthopsychiatry, 43:720-731.

GREENFIELD, P. (1974). "What we can learn from cultural variation in child care." Paper presented at the 140th meeting of the American Association for the Advancement of Science, San Francisco.

HOSTETLER, J., and HUNTINGTON, G. (1971). Children in Amish society. New York: Holt, Rinehart and Winston.

JAFFE, D. (n.d.). "The dynamics of couples in domestic communes." Unpublished manuscript.

KANTER, R.M. (1972). Commitment and community. Utopias and communes in sociological perspective. Cambridge, Mass.: Harvard University Press.

KENNISTON, K. (1965). The uncommitted: Alienated youth in American society. New York: Dell.

KLEIN, C. (1973). The single parent experience. New York: Walker.

MELVILLE, K. (1972). Communes in the counter culture. New York: William Morrow.

MUNCY, R. (1974). Sex and marriage in utopian communities. Baltimore: Penguin.

OAKLEY, A. (1974). Woman's work: The housewife past and present. New York: Pantheon.

SPIRO, M. (1965). Children of the kibbutz. New York: Schocken.

ZABLOCKI, B. (1971). The joyful community. Baltimore: Penguin.

CONCLUSIONS

JANE ROBERTS CHAPMAN

This volume has analyzed the status of women by looking at the complex of problems surrounding marital status. The legal, economic, and social status of women is tied to the status of wives, because most women are married for some portion of their lives, and society's legal and social institutions are predicated on that fact. On assuming this marital status, women profoundly affect their economic position, their legal rights, and their likelihood of becoming dependent upon a person or a public assistance program. Chapter 9, written by Margaret Gates, demonstrates that some of these effects continue long after the marriage is terminated by widowhood or divorce.

Opponents of equality for women have based much of their opposition on the contention that if women (most often referring to wives) gained equality they would lose a host of privileges and protections which they now enjoy. This book demonstrates that married women cannot lose those privileges and protections, because they do not have them. State and federal laws treat married women differently from married men—for example, they restrict the financial rights of women. But they do not counterbalance these restrictions with guarantees that married women will be supported by husbands. Even when states have "support" laws, they are not enforced (see Chapter 4, by Joan Krauskopf), because judges consider it improper to interfere in an ongoing marriage. Sheila B. Kamerman (Chapter 8) finds that U.S. public policies affecting "the family and its members are fragmented, inconsistent, and contradictory," with many aspects that reinforce women's dependency on husbands, or limit women's choices and options regarding major roles, or treat them inequitably.

Fifty-five percent of women are not in paid employment, and most are dependent on others for their livelihood. The influence of their dependency is far-reaching, touching all women. This is because the legal and social structure frequently assumes that all women are dependents whether they are or not. For example, for years married women were denied credit in their own names. It took several years of public pressure and passage of a federal law to begin to open up credit to married women who had their own incomes and were credit-worthy. As we learn in Susan Kinsley's Chapter 3, institutions such as the social security system base their benefit structure for working men on the presumption that married women are dependents of their husbands.

Some dependency is no doubt voluntary. But much of it is imposed by legal, cultural, economic, or psychological constraints. And it is difficult and perhaps meaningless to attempt to separate the dependency which is voluntary from that which is caused by social indoctrination, lack of job opportunity or training, or overwhelming child-rearing responsibilities. Mary King, Judith Ann Lipshutz, and Audrey Moore (Chapter 5) report that married women experience higher rates of mental illness than single women, and it is believed that it is the marital role itself "rather than any biological differences that causes psychological malaise."

The papers that constitute this book have delineated the nature and scope of women's dependency. In addition, the chapters set forth a variety of options that would reduce female dependency. Implicit in these discussions is the belief that dependency is a bad thing. Of course, if marriage is a loving partnership in which each contributes according to his or her preference and abilities and each receives not only equal benefits from their joint labor but also equal protection before the law, then the fact that one partner earns money and one does not is not necessarily invidious.

But most marriages are not this way. In fact, the best intentions in the world between two spouses can hardly make marriage such a partnership. The law, institutional structures, and other forces will put the woman in a disadvantaged position in the marriage whether she and her husband wish it or not. (A married man who does not engage in paid employment faces some of the disadvantages of a dependent wife, such as lack of social security coverage, but not the full range of legal disabilities faced by a nonworking wife.) Diann Holland Painter (Chapter 6) contrasts the situation of the middle-class wife with that of the women who insure the survival of their families by shifting their dependence from the traditional nuclear family arrangement to dependence on other types of structures. "They become dependent on kinship ties, friendship networks, and public assistance."

In her analysis of marriage, Joan Krauskopf (Chapter 4) points out that the low economic return for the effort invested is sufficient to discourage the wife who does not currently need money from obtaining training or employment. "Thus, we have a vicious circle of dependency forever revolving: channel women into a protected and dependent role; use their dependency and protection as a rationalization for keeping them dependent; channel them into the role because they are dependent."

If a woman lives in a substantial house that she co-owns and if she has access to a joint checking account and is obliged primarily to care for the home and children and to do pleasant things in the suburbs, it is more difficult to perceive her as a dependent or to perceive dependency as bad. But the papers presented in this book demonstrate that she can be rapidly reduced to poverty if the man from whom she derives her living is removed from the scene. This is the fearful side of the homemaker-breadwinner bargain.

Some dependency could be reduced by law change, but not all. If the property and domestic laws were reformed along the lines suggested by Krauskopf, a married woman would become a full partner in the economic matters of the marriage. If one spouse earned or otherwise secured assets, the other spouse would share in them. This would tend to establish the economic worth of the nonemployed spouse. But it would not eliminate the dependency problem, because a husband can share all his assets with a wife except his most useful one, his earning power. And despite equal legal and property rights within the marriage, a nonworking wife would still be dependent for her bread and butter on the ability and willingness of another person to earn it for her.

This book has set forth the barriers of various sorts that encourage women to be dependent and that impede their efforts to be independent. It also points out the kinds of policy changes needed for women to be equal in their marital relationships. The unmet policy needs range from social security reform to flex-time, from shelters for abused wives to new inheritance tax codes. But the unanswered question is whether there will be a constituency to press for these changes.

If the past is any guide to the future, the government will do no more than respond slowly to outside pressures. There is some doubt that state governments will even do that. A state legislator in Oklahoma in a public statement opposing the Equal Rights Amendment said, "Woman was not made from Adam's head so she could think." Reform efforts introduced into the legislative climate indicated by that remark will not be easy to implement. Jean Lipman-Blumen (Chapter 10), in observing the impact of divorce on society, notes that social change is clearly underway but that "social policy changes with glacial speed."

The women's movement has been criticized as being for working women only, especially professional working women. This is not now the case, if it ever was. Activist women's groups now operate on the premise set forth by Elizabeth Cady Stanton in a letter to Susan B. Anthony in 1853: "I feel, as never before, that this whole question of women's rights turns on the pivot of the marriage relations, and mark my word, sooner or later, it will be the topic for discussion." Establishing the economic value of a homemaker's duties and pressing for legal changes that would secure economic security for full-time homemakers have been objectives of NOW task forces and the National Commission on the Observance of International Women's Year and a host of other women's organizations.

Because of the widespread assumption that women are dependents and men are breadwinners and heads of household, women as a group cannot achieve equality until two things are achieved. First, the dependency of wives must be eliminated as a presumption from law, public programs and private institutions. Public programs and policies must be formulated and implemented in a more neutral fashion based on the notion that all adult citizens are equal individuals. Second, the level of actual (as opposed to legislated) economic, social, and psychological dependency must be significantly reduced. It would be simplistic to say that all women should be in the labor force. But we must move further in that direction if equality is to be achieved. Mary P. Rowe (Chapter 7) presents a persuasive case for the involvement of men in child-rearing, not only to reduce female dependency but also to improve the lives of men and children.

Dependency appears in its ugliest form in the homes in which husbands inflict violence on wives. Murray A. Straus (Chapter 2) says that the cultural norms and values that permit or encourage husbands' violence against their spouses reflect the male-dominant society of the Western world. The right to use force exists to provide the ultimate support for the existing power structure of the family, if those low in the hierarchy refuse to accept their place and roles.

One wonders why a woman would live with a man who beats her. One such wife said:

> I stay because I have nowhere else that I belong. I don't fight back because I am afraid to. I don't charge assault and battery because I went through that courtroom scene and was fined and admonished by the judge to "go home and mind your husband and never bring your domestic quarrels to my court again." [NOW, 1976:4]

This to me is the saddest of statements. Certainly violence has been done to other helpless people, such as prisoners, or slaves or children. But when a free, uninstitutionalized adult is beaten by a person who is supposed to be a loving, supportive family member and then says she endures it because she has no alternative, one reaches some sad conclusions about the family, the victim's self-view and society. If society cared about such women, there would be help for them and places for them to go.

A national poll of women's attitudes in 1975 found that, while most women still considered having a husband and family to be a very important goal in life, almost half felt that a partnership arrangement would be ideal (Roper Public Opinion Research Center, 1974). Some other signs of change in the legal-economic-social relationships between men and women are becoming evident. The project on alternative family styles at the University of California, Los Angeles (Chapter 11), investigates this trend noting that "change, variability, and flexibility in family arrangements is becoming the norm, not the exception to be explained." The expectation of the children discussed by Raphaela Best (Chapter 1) changed greatly over their grammar school years. The author attributes this largely to the impact of the women's movement and the alternatives it is making known to adult society. If these children foretell the men and women of the 1980s and 1990s, then our legal institutions and public policies must undergo change to accommodate them.

REFERENCES

National Organization for Women (1976). Do it now. Washington, D.C.: Author.

Roper Public Opinion Research Center (1974). The Virginia Slims American Women's Opinion Poll: A survey on the attitudes of women on marriage, divorce, the family and America's changing sexual morality (vol. 3). Williamstown, Mass.: Author.

STATISTICAL APPENDIX

The trends in marriage, childbearing, divorce, support, and remarriage are the basis of a number of the preceding chapters. Rather than repeat the statistics, which document these trends each time they were relevant, the editors decided to combine the most significant of these figures in the text which follows.

The number of marriages performed is declining, and people are tending to stay single longer prior to their first marriage. Whereas 28% of women aged 20 to 24 years were single in 1960, by 1974 this figure had jumped to 40%. College education is in part a factor delaying marriage among those under 25. Nearly three times as many women were enrolled in college in 1972 as in 1960.[1] The number of marriages performed (2,221,000 in 1974) would be even smaller were it not for the upturn in remarriages associated with the increase in the number of divorces in this period. Remarriage is more than twice as likely for divorced women than widowed women.

Of women over the age of 24, 86.9% are married. Women with a high school education, but no college, are more likely to be married than those with more education and income.

Out of over 55 million families, 47 million were husband-wife families in 1974. (A family is defined by the U.S. Bureau of the Census as two or more persons related by blood, marriage, or adoption and residing together.)

In 1974 the birth rate was 15 children per 1,000 people. This was 1% higher than the 1973 level, and the rise can be explained by increasing numbers of women in childbearing years, a phenomenon which will continue through 1980. The 1974 fertility rate was 1.9 children per woman. This is 1% lower than the 1973 level and 1.7 children lower than in 1957, when the rate started to decline steadily.

Births occurring outside marriage have doubled since 1950. In 1971, 11% of all first births were to unmarried women.

EDITORS' NOTE: Information in this Statistical Appendix was collected, reviewed, and organized by Susan Baird, Monica Melamid, and Molly Peter.

As of 1974, 42% of all mothers of school-age children held full-time jobs. Between 1960 and 1974 the labor force participation rate of wives with children age 5 years or younger rose 16 percentage points to 34%. More than one-third of the mothers whose children were under 6 years (in 1974) worked, most working full-time (U.S. Department of Labor, 1974:64).

On the average there are fewer children in families in which the mother is in the labor force. This is the case whether the family members are black or white, and whether it is a female-headed or a two-parent household. Black married women are more likely than white married women to be in the labor force.

Through the 1960s, there was an increase from 8% to 12% in the proportion of children under 18 years old living with their mothers only. By 1974, 1 out of 10 white children and 4 out of 10 black children were living in families with only their mothers.

Among families headed by women, 51% of all children under 18 had a mother in the labor force, compared with 38% of all children in husband-wife families. The labor force participation rate in 1974 for divorced or separated white female heads of families with children under 18 years was 68%, compared with 42% for white working wives with husband present.

Employed wives spent an average of 34 hours a week on household tasks, compared with 57 hours per week for women not employed outside the home (according to a 1968 study). The average time per week that a husband put into household chores was approximately four hours per week (U.S. Department of Agriculture, 1973:10).

The rate and number of divorces has climbed higher every year since 1932. In July 1974 the divorce rate was 4.7 per 1,000 population. The 1974 divorce rate was 4.5% higher than in 1973 and 109% higher than 1962. The highest proportion of those divorcing in 1971 were persons who had been married at least 20 years and who had married at a young age (men under 22 and women under 20 years old). More men than women who divorce will remarry (three-fourths compared with five-sixths). Remarriage accounts for the small proportion of the total population that is currently divorced (between 2% and 4%).

In 1974, 79% of all divorced women, including those who were not family heads, were in the labor force. Fifty-five percent of all separated women were in the labor force (U.S. Department of Labor, 1975:25).

Fourteen percent of divorced women are awarded alimony according to a survey sponsored by the National Commission on Observance of International Women's Year in 1975. A higher proportion of whites than blacks were receiving alimony and/or child-support payments.

The number of households headed by women accounted for one-fifth of all households in 1970. Such households increased by nearly a third from 1960 to 1973. Female household heads 65 years and over increased from 2.3 million in 1960 to 4.0 million in 1970, a 73% rise.

While male-headed poor families are declining, poor female-headed families are increasing rapidly. Forty-three percent of all poor families are female-headed. By 1972, 70% of poor nonwhite families were headed by women (Ross, 1976:141). The 1973 median annual income for female-headed families was $5,800, compared with $13,030 median income for all families (National Commission on the Observance of International Women's Year, 1976).

In one of the few available studies on support payments, the median child-support payments were found to be about $95 per month, or about $50 per child. Only one-fourth of the absent parents were paying 90% or more of the ordered amount, while one-half were making practically no payments (U.S. Department of Labor, 1975:46).

NOTE

1. Statistics and other information used in the narrative portion of the Statistical Appendix are drawn from publications of the U.S. Bureau of the Census, unless otherwise cited.

REFERENCES

National Commission on the Observance of International Women's Year (1976). "To form a more perfect union: Justice for American women." Washington, D.C.: U.S. Government Printing Office.

ROSS, H.L. (1976). "Poverty: Women and children last." Pp. 137-154 in J.R. Chapman (ed.), Economic independence for women: The foundation for equal rights (Sage Yearbooks in Women's Policy Studies, vol. 1). Beverly Hills, Calif.: Sage.

U.S. Department of Agriculture, Agricultural Research Service (1973). "Time and its dollar value in household work." Family Economics Review (fall).

U.S. Department of Labor, Bureau of Labor Statistics (1974). "Children of working mothers." Monthly Labor Review (March).

––– (1975). U.S. working women: A chartbook. Washington, D.C.: U.S. Government Printing Office.

TABLE 1: Marriage Laws as of October 1, 1973*

State or other jurisdiction	Age at which marriage can be contracted with parental consent		Age at which marriage can be contracted without parental consent		Common law marriage recognized	Physical examination and blood test for male and female			
						Maximum period between examination and issuance of marriage license	Scope of medical examination	Waiting period	
	Male	Female	Male	Female				Before issuance of license	After issuance of license
Alabama	17(a)	14(a)	21	18	★	30 da.	(b)	....	....
Alaska	18(c)	16(c)	19	18	....	30 da.	(b)	3 da.	....
Arizona	18(c)	16(c)	18	18	....	30 da.	(b)	(d)	....
Arkansas	17(c)	16(c)	21	18	....	30 da.	(b)	3 da.	....
California	18(a,e)	16(a,e)	21	18	....	30 da.	(b,f,g,h)	....	....
Colorado	16(e)	16(e)	18	18	★	30 da.	(b,g,i)	....	....
Connecticut	16(e)	16(e)	18	18	....	35 da.	(b)	4 da.	....
Delaware	18(c)	16(c)	18	18	....	30 da.	(b)	....	(j)
Florida	18(a,c)	16(a,c)	18	18	....	30 da.	(b)	3 da.	....
Georgia	18(c)	16(c)	18	18	★	30 da.	(b,f)	3 da.(k)	....
Hawaii	16	16	18	18	....	30 da.	(b)	....	....
Idaho	18(e)	16(e)	18	18	★	30 da.	(b)	3 da.(l)	....
Illinois	18(c)	16(c)	21	18	....	15 da.	(b,f,g)	....	....
Indiana	18(c)	16(c)	18	18	....	30 da.	(b,f)	3 da.	....
Iowa	18(c)	16(c)	18	18	★	20 da.	(b)	3 da.	....
Kansas	18(e)	18(e)	18	18	★	30 da.	(b)	3 da.	....
Kentucky	18(a,c)	16(a,c)	18	18	....	15 da.	(b,f)	3 da.	....
Louisiana	18(e)	18(e)	18	18	....	10 da.	(b)	....	72 hrs.
Maine	16(e)	16(e)	18	18	....	60 da.	(b)	5 da.	....
Maryland	16(c)	16(c)	18	18	....	.....	...	48 hrs.	....
Massachusetts	18(e)	16(e)	18	18	....	30 da.	(b)	3 da.	....
Michigan	(m)	16(c)	18	18	....	30 da.	(b)	3 da.	....
Minnesota	18(a)	16(n)	18	18	....	.....	...	5 da.	....
Mississippi	17(e)	15(e)	21	21	....	30 da.	(b)	3 da.	....
Missouri	15(e)	15(e)	21	18	....	15 da.	(b)	3 da.	....
Montana	18(e)	18(e)	18	18	★	20 da.	(b)	5 da.	....
Nebraska	18	16	19	19	....	30 da.	(b)	5 da.	....
Nevada	18(a,e)	16(a,e)	18	18	....	.....	...	....	....
New Hampshire	14(o)	13(o)	18	18	....	30 da.	(b)	5 da.	....
New Jersey	18(e)	16(e)	18	18	....	30 da.	(b)	72 hrs.	....
New Mexico	17(c)	16(c)	18	18	....	30 da.	(b)	72 hrs.	....
New York	16	14(p)	21	18	....	30 da.	(b,f)	....	24 hrs.(q)
North Carolina	16	16(c)	18	18	....	30 da.	(b,r,s)	(t)	....
North Dakota	18(u)	15	18	18	....	30 da.	(b,v)	....	....
Ohio	18(c)	16(c)	21(w)	21(w)	★	30 da.	(b)	5 da.	....
Oklahoma	18(c)	15(c)	18	18	★	30 da.	(b)	(x)	....
Oregon	18	15	18	18	....	30 da.(y)	(b,z)	7 da.	....
Pennsylvania	16(e)	16(e)	18	18	★	30 da.	(b,r)	3 da.	....
Rhode Island	18(e)	16(e)	18	18	★	40 da.	(b,s)	....	(aa)
South Carolina	16(c)	14(c)	18	18	★	.....	...	24 hrs.	....
South Dakota	18(c)	16(c)	18	18	....	20 da.	(b)	....	....
Tennessee	16(e)	16(e)	18	18	....	30 da.	(b)	3 da.(l)	....
Texas	16	14	18	18	★	21 da.	(b)	....	....
Utah	16(a)	14(a)	21	18	....	30 da.	(b)	....	....
Vermont	18(e)	16(e)	18	18	....	30 da.	(b)	....	5 da.
Virginia	18(a,c)	16(c)	18	18	....	30 da.	(b)	....	....
Washington	17(e)	17(e)	18	18	....	.....	(b,s,v)	3 da.	....
West Virginia	18(a)	16(a)	18	18	....	30 da.	(b)	....	5 da.
Wisconsin	(ab)	16	18	18	....	20 da.	(b)	5 da.	....
Wyoming	18	16	19	19	....	30 da.	(b)	....	....
Dist. of Columbia	18(a)	16(a)	21	18	★	30 da.	(b)	5 da.	....

*Prepared by the Women's Bureau, U.S. Department of Labor.
★Indicates common law marriage recognized.
(a) Parental consent not required if minor was previously married.
(b) Venereal diseases.
(c) Procedure established whereby younger parties may obtain license in case of pregnancy or birth of a child.
(d) Blood test must be on record for at least 48 hours before issuance of license.
(e) Procedure established whereby younger parties may obtain license in special circumstances.
(f) Sickle cell anemia.
(g) Rubella immunity.
(h) Tay-Sachs disease.
(i) Rh factor.
(j) Residents, 24 hours; nonresidents, 96 hours.
(k) Unless parties are 18 years of age or over, or female is pregnant, or applicants are the parents of a living child born out of wedlock.
(l) Unless parties are 18 years of age or over.
(m) No provision in law for parental consent for males.
(n) Permission of judge also required.
(o) Below age of consent and above minimum age, permission of judge, which is given only for special cause, also required.

(p) If under 16 years of age, consent of a family court judge also required.
(q) Marriage may not be solemnized within 3 days from date on which specimen for serological test was taken.
(r) Mental incompetence.
(s) Tuberculosis.
(t) Forty-eight hours if both are nonresidents of the State.
(u) Any unmarried male of the age of 18 years or upwards, and any unmarried female of the age of 15 years or upwards, and not otherwise disqualified, are capable of consenting to and consummating a marriage. If the male or the female is under the age of 18 years, a marriage license shall not be issued without the consent of the parents or guardian, if there are any.
(v) Feeblemindedness, imbecility, insanity, chronic alcoholism.
(w) Change to 18 becomes effective January 1, 1974.
(x) Seventy-two hours if one or both parties are below the age for marriage without parental consent.
(y) Maximum period between examination and expiration of marriage license.
(z) Feeblemindedness, mental illness, drug addiction, and chronic alcoholism.
(aa) If female is nonresident, must complete and sign license 5 days prior to marriage.
(ab) Male under 18 years may not marry.

SOURCE: *The Book of the States,* published by Council of State Governments. Prepared by the Women's Bureau, U.S. Department of Labor.

TABLE 2: Average *Daily* Time Contributed by Various Family Members in All Household Work

Number of children	Age of wife or youngest child	Time contributed by—									
		Nonemployed-wife households					Employed-wife households				
	Wife	Families in sample	Wife	Husband	Child 12-17[1]	Child 6-11[1]	Families in sample	Wife	Husband	Child 12-17[1]	Child 6-11[1]
		Number	Hours	Hours	Hours	Hours	Number	Hours	Hours	Hours	Hours
None	Under 25	16	5.1	.9	--	---	29	3.5	1.4	---	---
	25-39	20	5.9	1.2	--	---	25	3.6	1.4	---	---
	40-54	32	6.2	1.5	--	---	13	4.3	.8	---	--
	55 & over	39	5.4	2.0	---	---	11	4.3	1.1	---	--
	Youngest child										
1	12-17	22	7.0	2.0	1.2	---	24	5.0	1.8	1.1	--
	6-11	24	6.9	1.5	---	.4	21	5.7	1.2	---	.6
	2-5	28	6.8	1.7	--	--	18	4.6	1.4	--	---
	1	39	7.5	1.7	---	---	6	6.4	.5	--	---
	under 1	41	8.3	1.6	--	---	(2)	(2)	(2)	---	--
2	12-17	27	7.1	1.7	.9	---	19	4.8	1.7	1.2	---
	6-11	64	7.4	1.6	.8	.5	24	5.4	1.5	1.0	.5
	2-5	96	8.2	1.6	.8	.3	29	6.2	1.7	1.2	.3
	1	53	8.8	1.7	(3)	.4	10	6.2	3.5	(3)	(3)
	under 1	66	9.5	1.5	(3)	.3	7	7.7	1.6	(3)	(3)
3	12-17	26	6.7	1.1	1.0	---	17	3.8	1.5	1.1	---
	6-11	6.1	7.3	1.6	1.2	.6	27	6.3	1.4	1.4	.8
	2-5	72	8.0	1.4	1.1	.6	15	7.5	2.1	(3)	.4
	1	51	8.8	1.6	.4	.4	4	7.5	2.4	(3)	(3)
	under 1	32	10.1	1.5	(3)	.7	4	6.6	2.1	(3)	(3)
4	12-17	7	6.4	1.1	.9	---	9	6.1	1.2	1.4	---
	6-11	52	8.0	1.4	1.1	.6	18	5.3	.9	.8	.4
	2-5	35	9.1	1.4	.9	.5	(2)	(2)	(2)	(3)	(3)
	1	23	8.7	1.9	1.0	.5	(2)	(2)	(2)	(3)	(3)
	under 1	34	10.5	2.1	(3)	1.5	(2)	(2)	(2)	(3)	(3)
5-6	6-11	16	8.6	2.0	1.4	.6	(2)	(2)	(2)	(3)	(3)
	2-5	17	9.0	1.5	1.0	.5	(2)	(2)	(2)	(3)	(3)
	1	6	7.5	1.1	(3)	.4	(2)	(2)	(2)	(3)	(3)
	under 1	11	10.3	2.0	1.2	.8	(2)	(2)	(2)	(3)	(3)
7-9	2-5	10	8.8	2.1	1.2	.5	(2)	(2)	(2)	(3)	(3)
	under 1	4	11.7	1.9	(3)	.9	---	---	--	---	---

[1] Averages for children are for each child in family.
[2] Fewer than 4 families.
[3] Fewer than 4 children of designated ages.

SOURCE: Family Economics Review, fall 1973, Agricultural Research Service, U.S. Department of Agriculture. Data collected by N.Y. State College of Human Ecology, Cornell University, included 1,318 urban-suburban households, Syracuse, N.Y., 1967-1968, and 60 rural households, Cortland County, N.Y., 1971. Based on 1971 wage rates.

TABLE 3: The Status of Married Women, by State

Column categories (left to right):
- Age of Marriage
- Domicile
- Support
- Property Systems
- Wive may Engage in Business
- Support of Children During Marriage
- Custody*
- Grounds for Divorce
- Division of Property
- Alimony

Sub-column labels:

Age of Marriage:
- Same age for both sexes
- Different age when parental consent required
- Same age when consent not required
- Different age when consent not required
- Conclusively determined by husband's residence
- Married woman may establish own residence for specific purpose(s) not based on sex or marital status
- Right to establish residence not based on sex or marital status

Domicile:
- Mutual obligation
- Husband has primary duty of support
- Wife must support husband when he is in need

Support:
- Community property
- Separate property
- On same basis as husband

Property Systems:
- May not sell property
- May not contract to guarantee husband's debts
- Joint obligation

Wive may Engage in Business:
- Father has primary obligation
- Based on best interests of child

Support of Children During Marriage:
- Denial to party at fault in divorce
- Statutory preference for mother
- Either parent may be ordered to support

Custody*:
- Breakdown of marriage
- Standard fault grounds
- Incompatibility
- Separation
- Alcoholism or drug use

Grounds for Divorce:
- Court cannot make a distribution
- Court empowered to distribute community property

Division of Property:
- Joint ownership
- To either spouse
- To wife only

Alimony:
- No alimony

States (rows):
Alabama, Alaska, Arizona, Arkansas, California, Colorado, Connecticut, Delaware, Florida, Georgia, Hawaii, Idaho, Illinois, Indiana, Iowa, Kansas, Kentucky, Louisiana, Maine, Maryland, Massachusetts, Michigan, Minnesota, Mississippi

Missouri																									
Montana	• [1]																								
Nebraska																									
Nevada																									
New Hampshire	• [1]																								
New Jersey																									
New Mexico																									
New York																									
North Carolina																									
North Dakota																									
Ohio																									
Oklahoma																									
Oregon																									
Pennsylvania																									
Rhode Island																									
South Carolina																									
South Dakota																									
Tennessee																									
Texas																									
Utah																									
Vermont																									
Virginia																									
Washington																									
West Virginia																									
Wisconsin																									
Wyoming																									

1. Court approval required
2. Unless husband is non-resident
3. Except for divorce purposes
4. Equal obligation to support "spouse" in need
5. Equal control and management
6. Mother must assist if father unable
7. May consider causes of dissolution
8. Most custody statutes are non-discriminatory; however judges often show preference for the mother
9. Some young children presumed to need mother
10. Father may be ordered to support (often because of fault)
11. Alimony limited to 1/3 of husband's income
12. Alimony limited to 3 year term (renewable)
13. Alimony only if spouse unable to work
14. Non-discriminatory change passed both houses this session, awaiting Governor's signature

Sources: National ERA Task Force, Anita Miller, Director, Sacramento: A Commentary on the Effects of the Equal Rights
Amendment on State Laws and Institutions, Equal Rights Amendment Project, Anne K. Bingaman; ERA Confor-
mance: An Analysis of the California State Codes, Equal Rights Amendment Project; State-by-State Guide to Women's
Legal Rights, Shana Alexander; "The High Cost of Divorce", Business Week, February 10, 1975; Excerpt from A
Report on State Law Conformance to Equal Rights Principles, by The Women's Law Project Philadelphia.

Reprinted from: *Monitor*, California Commission on Status of Women, 1976.

TABLE 4: Poor Families by Sex and Race of Head (in percentages)

| | White Poor Families With Children Under 18 | | Nonwhite Poor Families With Children Under 18 | |
	Female Head	Male Head	Female Head	Male Head
1960	24.5	75.5	34.9	65.1
1961	23.6	76.4	35.7	64.3
1962	24.7	75.3	39.5	60.5
1963	26.5	73.5	41.9	58.1
1964	25.4	74.6	39.9	60.1
1965	30.3	69.7	41.6	58.4
1966	33.5	66.5	45.5	54.5
1967	32.9	67.1	51.1	48.9
1968	36.4	63.6	57.0	43.0
1969	40.1	59.9	59.2	40.8
1970	40.1	59.9	62.3	37.7
1971	41.4	58.6	64.6	35.4
1972	43.3	56.7	69.0	31.0

SOURCE: U.S. Bureau of the Census, *Current Population Reports,* Consumer Income Series P-60, Nos. 68, 76, 81, 86, and 88, "Characteristics of the Low-Income Population."

TABLE 5: Number of Female-Headed Families by Marital Status, 1960-1973 (Numbers in thousands)

| | | | | Change, 1970-73 | | Change, 1960-70 | |
Marital status	1973	1970	1960	Number	Percent	Number	Percent
Female family heads	6,607	5,515	4,196	1,092	19.8	1,319	31.4
Married, spouse absent	1,579	1,247	914	332	26.6	333	36.4
Separated	1,289	922	588	367	39.8	334	56.8
Other	290	325	326	−35	−10.8	−1	−.3
Widowed	2,468	2,265	2,093	203	9.0	172	8.2
Divorced	1,712	1,312	702	400	30.5	610	86.9
Single	848	691	487	157	22.7	204	41.9
Number of children under 18 per family	1.40	1.28	1.51	.12	9.4	−.23	−15.2

SOURCE: Population of U.S. Trends: Prospects 1950-1990, Series P-20, No. 225, March 1973.

TABLE 6: Median Age at Divorce and Remarriage

Race and year of birth	Median age of woman at divorce after first marriage				Women married twice		
	Total divorced after first marriage	Married--			Median age at remarriage after first marriage ended in--		Median age at second divorce
		Once	Twice	3 or more times	Divorce	Widowhood	
Total born in 1900 to 1954..........	27.1	31.6	25.8	25.0	29.6	40.6	38.1
RACE							
White...................	27.0	31.8	25.8	24.9	29.4	40.9	38.3
Negro..................	27.7	30.5	26.2	25.7	30.7	37.9	37.5
Other.................	(B)	(B)	(B)	(B)	(B)	(B)	(B)
YEAR OF BIRTH[1]							
1940 to 1944...........	24.6	26.1	22.8	(B)	25.1	(B)	(B)
1935 to 1939...........	26.3	30.2	24.5	22.8	27.2	(B)	(B)
1930 to 1934...........	27.8	34.2	26.1	23.4	29.8	32.6	(B)
1925 to 1929...........	28.8	37.0	27.0	24.1	31.5	33.7	39.1
1920 to 1924...........	29.6	39.0	27.6	25.9	32.1	38.2	(B)
1915 to 1919...........	31.4	40.2	29.9	26.9	34.5	42.2	(B)
1910 to 1914...........	33.3	43.2	31.5	28.3	36.6	45.1	(B)
1905 to 1909...........	32.0	44.1	29.9	(B)	36.5	47.3	(B)
1900 to 1904...........	33.2	(B)	31.4	(B)	39.3	46.8	(B)

(B) Base is too small to show derived figures.

1. Women born in 1945 to 1954 are included on the preceding lines but are omitted on the lines below because of their brief exposure to divorce and remarriage.

SOURCE: U.S. Bureau of the Census, Current Population Reports, p. 20, No. 239, September 1972.

TABLE 7: Collection of Alimony and Child Support

Years since court order	Number of open cases	Full Compliance	Partial Compliance	No Compliance	Non-paying fathers against whom legal action was taken
One	163	38%	20%	42%	19%
Two	163	28	20	52	32
Three	161	26	14	60	21
Four	161	22	11	67	18
Five	160	19	14	67	9
Six	158	17	12	71	6
Seven	157	17	12	71	4
Eight	155	17	8	75	2
Nine	155	17	8	75	0
Ten	149	13	8	79	1

SOURCE: Citizen's Advisory Council on the Status of Women, Department of Labor Building, "The Equal Rights Amendment and Alimony and Child Support Laws," p. 8, January 1972.

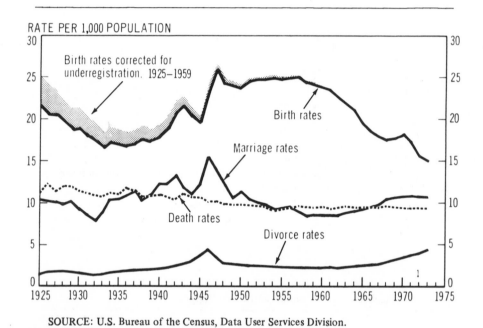

RATE PER 1,000 POPULATION

Birth rates corrected for underregistration. 1925–1959

Birth rates

Marriage rates

Death rates

Divorce rates

SOURCE: U.S. Bureau of the Census, Data User Services Division.

FIGURE 1: Birth, Marriage, Death, and Divorce Rates, 1925-1975

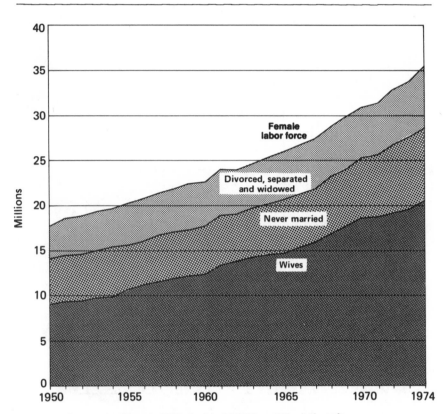

Note: Data are for March in 1950, April in 1951-55, and March thereafter.

The number of married women in the labor force has more than doubled since 1950.

SOURCE: U.S. Department of Labor, Bureau of Labor Statistics, *U.S. Working Women: A Chartbook,* Bureau of Labor Statistics Bulletin 1880 (Washington, D.C.: U.S. Government Printing Office, 1975).

FIGURE 2: Women in the Labor Force by Marital Status, 1950-1974

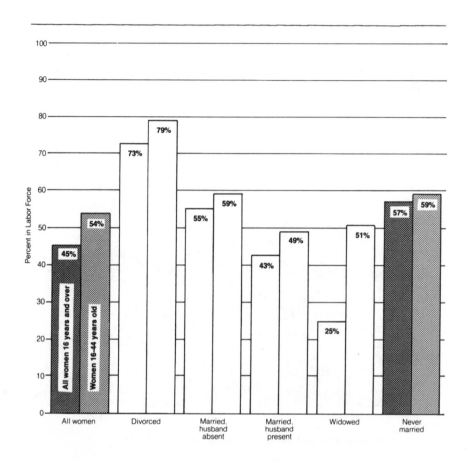

As a group, divorced women are more likely to be in the labor force than women of any other marital status. Widows are the least likely to be workers, but this is largely attributable to age.

SOURCE: U.S. Department of Labor, Bureau of Labor Statistics, *U.S. Working Women: A Chartbook,* Bureau of Labor Statistics Bulletin 1880 (Washington, D.C.: U.S. Government Printing Office, 1975).

FIGURE 3: Labor Force Participation Rates of Women by Marital Status and Age, March 1974

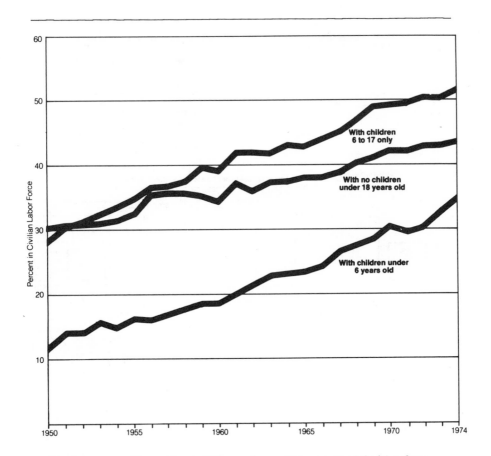

Married women with or without children under age 18 have entered the labor force in increasing proportions over the past quarter century; the pace of the increase for women with preschool age children has accelerated in the past few years.

SOURCE: U.S. Department of Labor, Bureau of Labor Statistics, *U.S. Working Women: A Chartbook,* Bureau of Labor Statistics Bulletin 1880 (Washington, D.C.: U.S. Government Printing Office, 1975).

FIGURE 4: Labor Force Participation Rates of Married Women by Presence and Age of Children, 1950-1974

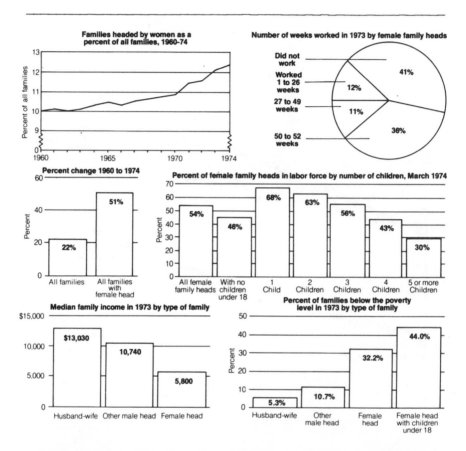

Families headed by women account for a significant and growing share of all American families. On average, half of the women who head families are in the labor force, but proportionately more female than male family heads are below the poverty level.

SOURCE: U.S. Department of Labor, Bureau of Labor Statistics, *U.S. Working Women: A Chartbook,* Bureau of Labor Statistics Bulletin 1880 (Washington, D.C.: U.S. Government Printing Office, 1975).

FIGURE 5: Summary Indicators for Families Headed by Women,
Selected Periods, 1960-1974

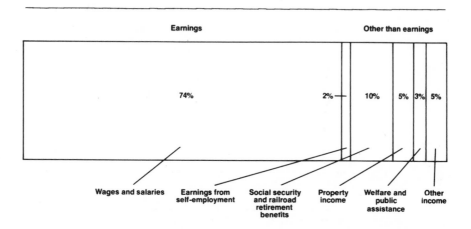

Of the aggregate income of women in 1973, more than 75% was from earnings, about 10% was from social security and similar benefits, and 3% was from welfare and public assistance payments.

SOURCE: U.S. Department of Labor, Bureau of Labor Statistics, *U.S. Working Women: A Chartbook,* Bureau of Labor Statistics Bulletin 1880 (Washington, D.C.: U.S. Government Printing Office, 1975).

FIGURE 6: Income of Women by Source, 1973

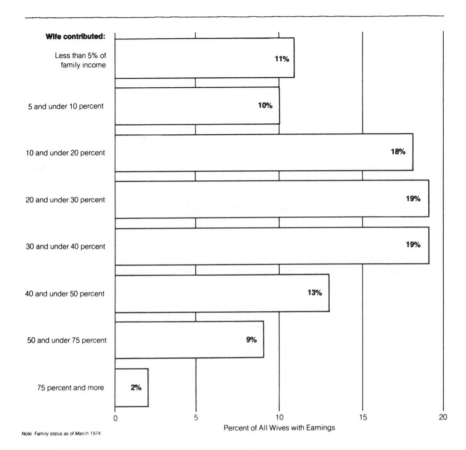

In families where the wife was an earner, she most commonly contributed between 20% and 40% of the family income.

SOURCE: U.S. Department of Labor, Bureau of Labor Statistics, *U.S. Working Women: A Chartbook,* Bureau of Labor Statistics Bulletin 1880 (Washington, D.C.: U.S. Government Printing Office, 1975).

FIGURE 7: Wives with Earnings by Percent of 1973 Family Income

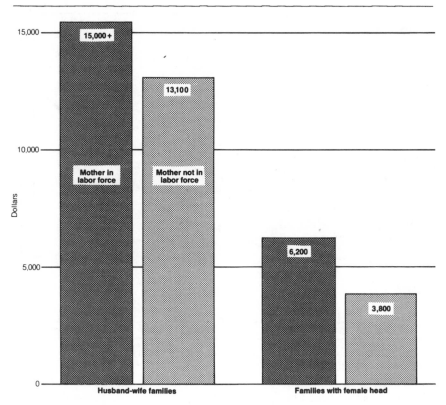

Note: Numbers rounded to nearest $100

Children of working mothers are typically in higher income families.

SOURCE: U.S. Department of Labor, Bureau of Labor Statistics, *U.S. Working Women: A Chartbook,* Bureau of Labor Statistics Bulletin 1880 (Washington, D.C.: U.S. Government Printing Office, 1975).

FIGURE 8: Median 1973 Incomes of Families with Children by Type of Family and Labor Force Status of Mother, March 1974

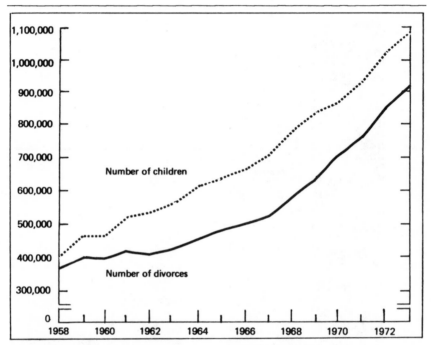

SOURCE: Bureau of Census, Monthly Vital Statistics: Summary Report,
Final Divorce Statistics: 1973, vol. 24.

FIGURE 9: Divorces and Children Involved, 1958-1973

THE CONTRIBUTORS

JESSIE BERNARD is Professor Emerita of Sociology at Pennsylvania State University. In 1974-1975 she was Visiting Research Scholar at the National Institute of Education, Washington, D.C. In 1975-1976 she was Scholar-in-Residence at the U.S. Civil Rights Commission, Washington, D.C. Among her awards are an Honorary Doctor of Humanities, Washington University, May 1976; the Jessie Bernard Award, given annually by the American Sociological Association; and the Outstanding Achievement Award, American Association of University Women, 1976. Her extensive publications in the field of family and community organization include *The Future of Marriage, The Future of Motherhood, The Sociology of Community,* and *Women, Wives, Mothers: Values and Options.*

RAPHAELA BEST is a reading specialist in the Montgomery County Maryland School System. She taught courses in reading instruction at the University of Virginia and was for a time consultant to the Central Atlantic Regional Educational Laboratory (CAREL) in Washington, D.C. She is also an anthropologist and did a full year's participant-observation study of primary aged school children in an urban school, which is reported in a forthcoming work, *Winners, Losers, and Girls: Sex Roles and Socialization in Early Childhood,* coauthored with Jessie Bernard.

JANE ROBERTS CHAPMAN is a founder and Co-Director of the Center for Women Policy Studies, Washington, D.C., and an editor of the Sage Yearbooks in Women's Policy Studies. She is a coordinator of the National Women's Agenda Task Force on Women and Economic Power. Her recent publications include "Women's Access to Credit" (1975), "Essays in the Social Sciences: Economics"

(1975), "Sex Discrimination in Credit: The Backlash of Economic Dependency" (1976), and "How Family Law Affects You" (1976).

MARGARET GATES, a founder and Co-Director of the Center for Women Policy Studies, is an attorney and Adjunct Professor of Law at the Georgetown University Law Center. Her recent publications include "Credit Discrimination Against Women: Causes and Solutions" (1974), "Women and Policing: A Legal Analysis" (1974), Rape and Its Victims: A Report for Citizens, Health Facilities, and Criminal Justice Agencies (1975), and "Occupational Segregation and the Law" (1976).

SHEILA B. KAMERMAN is Co-Director, Cross-National Studies of Social Services and Family Policy, and Director, Working Mothers Research Project, Columbia University School of Social Work. In addition to articles on social services and family policy, she is coauthor of *Not for the Poor Alone* (1973), *Social Services in the United States* (1976), and the forthcoming *Social Services in International Perspective.* She is also the author of *Child Care Programs in Nine Countries.*

MARY E. KING has been an independent consultant and president of a Washington-based management consulting firm since 1972. Ms. King's research largely involves health services and criminal justice systems, including aspects of those fields pertaining specifically to women. Among her writings for a variety of publications, the one of which she is most proud is a manifesto on women in the civil rights movement written in 1965.

SUSAN KINSLEY received a B.A. in 1974 from Harvard University, where she was an editor of *The Harvard Crimson.* She is currently in her final year at Georgetown University Law Center. She has worked at the Center for Women Policy Studies and the Office for Civil Rights, U.S. Department of Health, Education, and Welfare.

MADELEIN KORNFEIN has been a Research Associate with the Family Lifestyles Project since its inception. She received her M.A. in sociology from the University of California, Los Angeles, and was instrumental in establishing child-care facilities on that campus. She has lived communally and is currently a member of a city-wide citizen's committee studying the implications of zoning laws on communal households in residential neighborhoods.

JOAN M. KRAUSKOPF, Professor of Law at the University of Missouri-Columbia, taught family law for many years and published extensively in the areas of family law and sex discrimination. She has been a member of the Missouri Governor's Committee on Children and Youth (1972-1974); Missouri State Advisory Committee to the United States Civil Rights Commission; active member of Missouri Bar Family Law Committee, which drafted and obtained passage of the Missouri Divorce Reform Act, and Chairperson, Missouri Bar Committee on the Uniform Interstate Child Custody Jurisdiction Act.

JEAN LIPMAN-BLUMEN is the Director of the Women's Research Program at the National Institute of Education in Washington, D.C. She has published widely in the fields of sex roles, role theory, and divorce.

JUDITH ANN LIPSHUTZ graduated from Mount Holyoke College in 1975. She is currently a research assistant at Mary King Associates, Inc., and is a charter organizer for the National Women's Health Network. She recently coauthored an article in *The Woman Offender Report* entitled "Health Services for Women Prisoners."

JOAN C. MARTIN is a Ph.D. student in the Department of Psychology at the University of California, Los Angeles, and has served the Family Lifestyles Project since its beginning as a Research Associate developing the observational measures in training the Home-Observation Staff. Past research experience includes social, physiological, personality, and animal behavior areas within psychology as well as four years in archaeology. She is currently preparing her dissertation research in communal child rearing.

AUDREY MOORE is an independent consultant in the areas of health, education, and management. She was formerly with a comprehensive health planning agency and currently is a consultant to the U.S. Public Health Service and to the Secretary's Advisory Committee on the Rights and Responsibilities of Women, U.S. Department of Health, Education, and Welfare.

DIANN HOLLAND PAINTER is Assistant Professor of Economics at Wellesley College. Her special area of concentration is economic development, with particular reference to the problems of industrialization and economic integration in West Africa. Her current research is focused on economic problems of black women in America. She recently published an article entitled "The Black Woman in American Society" in *Current History* (1976).

MARY POTTER ROWE is Special Assistant to the President and Chancellor of the Massachusetts Institute of Technology, where she is an institute ombudsperson and also teaches. She is a well-known authority on child-care economics and has published numerous articles on day-care, androgyny, and subtle discrimination against women and minorities. At present she is mainly concerned with innovative mediation techniques in large organizations.

MURRAY A. STRAUS is Professor of Sociology at the University of New Hampshire. He is the author, coauthor, or editor of five books and over 70 journal articles. His books include *Violence in the Family* (1974), *Family Problem Solving* (1971), and *Family Measurement Techniques* (1969). He was President of the National Council on Family Relations in 1973-1974 and Vice-President of the Eastern Sociological Society for 1976-1977. He is currently studying the factors associated with husband-wife physical violence in a nationally representative sample of 2,100 families.

THOMAS S. WEISNER is Assistant Professor of Anthropology, Departments of Psychiatry and Anthropology, at the University of California, Los Angeles. He is also the Co-Principle Investigator of the Family Lifestyles Project. His recent publications include "Experimental Family Lifestyles: A Child's-Eye View," "My Brother's Keeper: Child and Sibling Caretaking" (with Ronald Gallimore), and "Urban-Rural Differences in African Children's Performance on Cognitive and Memory Tasks."

DATE DUE

APR 1 6 1996			
NOV 1 8 1996			
MAR 1 3 1998			

HIGHSMITH 45-102   PRINTED IN U.S.A.